METHUEN'S
MANUALS OF MODERN PSYCHOLOGY
General Editor: H. J. Butcher

The Psychology of Thinking

The Psychology of Thinking

NEIL BOLTON

METHUEN & CO LTD
11 New Fetter Lane London EC4

First published 1972
© *1972 Neil Bolton*
Printed in Great Britain by
T & A Constable Ltd
Edinburgh

SBN 416 66000 2

Distributed in the USA by
HARPER & ROW PUBLISHERS, INC.
BARNES & NOBLE IMPORT DIVISION

Contents

Acknowledgements

I would like to thank Arthur Still, John Findlay and David Hargreaves for their comments on certain chapters. My thanks are also due to the following: G. A. Miller, E. Gallanter and K. H. Pribram and Holt, Rinehart & Winston, Inc. for permission to reproduce Figure 3; J. P. Guilford and the American Psychological Association for permission to reproduce Figure 7; N. Chomsky and Harcourt Brace Jovanovich, Inc. for permission to reproduce Figure 8; M. Merleau-Ponty, the Humanities Press Inc. and Routledge & Kegan Paul Ltd. for permission to quote the passage on p. 231.

of natural, mechanical laws. Thus, the causal laws, to which thought must conform in order to satisfy the ideal norms of logic, are not the same as the norms themselves, and psychologism confuses this fundamental and essential difference.

A further objection to psychologism revolves around the idea that if the source of logical laws is to be found in psychological facts, then logical laws would have to have psychological content; they would have to be laws of psychological facts as well as presupposing the existence of these facts. But, Husserl says, no logical law implies a 'matter of fact'. An analysis of the real meaning of logical laws shows that they are not laws of actual mental life. The psychologistic interpretation therefore does violence to the meaning of logical laws which refer generally to any terms or propositions. Of course, our knowledge of the laws is a psychologically conditioned event, but this does not signify that the laws themselves arise from experience.

Another charge which Husserl lays against psychologism is that it leads to 'sceptical relativism', which, for him, was a self-defeating position. Understood broadly, the doctrine of sceptical relativism states that truth is relative because dependent upon the facts of human constitution and experience. These facts vary from place to place and from time to time; therefore our perception of truth varies in response to changing historical and social circumstances. Consequently, there is no absolute and universal truth, but merely 'points of view' of equal validity in so far as these viewpoints faithfully express particular sets of circumstances. Husserl objects to this view which, he says, makes man, in all his instability, the measure of everything. And for him, relativism was a contradictory position, since it denies the possibility of all absolute knowledge while asserting its own absolute truth. For to state that 'there is no absolute and universal truth' is either to state an absolute and universal truth or to state a probability, in which case there may well be absolute truths.

The distinction which appears to be crucial to Husserl's attack on psychologism is that between two types of thinking corresponding to two types of knowledge. On the one hand, there is knowledge gained by induction or abstraction from experience, and, on the other, there is knowledge acquired through 'direct intuition' or insight. The former is the realm of the empirical sciences – physics, biology, psychology, etc. – and the laws of these sciences can only be stated in terms of probabilities. But certain and absolutely self-evident knowledge can be achieved in the domain of purely conceptual knowledge, which includes the laws of logic and pure mathematics. The proof that justifies these is not obtained from induction but from insight, so that a logical law is the one and only truth, which excludes all other possibilities. The upshot of this distinction seems to be to separate logic completely from psychological phenomena, but, that this cannot be, since logical relations are given to us in experience, was recognized by Husserl in subsequent work (e.g. Husserl, 1901, 1929). In these studies Husserl developed the idea that what was needed was a psychology of the ways in which we experience logical relations, a psychology of thinking which would describe the processes in which the entities studied in pure logic are presented to conscious experience. But he insisted that he was not concerned with actual, individual experience, as psychology must be. Rather, his objective was to describe the ideal types of logical experience corresponding to the ideal logical laws. As Spiegelberg (1965) points out, this study of the pure types or essences of these experiences, a study which Husserl came to designate as 'phenomenology', was to be neutral towards the question of what went on in actual cases. This was to remain the province of empirical psychology. Phenomenology, in its Husserlian form, does not therefore study factual relationships, but aims at studying essential relationships that can be understood independently of actual cases. Thus, logic is independent of empirical psychology, which deals with causes and effects, but there is a close relationship between logic and phenomenological psychology since, in Husserl's philosophy, there is a parallelism between the structures of the subjective act and the structures of the logical entities to which the act refers.

The dichotomy which this philosophy postulates between the empirical and the rational is very clearly illustrated in Husserl's (1900) discussion of the biological principle of adaptation. He contests the theory that a progressive increase in rational thinking is due to an increase in an organism's adaptation to its environment. This, he believes, represents the same kind of confusion of logical and empirical laws that was evident in psychologism. The principle of establishing the most general laws, which is the goal of the sciences, is a purely ideal principle, and one which cannot be reduced to social and psychological facts. It is not correct, therefore, to say, as theorists who see the source of rationality in adaptation do, that life – whether conceptualized biologically or psychologically – is actually governed by this principle, because this principle is an ideal and not a natural law. Our factual thinking does not proceed according to ideals, because ideals are not natural forces. It is by illicitly converting an ideal principle into an actual law that adaptation theorists can explain the ideal by the actual, the idea of rationality by the facts of adaptation. Husserl maintains that it is an error to level out the difference between logical and natural thought, for logical thinking has to do with necessary relationships between propositions, whereas natural thinking derives from experience in all its contingency. Adaptation cannot therefore account for rational thinking because the two phenomena belong to two different realms of discourse.

Husserl's viewpoint clearly emphasizes the discontinuity between logic and psychology, underlining, as it does, how logical thinking differs from thinking guided by experience. It should be noted that the theory which Husserl had in mind when attacking psychologism was the associationist theory of thinking put forward by the British empiricist philosophers. Before attempting to evaluate Husserl's contribution, it is desirable that this theory should be stated.

THE ASSOCIATIONIST THEORY OF THINKING

This theory could justifiably be called the traditional theory of thinking. The principles of association were first formulated by Aristotle; they were developed, in rather different ways, by philosophers such as Hobbes, Locke, Hume, James Mill and John Stuart Mill, and they have been adopted by psychologists who view thinking as the learning of conditioned responses. The importance of this movement may be judged from Humphrey's (1963) remark that 'the history of the psychology of thinking consists largely of an unsuccessful revolt against the doctrine of association' (p. 28). The theory has suffered many modifications in the course of its long history, but, for the purpose of this chapter, it is only necessary to expound the two basic principles common to most versions.

The first principle asserts the derivation of ideas from sensory impressions. Locke (1690) held that all knowledge derives from experience and that there are two kinds of experience, that which arises directly from our sensations and that constituted by the operation of the mind in reflection. Locke had no hesitation in saying that our first ideas are provided by sensation, while those which we owe to reflection come later: 'These alone, so far as I can discover, are the windows by which the light is let into this dark room; for methinks the understanding is not much unlike a closet wholly shut from light, with only some little opening left, to let in some external visible resemblances, or ideas of things without' (p. 91). This notion was taken up by Hume (1739), who agreed with Locke in maintaining that the first elements of all knowledge are simple perceptions which are received passively by us. However, Hume divided perceptions into two kinds which he called 'impressions' and 'ideas'. The difference between them consists in the degree of force or liveliness with which they strike the mind. Those perceptions which enter the mind with more force he terms impressions; ideas, on the other hand, are 'but the faint images of impressions in thinking and reasoning' (p. 45). The principle that all ideas are derived, in the first instance, from sensations continued to influence later thinkers, such as James Mill (1829), and receives its modern formulation in the definition of thinking as the activity of stimulus-selection and classification. This is the theory of abstraction and it will be given a more detailed and critical treatment in Chapter 4.

If sensations or stimuli are the building-blocks of perception and thinking, the discrete elements or atoms which, when combined, form a percept or a thought, the question naturally arises: how are they combined? The answer is contained in the second basic principle of this school, the principle of association. In his essay on memory, Aristotle (1952, vol. 3) argued that recollection occurs because processes follow one another in an orderly manner; three principles govern this orderly appearance, contiguity, similarity and contrast. According to the principle of association by contiguity, one mental event will call up others which occurred previously at the same time; according to the principle of similarity, a mental event will reinstate another one like it, and according to that of contrast, one which is its opposite. The empiricist philosophers differed among themselves about the importance of each of these principles, both Hartley (1749) and James Mill (1829) believing that the principles of similarity and contrast could be reduced to the fundamental law of contiguity, for example, whilst Spencer (1855) thought the principle of similarity was the fundamental one.

With the foundation of behaviourism, the term 'association' was replaced by the notion of 'conditioned reflex'. Theories of thinking based upon the notion of association or conditioning are currently still in vogue; witness, for example, Underwood (1952), Galanter and Gestenhaber (1956) and Cofer (1957). The terminology has, of course, changed. It is not now processes or ideas that are associated, but responses. Underwood carries forward the tradition of associationism when, after defining thinking as the understanding of relationships, he says that, for the perception of relationships among stimuli, the appropriate responses to those stimuli should be contiguous.

The chief spokesman for this school of thought on the question of the nature of logical thinking was J. S. Mill, or at least it was Mill whom

Husserl had in mind when attacking psychologism. As Anschutz (1949) has pointed out, Mill's opinions on this issue were by no means consistent, but the general tenor of his work is in line with the view that all knowledge is derived from experience. Thus logic is restricted to knowledge which consists of inferences from truths previously known. It is the science of proof or evidence, or 'the science of the operations of the understanding which are subservient to the estimation of evidence' (Mill, 1874, p. 6). Thus, says Mill, when a logician inquires about the meaning of a proposition he is asking whether it conforms to the facts of experience, because all knowledge, including logical laws, is derived from experience. His psychologism can be seen in his discussion of the two axioms of contradiction and of the excluded middle. The first axiom asserts that an affirmative proposition and the corresponding negative proposition cannot both be true. Mill considers this to be, 'like other axioms', one of our first and most familiar generalizations from experience. 'The original foundation of it, I take to be, that belief and disbelief are two different mental states, excluding one another. This we know by the simplest observation of our own minds' (p. 185). Generalization from experience also accounts for the principle of the excluded middle which states that one of two contradictory statements must be true. Mill registers his surprise that anyone should ever have made this generalization from experience, since one can think of statements which are neither true nor false but meaningless, for example, 'Abracadabra is a second intention'.

Many voices have been raised against the doctrine that thinking consists of fortuitous associations between ideas or responses, but perhaps the principal objection to this theory is that thought is directed and proceeds according to a purpose. Logical thinking is not reducible to a collection of associations but entails necessary connection between its component parts. Blanshard (1939) has argued forcibly for this idea. He quotes as an example Thackeray's story of the Abbé and the nobleman. The Abbé, talking among friends, has just said 'Do you know, ladies, my first penitent was a murderer', and a nobleman of the neighbourhood, entering the room at the moment, exclaims: 'You there, Abbé. Why, ladies, I was the Abbé's first penitent, and I promise you my confession astounded him'. According to Blanshard, given the premises, 'The first penitent was a murderer' and 'X was the first penitent', nothing more need be said as 'the circle of thought completes itself on the instant. And the point to be noted here is that this movement is governed by seen necessity' (p. 458). Again, 'we can watch our thought burgeoning; we can see that it develops as it does because it must, because it is being laid under compulsion by a necessity immanent in the matter before it' (p. 458).

That associationism is quite incapable of explaining the foundation of the necessary connections of logical thinking through an appeal to experience, in Mill's sense of the word, is apparent from the examples of psychologism which Mill provides. His reduction of the axiom of contradiction to our experience that belief and disbelief are two entirely different mental states is refuted by the simple observation that people often do hold contradictory beliefs without any recognition of their doing so. Now this, on Mill's theory that belief and disbelief are mutually exclusive mental states, would be impossible. If it is answered that the individual must recognize these incompatible states, so that he observes them to be contradictory, then we are now presupposing that which we have to explain, for why should the person grant to this recognition its privileged status? Why should he feel compelled to recognize the contradiction? Similarly, in his treatment of the axiom of the excluded middle, Mill misinterprets the nature of logical propositions, which are not abstractions from experience of actual things and events, but, as Husserl emphasizes, have to do with relations which are independent of actual existents.

Husserl's analyses help us to see the limitations of Mill's psychologism and the associationist theory of thinking in general, but it may be questioned whether they advance us nearer to an understanding of the relationship between the subject and the rules he uses, which, it was suggested, is the most basic question facing the psychology of thinking. On the contrary, it seems that the solution to this problem is even more difficult because of Husserl's insistence that the logical be divorced from questions of empirical psychology. As Natorp (reported by Farber, 1943) was quick to point out, the central problem for Husserl, and one which he never resolved, was that, having taken the side of the ideal or logical as against the real or psychological, there appeared to be no relationship between the two and the latter – that which is psychological, empirical and real – remained an incomprehensible, irrational residue. In short, Husserl's solution to the problem was the Platonic one, namely, the view that logic consists of a system of universal laws existing independently of experience and non-psychological in origin. Thus, whilst associationism is unable to distinguish rational from senseless thinking, Husserlian idealism seems quite unable to account for the *transition* from the senseless to the sensible. Mill and Husserl represent the two extremes, between which subsequent theories have steered their course. With what success we shall attempt to assess.

THE GESTALT THEORY OF THINKING

The first major challenge to the associationist theory of thinking came with the formulation of Gestalt psychology. Associationism was based upon an atomistic theory of perception in which sensations were conceptualized as the building-blocks of complex mental processes. Gestalt theory rejected the atomistic bias of associationism in favour of the view that all psychological processes – learning, perception, emotion, and thinking – do not consist of independent elements, but are determined in the situation as a whole. Gestalt psychologists were led to this conclusion by their experiments on perceptual processes which revealed the inadequacies of the traditional perspective.

For the Gestalt psychologist the distinction between a sensation and a percept is dissolved by the recognition that they both involve perceptual processes which differ only in complexity. A so-called sensation of brightness, for example, is never seen in itself and independent of things; we never see a sensation of brightness but, rather, we see a bright object. As Köhler (1930) points out, the starting-point for Gestalt theory was the observation that sensory fields are replete with qualities and properties which one neglects if one takes 'sensations' as their sole content. These properties can only be discovered if we analyse the perceptual field. This notion is stated clearly in Wertheimer's (1923) monograph, in which he formulated the basic laws which govern our visual field, the laws of proximity, similarity, common-fate and closure. Wertheimer demonstrated that we do not react in uniform or constant ways to specific stimuli, as though they were isolated from one another, but that the nature of the setting in which they are found determines the way in which they are perceived. One of the most fundamental of the laws of perception is that a perceptual field is necessarily organized into figure and ground. This is most convincingly demonstrated in those perceptual fields in which figure and ground can alternate, for example, Rubin's 'wife-mother-in-law' drawing, but the principle is implicit in Wertheimer's laws of organization. All the experiments of the Gestalt psychologists deny the basic premise of associationist sensationalism in their demonstration that 'the whole is other than the sum of its parts'.

The Gestalt psychologists drew important theoretical conclusions from these experiments. They concluded that it is not the self or any mental process which brings about the various forms of organization. The observer is unaware of how one stimulus influences another, so that we cannot appeal to his consciousness. Accordingly, Gestalt psychologists assume that the interaction occurs among the brain-correlates of the perceptual facts in question. Thus, the theory asserts that psychological and neurophysiological processes are parallel or isomorphic. Stimuli in the perceptual field interact with one another in lawful ways and, in order to account for this fact, we must postulate that the brain functions as a field. Köhler (1940), following the line of reasoning used by Faraday in his investigations of electrodynamic interactions, suggests that, although the physiological correlate of a percept may be said to have a circumscribed, local existence, it nevertheless acts as a dynamic agent and extends into the surrounding tissue, and that, by this extension, its presence is represented beyond its circumscribed locus. In this way we can account for the dynamic organization of perception and other processes. This isomorphism, a term which signifies equality of structure, makes the assumption that the processes of organization occurring in the brain are identical with the structural processes discernible in perception and thinking. It is the assumed structural identity of these two processes which makes possible a physical-physiological explanation of psychological organization. As Koffka (1935, p. 63) says:

> And now, with the tool of a thorough-going isomorphism in our hands, we return to our balance sheet which we drew up after stating the reasons why, when we come to fundamentals, we must choose a physiological field rather than the behavioural environment as our fundamental category. . . . We are no longer losing the advantage gained by the introduction of the behavioural environment, for we construct our physiological field in accordance with, and directed by, the observed properties of it. Thus we have good reason for introducing and keeping the behavioural environment, even though we look ultimately for physiological explanations.

The same viewpoint is expressed forcibly by Köhler (1940).

The now-classical experiments on thinking in the Gestalt tradition are those by Köhler (1925) on problem-solving in apes, studies by Wertheimer (1945) on complex reasoning processes in humans, and Duncker's (1945) work on factors influencing flexibility or the lack of it (functional fixedness) in problem-solving. The theory underlying this work is most clearly stated by Wertheimer. In opposition to both associationism and logical theory which, he maintains, ignore the structural nature of living thinking, Gestalt theory goes directly to these essential, structural processes. It is argued that when a problem is perceived, structural strains and stresses are established which, if thinking continues, yield vectors in the direction of improvement. The solution of the problem represents a 'good structure', one in which there is harmony between the parts of the field. It can thus be seen that, in place of the isolated elements of the associationists, Gestalt psychology postulates that perceptual processes and factors of past experience exist in interrelationship to form a system, an organized whole or configuration. It is when an existing structure suffers stress, i.e. when the parts do not fit together, that what we call thinking ensues. Thinking is thus the process of reorganization which follows from the tension created by the organism's perception of a problem. The successful accomplishment of this reorganization, when one solves the problem, signifies that insight has been acquired. Insight is that moment of sudden illumination, the 'Aha-experience', when aspects of the situation 'fall into place'. It is insight that distinguishes thinking from blind associations and habits.

We can appreciate readily how closely this theory of thinking is related to Gestalt views on the essentially organized nature of perception and to the isomorphism of psychological and physiological facts. In the first place, it is assumed that perception provides the structures that are utilized in the thinking process. As Helson (1926, p. 54) points out: 'For thinking to progress along logical lines it must proceed within a structure, and this structure is very often furnished in perception. The relation of objects to one another are given in phenomenal configurations won in perception'. This amounts to saying that perception provides the material for thinking, but, whereas for the associationist this material consisted of discrete elements, for the Gestalt theorist the material is already structured and consequently plays some part in determining the direction of thinking. Secondly, the relationship of this theory of thinking to the doctrine of isomorphism is implicit in Wertheimer's dictum that 'structural reasons become causes in the process' (Wertheimer, 1945, p. 239). This can be interpreted to mean that the lack of equilibrium, which stimulates thinking and of which we are conscious when we recognize a problem, is paralleled by a lack of equilibrium in the cortical field and the creation of vectors of a neurophysiological nature which result in the solution of the problem.

Does this theory resolve the question of the relationship between logic and psychology? Koffka (1935) believed that it did. He held that Gestalt psychology overcomes Husserl's objection to a psychological explanation of thinking. Husserl's argument, according to Koffka, rests upon the assumption that psychological relations are merely factual or external. Koffka is quite willing to concede that a psychologism based upon this assumption has indeed been refuted by Husserl.

B

But this refutation does not affect our psychologism – if our theory can rightly be given this name – since in our theory psychological and physiological, or rather psychophysical, processes are organized according to intrinsic or internal relations. This point can only be alluded to. It means that in our theory psychology and logic, existence and substance, even, to some extent, reality and truth, no longer belong to entirely different realms or universes of discourse between which no intelligible relationship exists. (pp. 570-1)

For Gestalt psychology, as we have seen, there are no absolutely unordered data in perception which must needs be associated in order to bring meaningful connections out of chaos. Koffka rejects this assumption when he states that psychophysical processes are organized according to intrinsic or internal relations. In other words, from the outset our perceptions and thoughts consist of organized wholes, whose elements are interdependent by the very fact that they are perceived as wholes. Thus the relationships between these elements are not fortuitous and external but necessary and internal. In all thinking, the problem and the answer to it are not matters of chance; the solution fits the problem like a key fits a lock. The problem creates tension in the system and the correct answer restores equilibrium. In reasoning we experience this process as a necessary and orderly affair: the solution achieves a restructuring of the field in the simplest or only possible way.

Gestalt theory can, therefore, unlike the associationism it was designed to replace, claim to give an adequate explanation of logical thinking. This is Wertheimer's conclusion in his book, *Productive Thinking* (1945). By emphasizing the structural nature of thinking the theory avoids the pitfalls of both associationism and logicism, for it is recognized that necessary relationships are achieved in problem-solving and, at the same time, that they are achieved *by* living thought and not *in* some extra-empirical realm. Indeed, Wertheimer characterizes the traditional laws of logic, the laws of identity, contradiction, and so on, as 'merely limiting cases' (p. 255) because they are blind to the structure of living thought. For example, in traditional logic the term 'and' may combine any two things or propositions, whether or not they belong to each other structurally. Thus, in the statement, 'Two is smaller than three *and* the snow is white', the actual content of each statement means nothing to the actual content of the other. But, Wertheimer says, this empty 'and' is merely an extreme case. In living thought 'and' is not generally used in this way. Instead, there is the 'and' that combines two things which belong to each other, or there is the 'and' that states two things are together which should not be together. These 'ands' involve real relations, the existence of specific wholes and of their dynamics. And it is the same story with other traditional logical terms, which, according to Wertheimer, are extreme forms which are indifferent to the structural relatedness of living thought. We need, therefore, to develop a logic which deals with the logical features and rules of dynamic events, a logic of experience and the ways in which experience is structured.

That Gestalt psychology was of immense importance to the psychology of thinking cannot be denied and will be evident from subsequent chapters. The idea that the task of the psychologist is to analyse the structural relations evident in thinking signified a major departure from the traditional schools of logicism and associationism. However, the theory's importance stems, not from a wholesale acceptance of the Gestalt postulates by subsequent workers, but rather from their desire to recast the insights of the Gestalt psychologists into a more dynamic form. There are, in fact, grave doubts as to whether the Gestalt postulates, as they stand, afford a firm basis for understanding the nature and development of structured thinking. At one moment in his classic study of productive thinking, Wertheimer (1945) cautions the reader not to misunderstand the meaning of Gestalt theory. He says (p. 243) that 'when a picture is given here of the inner, structural dynamics in the determination of processes, it does not mean that in this development man is merely passive'. On the contrary, it is assumed that problem-solving will be aided considerably by attitudes, such as openmindedness and the desire for improvement. But, given the assumptions essential to the theory, it seems impossible not to 'misunderstand' it in the way that Wertheimer indicates. Thinking, it is argued, is determined by imbalances in perceptual and mnemonic configurations creating vectors which result in the solution of the problem. There is no mention here of how the activity of the person contributes materially to the attainment of a necessary answer. It is symptomatic of Gestalt theory's primary concern with perception that Wertheimer should mention attitudinal factors, and not actions which the individual performs on the problem-material, as a defence against the charge of passivity. Of course, the theory insists upon the influence on thinking of experience, both past and present, but this is perceptual experience, which for the Gestalt psychologists serves the same function in the thinking process as the sensations of the associationist. As Piaget (1950) puts it:

In attempting to reduce the mechanisms of intelligence to those characterizing perceptual structures, which are in turn reducible to 'physical Gestalten', the Gestalt theory reverts essentially to classical empiricism, although by far more refined methods. The only difference (and considerable though it is, it has little weight in the face of such a reduction) is that the new doctrine replaces 'associations' by 'structured wholes'. But in both cases operational activity in sensory processes fades into pure receptivity and abdicates in favour of the passivity of automatic mechanisms. (p. 64)

There are those who think this criticism unjustified. Merleau-Ponty (1964), for example, points out that Gestalt psychologists, far from minimizing the role of experience, actually describe the development of different structures throughout human development (Koffka, 1928, 1935). He remarks that to the Gestalt psychologist the accumulation of experience makes possible a restructuring which will re-establish the equilibrium between the organism and its environment at another level. This is an on-going process, since new perceptual forms change the state of the organism with the result that subsequent perceptions interact with these changed organic conditions to originate other new forms, and so development continues. But one still might ask: how are we to describe this function of relating and restructuring the experience given in perception into new forms? Here, Gestalt psychologists have little to offer, other than making use of such terms as 'insight' and 'restructuring', which seem to do nothing more than draw a discrete veil over the process which is central to the psychology of thinking. Gestalt psychologists themselves came to recognize this deficiency, and Duncker's (1945) monograph on functional fixedness was an attempt to rectify this state of affairs by an investigation of the ways in which fixation on the customary uses of objects can limit the ability to solve problems which require looking at things in different and novel ways. This work has not, however, been taken up to any great extent and one reason for this may be the recognition that the Gestalt concepts themselves are not very useful for analysing the process and development of thinking. Indeed, although Piaget accuses the theory of falling into the same error as associationism, there is a sense, also, in which Gestalt theory is open to much the same criticism as was made against Husserl's ideas. For the perceptual configurations of the Gestalt psychologists are 'given' to the thinker rather like the way in which the ideal logical laws are present in the Husserlian conception. Admittedly, the former change in the course of the organism's growth, whilst the latter are fixed and immutable, but there is still the problem of how the thinker makes use of these 'givens' as he struggles to make his thoughts clear. For Husserl, the answer was 'direct intuition', for the Gestalt psychologists, 'insight'. With both theories the explanation of thinking appears to come to a full stop.

The problem of the relationship between logic and the psychology of thinking remains. How is it possible to describe and explain the development of thinking and at the same time do justice to the necessary relationships described by the laws of logic and of which we are aware in our acts of reasoning? None of the theoretical standpoints considered so far has been able to solve this problem, logicism, associationism and Gestalt theory all suffering from some limitation. But Gestalt theory, with its concept of structure, has, I believe, prepared the ground for a solution of the problem which goes some way towards accounting both for the reality of concrete experience and the reality of logical forms.

PIAGET'S THEORY

This problem has been of central concern to Piaget, who, armed with an awareness of the difficulties involved, has proposed that logic and psychology may be reconciled if we accept the hypothesis that 'the intrinsic features of logic have their origin in the activities of the subject' (Beth and Piaget, 1966, p. 136). Piaget has outlined his views in his *Traité de Logique* (Piaget, 1949), in *Logic and Psychology* (Piaget, 1953) and, more fully, in *Mathematical Epistemology and Psychology* (Beth and Piaget, 1966). He has given his position the formal title of 'operationalism', after the notion of Bridgman (1927) that to define something in science is to specify what operations the scientist carries out. According to Piaget, the concept of 'operation' serves as a link between logic and psychology, since, on the one hand, operations are actual, psychological activities, and on the other, they play an indispensable part in logic, which can be regarded as a system of symbolic manipulations.

Piaget (1953) proposes that there are three major alternatives to operationalism. The first of these is 'Platonism', which sees logic as a system of universals existing independently of experience and non-psychological in origin. We have met this view in the consideration of Husserl's theory and concluded, as does Piaget, that this doctrine fails to explain how the mind comes to discover such universals. The second doctrine Piaget calls 'conventionalism'. This states that logic is nothing but a system of conventions or generally accepted rules. A thorough-going, associationist empiricism, such as Mill's, would support this idea, but, as Husserl's critique of this type of psychologism demonstrated, this interpretation distorts the true meaning of logical laws. Conventionalism has, therefore, been replaced by the point of view of logical positivism (e.g. Ayer, 1946), which distinguishes empirical truths, or non-tautological relationships, and tautologies, or purely syntactical relationships. On this theory, logic is a 'well-formed language' which expresses the empirical properties of objects as these are presented in perception; logical relationships are therefore linguistic expressions which translate and code our observations of objects and events. Piaget opposes this thesis by denying that these observations can be experienced apart from logical relationships, for the latter provide the means whereby empirical truths are attained. As an example, he cites his experiments showing that, before the child is able to perceive the horizontal correctly, he must construct a spatial framework of reference, whose construction entails the use of logical operations. He could as easily have quoted from other experiments which are designed to illustrate the basic tenet of operationalism – that intellectual development proceeds and empirical truths are reached through operations carried out either on objects directly or indirectly and symbolically. Thus, from this perspective it is false to separate perceptual 'facts' from operations, since perception itself presupposes forms of organization which interact with operations throughout development. Because of this interaction the child is not given a ready-made logic by his perceptions but must construct logical relationships in the course of his transactions with the world.

What precisely does Piaget mean by an operation? In answering this it is first necessary to emphasize the importance that he attaches to action in the development of thinking. This will be discussed in a more concrete way in the next chapter, but, for the time being, note that in Piaget's system the development of intelligence begins with the infant actively exploring his environment and building up cognitive structures through the co-ordination of actions. To this, the first period of mental development, Piaget gives the name of sensori-motor development, indicating that progress occurs through the inter-relating of actions which the child performs. However, there comes a stage at which the child becomes capable of combining and co-ordinating actions internally, that is, without the necessity of actually carrying them out; so, for example, if there were an obstacle in the way of a door opening fully, the child would initially have to carry out the action of opening the door to discover the impediment, but at a later age will be able to carry out this action in his mind, so that he will know he must remove the obstacle before opening the door. Piaget calls such internalized actions operations when, in the course of subsequent development, they become organized into cognitive systems or structures. An operation represents an action and, just as actions become coordinated, so do operations develop into stable cognitive structures. The most significant operations for the developmental psychology of thinking are logical operations, such as classification, relation and implication. These, according to Piaget, must of necessity form into logical systems, since the existence of one presupposes and is dependent upon the existence of others. Thus, for example, in order to classify, one must have a general ability to form other classes, one must be able to add classes together, or subtract one class from another, and so on. One cannot consider the isolated operation, since this acquires its meaning from the system to which it belongs. This reiterates Gestalt theory about the relations of part and whole, but whereas the units of this theory had the passive quality of automatic mechanisms, the operations of Piagetian psychology emerge from the simple sensorimotor activities of the infant and are capable of being further transformed throughout development.

Thus operationalism insists that logical operations develop from experience but it is essential to bear in mind that this is an experience which has to do with actions which the subject carries out on the objects around him. Accordingly, Piaget makes the distinction between 'physical experience' and logico-mathematical experience. For example, when a child discovers that a big pebble is heavier than a small one, we can speak of an experience of a physical type, since, while the child is weighing the pebbles in his hands, he discovers a property which already belonged to the pebbles before his action. On the other hand, when he puts five pebbles in a row and discovers that the number 'five' remains the same whether he counts from left to right or from right to left, this experience is of a logico-mathematical nature because it does not relate to the pebbles themselves, but to the relations between the activity of ordering and forming a sum. What the child discovers is thus not a property of the pebbles as such but that the result of the operation of addition is independent of the order followed. This is, therefore, an abstraction from experience, but it is an abstraction from actions and not from objects. In the course of development these actions are internalized as operations, and it comes about that these operations can sooner or later be carried out symbolically without further attention being paid to objects themselves. In this manner arise logic and mathematics which have to do with the manipulation of symbols without reference to specific objects.

Piaget emphasizes that this logico-mathematical experience is not to be confused with 'psychological experience', in which we discover through introspection properties of the subject's experience and behaviour, for example, that by working too long we become tired or that the action of ordering is difficult, and so on. Logico-mathematical experience is not concerned with such individual phenomena, but with the results of action in so far as they are objective and necessary, in other words, in so far as these results are separated from the individual and common to every subject carrying out the same action. A second important difference between logico-mathematical and psychological experience is that the latter may include any actions (for example, laughing or sneezing) whilst the former only includes actions which, once internalized, will be transformed into operations. Here, Piaget makes a fundamental point about the nature of those actions which become internalized as operations and which therefore provide the structures of logico-mathematical experience. He says (Beth and Piaget, 1966, p. 235):

> In fact, actions such as combining (or separating), ordering (in one direction or in the complementary direction), putting into correspondence, etc., actions which form the starting point of the elementary operations of classes and relations, are not simply actions capable of being performed on external objects: they are primarily actions whose schemes express the general co-ordination of all actions, for every action (from simple reflexes to actions which are learnt such as picking a flower or lighting a pipe) presupposes at least one of the co-ordinations consisting of the ordering of successive movements or the combining of elements etc. This is why such schemes have a completely general significance and are not characteristic merely of one or another of the actions of a single individual.

Piaget is asserting that all actions can be regarded as expressing, in however elementary a way, certain general features. The key word is 'co-ordination', which signifies the relating of actions into a whole. All activities, says Piaget, involve ordering and combining movements and there are general laws by which such co-ordinations are effected. These are general both in the sense that all actions exemplify them in various degrees of elaboration and in the sense that they are common to all subjects. At the sensori-motor level the rules are enacted and remain implicit in the infant's activities, but at a later stage, through the internalization of actions and the formation of operations, we become capable of making explicit, conscious use of these rules and become aware of them as a system of possible transformations.

The formal necessity inherent in logical and mathematical thinking may be accounted for, on this way of reasoning, by the fact that the actions and operations which are co-ordinated are not the peculiar actions of individual subjects but are actions common to all subjects; Piaget describes them (Beth and Piaget, p. 238) as 'the most general co-ordinations of every system of actions, thus expressing what is common to all subjects, and therefore referring to the universal or epistemic subject and not the individual one'. These general schemes of action, the roots of which must be sought in the nervous and biological organization of the subject, lay the foundation for the development of the higher mental processes. The fact that logical laws are universal laws, in the sense that they relate to any objects whatever, is explained by their being rooted in the actions common to all subjects, whilst these actions themselves are rooted in the neurophysiological organization of man.

Putting this conclusion in a slightly different form, one might say that logical laws are self-evident because they are expressions of the essential structures of action. On the issue of 'self-evidence' Piaget is anxious to find a path between Platonism, which asserts that the self-evident rules are given once and for all and are thus independent of experience, and relativism, which assumes them to be dependent upon circumstances and thus self-evident in only the most restricted sense. In the first place, he distinguishes between the problems of self-evidence which arise in connection with physical experience and those connected with logico-mathematical experience. In the former, although physical truth is assessed by the use of logico-mathematical thinking and the concordance of empirical data with such thinking, that which is seen as self-evident at one time may be regarded as quite false at another. On the other hand, in logico-mathematical thinking, that which is self-evident at one time, for instance, the axioms of Euclidian geometry, is not refuted by new advances but takes its place within a more general system. Thus non-Euclidean geometry has not abolished Euclidean self-evidence, but has only limited its generality. It is true, therefore, that there is a succession of varieties of self-evidence but, in the logical field, this should be conceived as a process of integration in which the general framework is expanded to include previous schemes as particular cases. Piaget maintains that this principle is apparent, not only in the history of logic and mathematics, but also

B*

in the development of individuals, where the cognitive structures of one stage are integrated into those of the next.

Logical operations develop from sensori-motor actions which, in turn, are determined by the structural properties of the nervous system. But, if logical operations are a continuation of sensori-motor activity, the question immediately arises: how can novel structures develop when the course of development appears to be predetermined in this way? Piaget recognizes that this consideration is crucial to his theory, and that, if he cannot account for novelty, his theory runs the risk of ending with the absurd conclusion that the whole of logic and mathematics is contained preformed in advance in the co-ordination of actions, just as preformist embryologists thought they had discovered an homunculus in the spermatozoa or the ova. In answering this question, he makes the distinction between an invention and a discovery. He defines an invention (Beth and Piaget, p. 204) as the creation of a new and free combination, not realized up to then either in nature or in the subject's mind, although the elements that have been combined may have been already known. A discovery, on the other hand, is the process by which a subject becomes aware of an object till then unknown to him, but which existed in the same form before his discovery of it. America was discovered; Esperanto was invented. Now, according to Piaget, mathematical constructions and creations cannot be reduced to either discoveries or inventions. A mathematical creation is not an invention, for the new elements in the creation are not 'free' in the sense that they might be different; there is, for instance, an element of arbitrariness in the invention of Esperanto, since other artificial languages could be and have been invented. At the same time, mathematical creation is not discovery in the sense defined above, because the created structure is not the same as the one from which it was derived. Thus, when the child discovers that the result of an addition is independent of the order followed, the creative process consists of translating a succession of material actions into a system of internalized operations. This is more than discovery, since there is a reconstruction on a new level of cognitive functioning and the attainment of a more general structure. Piaget is thus led to state that the relationship between the early sensori-motor stage and later stages consists of the latter actualizing the possibilities inherent in the former. This means that the elementary sensori-motor structures involve a whole series of possible developments and that the novelty of later structures consists in the actualization of some of them. These later, novel structures are at once new and non-arbitrary; they are new, because they are not contained in the earlier structures, and they are non-arbitrary, 'because they are contained in a predetermined framework of possibilities' (Beth and Piaget, p. 303). The paradox of logico-mathematical creation is that the subject actively constructs the solution of the problem and yet experiences the solution as a necessary result of his activities.

The task that Piaget has set himself, therefore, is to describe the emergence of the structures of logico-mathematical thinking from the sensori-motor activities of the infant. The theory would be incomplete, however, if he did not also explain *why* structures develop as they do. What, in brief, causes the progression from simpler to more complex and general levels? With this question we are beginning to exceed the bounds of this chapter, but Piaget's answer to it can be given in outline. In fact, his views on this issue are implicit in the contention, stated above, that the more advanced structures actualize the possibilities inherent in the simpler ones. If this is the case, then a principle is called for which will explain how structures develop from one another in a non-arbitrary and definite manner. For Piaget, this principle is the idea of 'equilibration'. He maintains that the organism attempts to establish a state of equilibrium or balance with its environment; when this is attained we may speak of the organism being adapted to its environment. This is regarded, not as a closed, but as an open and dynamic equilibrium, and, Piaget (1950) argues, there is an autonomous tendency for development to progress from relatively unstable to more and more stable forms of adaptation, presumably within the limits set by the organism's physical capacities. Thus, to take an extreme case, the adaptation of the subject who can think in abstract terms and hypothetically is more stable than that of the sensori-motor subject, since the latter is governed by the here and now and by the immediate consequences of his actions, while the former can range freely in his thoughts over the past, present and future. The development of adaptation and the development of the logical structures of thinking are, on this view, parallel, since both arise through the process of 'equilibration'.

We are now in a position to state Piaget's views on the relationship between logic and psychology. He does not assert that one is reducible to the other, but, rather, that logic is the formal study of operational structures, whilst the psychology of thinking studies their real functioning and development (Piaget, 1949). Logic is concerned with the problems of formal deductions from axioms while psychology studies the development of logical structures. There is thus a complete independence of methods and a *possible* correspondence of problems; a methodological independence, since one cannot invoke psychological facts to solve problems of formal logic, nor formal logical procedures to explain the necessity inherent in logical laws or the development of structures which account for this necessity; and a possible correspondence of problems, since the problems solved by formal logic can correspond to psychological questions, for instance, each axiomatically derived structure corresponds to a real, psychological structure, either one common to all thinking at a certain stage of development or, at least, to a structure in the mind of the logician, and, conversely, every structure attained by the constructions of the individual can be understood in formal terms. Therefore, logic and psychology reflect one another, because, while remaining autonomous in their methods, they are complementary. Consequently, since each discipline raises problems for the other, it is the task of empirical research, in which psychologists and logicians collaborate, to study these common problems.

Bruner (in Harms, 1960) has suggested that this is a circular argument, for, having described thought structures in terms of formal logic, how can we then establish parallels between the laws of logic and the laws of thought? To be sure, there is a limitation imposed by looking at thinking through the language of formal logic, since the language we choose will determine what we find. But this is a general condition of all inquiry and hardly, therefore, a criticism that can be levelled against the choice of a logical language in particular. However, the major misconception underlying the criticism of circularity is that it ignores the fact that the methods of the two disciplines are radically different, the one being empirical, the other formal. Thus, there is nothing circular about verifying results obtained by two different methods against one another. Complementariness is, at least in principle, sought for, and not merely assumed. Bruner agrees with Piaget, though, that formal logic is a very powerful tool for analysing thinking because of the interconnectedness of its propositions; for example, if the child asserts one logical relationship, we can inquire whether he understands the full logical implications of the assertion by making use of the interconnected formal rules of logic. But, says Bruner (p. 26), 'this finding is certainly not correspondence of logic and thought any more than that between behaviour and geometry by virtue of the fact that for a person to walk from A to C, the two separated by region B, he must follow the route ABC'. But let us try to be clear on this point. It is not, as Bruner seems to maintain, simply the interconnectedness of formal logic which ensures its usefulness, since a formal system can contain many highly connected propositions and still be quite irrelevant to actual thought. Indeed, it is difficult to understand how the analyses of formal logic can be so useful if there is not some correspondence with the psychology of thinking, if, in short, formal logic is not a language which corresponds well to the reality of human thinking. As Piaget points out (Beth and Piaget, p. 311), it is not a question of using the language of formal logic to describe thought structures merely because this is a convenient and precise language or a stimulus to the imagination. The fundamental reason for this usage is that 'the logician's thought is the most articulated form of human thought'. This means that there is a continuity between ordinary and logical thought and that the latter can be used in the study of the former precisely because of its power to articulate and formalize those very psychological processes upon which it is based.

DISCUSSION

The question posed at the beginning of this chapter concerned the nature of the rules in the process of thinking. We have looked at a number of answers to this question of how the thinker makes use of such rules and how these rules are derived. The choice appears to be between, on the one hand, the doctrine that rules exist *a priori* and, on the other, various versions of the idea that such rules are derived from experience and arise in the course of development. The former is hardly a satisfactory standpoint for the psychology of thinking since it leaves the question of the relationship between the existing subject and the rules an unsolvable mystery, but the doctrine's central insight, especially evident in Husserl's writings, that logical rules are, in some sense, necessary and self-evident, does pose a problem for psychological theories. Of these, associationism and Gestalt theory seem to offer inadequate or incomplete solutions, the former because, essentially, it has no means of accounting for the necessary relationships of reasoning, the latter because it is unable to account for the development of cognitive structures (to which necessary relationships are due) and for the role of the actions of the individual in problem-solving. The most plausible thesis is an operational theory of thinking which regards cognitive structures as systems of internalized actions (operations) and which can, therefore, explain both the development of thinking and the fact that solutions to problems are necessary and not fortuitous.

Before we consider Piaget's operationalism in greater detail, however, there are a number of major issues which arise from a comparison of his views with other theories already outlined. No attempt will be made, for the moment, to evaluate opinion on these issues; rather, they are stated simply to provide a framework for viewing the more detailed exposition of Piaget's theory.

The similarities between the operationalisms of Dewey and Piaget are striking. Besides the common emphasis upon activity, rather than sensations or perceptions, there is the parallel between Piaget's 'internalization of actions' and Dewey's distinction between operations overtly performed and those symbolically executed; both theorists regard logical forms as originating in action and the operations of inquiry and both make a distinction between physical and logico-mathematical experience, the latter deriving from abstraction from actions and, therefore, as Dewey says, testable only by its non-incompatibility with other operations. But there are also very basic differences between them. In the first place, Dewey would, no doubt, reject Piaget's notion of the 'epistemic subject' and the idea that sensori-motor activities constitute a predetermined framework of possibilities for intellectual development. Dewey would in all probability assert that this idea is nothing but a resurrection of rationalist conceptions of innate properties of the mind and argue, instead, that the worth of ideas is not to be tested by their conformity to an *a priori* framework but by the consequences of their operation.

> Conception and systems of conceptions, ends in view and plans, are constantly making and remaking as fast as those already in use reveal their weaknesses, defects and positive values. There is no predestined course they must follow. Human experience consciously guided by ideas evolves its own standards and measures and each new experience constructed by their means is an opportunity for new ideas and ideals.
>
> (Dewey, 1930, p. 161)

It is apparent from these views that operationalism by itself does not resolve the conflict between empiricism and rationalism; it results merely in a reformulation of the problem. A second difference between Piaget and Dewey concerns the role of language, or, more generally, symbols, in the development of thinking. Piaget characteristically speaks about the internalization of actions, giving the impression that symbols themselves play, at most, a subsidiary role. For Dewey, on the other hand, it is the invention of symbols which enables us to carry out internalized operations and thus to begin to think. He distinguishes two kinds of symbols, those tied to particular contexts – mainly, one supposes, words – and the technical symbols of scientific thinking. Again we are confronted with a major issue, for some theorists have claimed that thinking is dependent upon language, while others have asserted its independence.

Piaget's theory agrees with Gestalt theory in the importance it attaches to the concept of structure and to equilibrium as the driving force of thinking, although in Piaget's theory the parts of the structure are conceived as actions and operations. However, a most important difference between the two theories centres around their conceptions of the nature of logical rules. Wertheimer (1945) suggested that we need to develop a logic of experience which would reflect the structures of living thought. But there is a fundamental difference between the two positions. In Piaget's case, the laws discernible in thinking derive their universality from being abstractions from actions common to all men, and therefore they are ultimately independent of particular situations. For Wertheimer, on the other hand, logical terms derive their different meanings from the various contexts in which they occur and they will only be universal in so far as these contexts are universal. At this point one can argue either that there are certain preoccupations common to all men or that the diversity of human environments and purposes precludes the existence of universal laws of thinking. This is a weighty question. However, it may be given a somewhat more empirical formulation. A major issue which emerges from a comparison of Wertheimer's and Piaget's views concerns the relative influence of situational and operational factors. To what extent, for instance, do language, social norms and structures, and the technologies of different societies influence the development of operational thinking and how do they exert their influence? These questions can, of course, be investigated by cross-cultural studies.

Piaget argues that the development of logical thinking is due to the progressive adaptation of the human organism to its environment. Husserl (1900), on the other hand, has contested the view that the facts of adaptation can be used to explain the laws of logical thinking, since this amounts to confusing actual cases with ideal principles. It has been argued that Husserl has drawn too sharp and drastic a distinction between the ideal and the real, but, at the same time, it must be admitted that it is by no means obvious why, in Piaget's scheme, progressive adaptation and the development of logical structures should be parallel. On the contrary, it seems that the correspondence of the two is impossible, if adaptation implies some form of adjustment to the demands of particular situations and if, as Piaget assumes, logical structures are universal and thus independent of particular contexts. Clearly, Piaget's views on this issue need to be examined more fully before any evaluation can be made, but, since this seems to be an assumption basic to his whole theory, it is evident that particular attention must be given to the way in which he states the relationship between adaptation and the development of logical rules.

This review of theories of the relationship between logic and psychology thus leads to the general conclusion that, although operationalism appears to be the most plausible thesis, there are a number of basic questions which must be directed towards Piaget's theory. This discussion indicates four questions. Does the development of logical thinking inevitably follow a course determined by the universal nature of sensori-motor actions? What is the relationship of language and other symbolic forms to the development of thinking? Are logical rules universal or dependent upon particular contexts? And how can the facts of adaptation account for the development of logical thinking? We shall return to these questions in our assessment of Piaget's theory and the work which it has inspired.

In summary, thinking may be defined as problem-solving but the essential feature of this activity, if it is to qualify as reasoning or logical thinking, is an adherence to certain rules. A central problem for the psychology of thinking is, therefore, to account for the relationship between the psychological subject and these rules, which confer upon his thinking the qualities of rigour and necessity. Formal logic has long been concerned with the elaboration of rules of reasoning, so that the question may be recast into the form: what is the relationship between logic and psychology? Husserl advanced the argument that logical laws deal with absolutely necessary and self-evident relationships, with the result that psychology, which is an empirical discipline whose laws can only be expressed as probabilities, is not in a position to explain these relationships. This argument, convincing as it may be against associationist psychology, loses its force in relation to Gestalt psychology, which replaced atomistic associations by the concept of structure: the interrelations of parts of a structure are necessary and not fortuitous. However, Gestalt psychology itself had no place for the operational activity of the subject in problem-solving and tended to reduce intelligence to perceptual structures. Piaget's solution to this problem is to insist that 'the intrinsic features of logic have their origins in the activity of the subject'. His theory retains the Gestalt notion of structure (although the parts are now conceived as actions and operations), but he suggests that structures develop through a process of abstraction from one's actions. This development is seen as an actualization of the possibilities inherent in the elementary structures provided by sensori-motor experience.

2

The developmental theory
of Jean Piaget

Piaget began his career as a zoologist, studying the behaviour of molluscs and, especially, the ways in which these creatures adapt to their different environments. At the same time, he informs us (in Tanner and Inhelder, 1956a), he was taking a lively interest in problems of knowledge, logic and the history of the sciences. Feeling that the approaches of philosophers to these problems were far too speculative and not sufficiently experimental, he decided to spend 'four or five years' studying the development of logical thinking in the child. This interim study has turned out to be his life's work, spanning a period of some forty years. Piaget's work during this period has taken many forms and has been concerned with diverse problems, but there is a remarkable continuity in this research, a continuity which originates in his initial interest in problems of biology and the philosophy of knowledge. These constitute a dialectic underlying all the theory and research, for, on the one hand, there are the facts pertaining to man as a physical organism – the facts of biology and neurophysiology which indicate that man is equipped with a certain physico-chemical structure and that he must adapt to his environment in order to survive, while, on the other hand, are the constructions of man the thinker – the social and physical sciences themselves, logic, mathematics, social conventions and laws. The philosophical problem, which arises from the confrontation of these two sets of data, is, broadly stated: how do we formulate the relationship between human achievements, which include scientific laws and generalizations, and those conditions which science asserts determine our experience and behaviour? The research which Piaget has undertaken represents an attempt to answer this question – the question of the nature and status of human knowledge – by experiment and observation, but there is implicit in this research a particular way of formulating the nature of this dialectic and, by generalization, a particular conception of the nature of explanation in psychology.

Piaget has recently made explicit his views on the question of explanation (Piaget, Fraisse and Reuchlin, 1968). He identifies seven main types of explanation. The first four of these are reductionist, differing principally in the type of substrate to which psychological processes are reduced. Thus, we have explanation by reduction to a psychogenetic principle, as, for instance, with the Freudian notion that adult personality is largely a result of identifications made during childhood, reduction to social structure and conditions, reduction to physical and to organic processes. The second group of explanations are, Piaget believes, complementary to reductionist models. These include behavioural explanations of the type favoured by Hull or Skinner, in which consequences are deduced from certain principles but no assumptions are made about the kind of reductionism, to which behavioural laws will eventually be submitted; a second non-reductionist explanation is the genetic, which consists, as in Piaget's own work on the development of operational structures, in tracing the development of processes as a result of the transactions of the subject with his environment; and, finally, there is explanation based upon abstract models, in which a formal scheme, such as probability theory, information theory or formal logic, is used to make deductions, often novel and unexpected, which can then be tested against actual behaviour.

Piaget argues that it is not a question of deciding that one, and one only, of these methods is correct. Rather, he believes that a psychological explanation must be both reductionist and abstract for the reasons that the problem facing such an explanation is to find a means of accounting for the uniqueness of conscious events while at the same time allowing for the eventual reduction of these events to their factual origins. The uniqueness of conscious events is evident from the fact that we cannot appeal to the laws of neurophysiology to explain the validity of the law of relativity, or why $2 + 2 = 4$, or why the individual normally obeys social conventions. But equally there is no doubt that the recognition of all these truths is dependent upon a system of nervous connections, so that the formulation and acceptance of these truths must be consistent with laws which neurophysiology and biology will elaborate. Piaget maintains, then, that the adoption of abstract models, such as logic and probability theory, is indispensable for understanding the uniqueness of conscious constructions, but that this does not preclude the reduction of these to their physical and organic bases.

What is the peculiar nature of these constructions? Piaget observes that the truth of $2+2 = 4$ is not the 'cause' of the truth of $4-2 = 2$ in the same way that a cannon causes the movement of billiard balls or a stimulus is one of the causes of a reaction. In the same way, the value attributed to an aim or moral obligation is not the 'cause' of an action connected with the obligation. In both cases we talk, not of causes, but of implications, and this is because consciousness consists of systems of relations or meanings. There are deductive, implicational systems which receive expression in logic and mathematics, as well as aesthetic implications and valuational implications, formalized in systems of ethics, law and social conventions. In all these instances, says Piaget, consciousness is essential in order to judge truth and value, that is, to reach the implications which specifically characterize them. The fruit of this argument is, then, the assertion that the idea of causality does not apply to consciousness, since one state of consciousness implies rather than causes another. We are now in a position to understand the virtue of abstract models for the description of conscious events; it lies precisely in the fact that they disregard questions of causality which characterize the various reductionist explanations. Abstract models themselves operate with implications and deductions; they can be valid independent of any reference to concrete, causal agencies, and can, therefore, be powerful tools in analysing conscious processes.

But if implication is the form of explanation applicable to conscious constructions and causality that appropriate to physical and physiological systems, it would appear that they are mutually exclusive and cannot, therefore, be related. Piaget's solution to this dilemma is to suggest that the two sets of data are ultimately reconcilable, since the relationship between systems of implication and systems of causality is that of isomorphism. The clearest example of such isomorphism is provided by electronic computers which are capable of solving complex problems. Each operation which the computer uses is parallel or isomorphic with a logical or mathematical operation, so that there is complete isomorphism between the conscious system of operations and the mechanical system. The machine itself is contructed according to the principles of electronics and engineering and is therefore governed by causality; on the other hand, the truth or falsehood of the propositions is a matter for conscious evaluation by means of the rules of implication of deductive reasoning. Piaget is fond of pointing to the research of McCulloch and Pitts (1943) which appears to demonstrate the isomorphism of nervous functioning with the relational system of propositional logic. This work, he maintains, holds out the hope that we shall eventually be able to describe the complete isomorphism between neurophysiological processes and those logico-mathematical operations which represent the highest achievements of human thought.

However, the doctrine of isomorphism between physical-causal and conscious-implicational data does not answer the question of how higher levels of thinking develop from elementary biological mechanisms. If the brain and consciousness can be compared to a computer in the sense that mechanical and deductive-implicational analyses are complementary, we have still to account for the development of these parallel physical and psychological operations. Indeed, this is Piaget's central concern, for he has stated on a number of occasions (e.g. Piaget, 1950, 1967) that his work is directed at explaining how superior levels of scientific thinking arise from biological mechanisms. This is the novel way in which he has framed the question of the nature and status of human knowledge – the question of epistemology which has been traditionally answered by pure speculation. Piaget insists that this is an empirical question and, to understand the full implications of his psychological theory and research, it is essential to bear in mind his dual concern with problems of biology and epistemology. But it is clearly not sufficient to point to an isomorphism of causality and implication to account for the development of psychophysiological structures, since we require dynamic concepts to explain their emergence. Thus, although it is necessary to construct abstract models to analyse conscious constructions and reductionist models to account for the causation of physical and organic systems, we also require developmental or genetic concepts. The explanation of thinking requires that we pursue three complementary lines of inquiry; we need concepts dealing with physical and neurophysiological processes, abstract models to handle implicational relations, and genetic concepts to explain how such implicational thinking develops. For Piaget, the results of these approaches will eventually prove complementary, since he affirms that genetic concepts explain the development of structures, which can be described either in physical-causal or in conscious-implicational terms. The genetic concepts are, therefore, fundamental, in so far as it is their task to account for the dynamics of physical systems and the dynamics of conscious experience. Consequently, our exposition of Piaget's theory must begin with a discussion aimed at discovering just how Piaget proposes that such concepts can fulfil this function.

THE BASIC DEVELOPMENTAL CONCEPTS

Adaptation

In his early studies of the behaviour of molluscs Piaget had become interested in the ways in which they adapted to their environment. His theory of thinking takes a cue from biology in that adaptation is accepted as a principle which holds for both biology and psychology. One of the most fundamental functions of living matter is that of incorporating into its structure nutrition-providing elements from the outside. The organism sustains itself and grows by means of such transactions with the environment. Piaget noted that there are certain invariant attributes of this kind of functioning. First, the organism must transform the substances it takes in in order to incorporate their food values into its system. New elements cannot be incorporated without being changed in some way. The process of changing elements in the environment in such a way that they can be incorporated into the structure of the organism is called *assimilation*. The manner in which the element is changed may vary, but the process as such always occurs when adaptation takes place. Secondly, in assimilating foodstuffs the organism is also adjusting itself to them – it may secrete digestive juices, open its mouth, and so on. Just as objects are adjusted to the peculiar nature of the organism, as in assimilation, so also must the organism adjust itself to the demands of the object. This latter process is called *accommodation*. However, although assimilation and accommodation can be distinguished conceptually and this distinction serves a useful purpose, in reality they are indissociable: every assimilation involves an accommodation and, conversely, every accommodation involves assimilation.

The continuity between biological and intellectual functioning is provided for in Piaget's system by the proposition that intellectual functioning is also characterized by the processes of assimilation and accommodation. Assimilation in the intellectual sphere refers to the fact that every cognitive encounter with an environmental object or event necessarily involves some kind of cognitive structuring of that object or event in accordance with the nature of the organism's existing intellectual organization. Thus every act of intelligence, however rudimentary, presupposes an interpretation of something in external reality, that is, an assimilation of that something to some kind of meaning system in the organism's cognitive organization. At the same time, in every cognition there has to be some 'coming to grips' with or accommodation to the properties of the thing apprehended. The essence of accommodation consists in adapting oneself to the requirements and demands which the world of objects imposes upon one. Although in reality assimilation and accommodation are indissociable, behaviour may show different degrees of one or the other. A simple accommodation to external reality signifies an imitation of or a conformity to the external event without the degree of assimilation necessary for a meaningful interaction of subject and object. At the other extreme, simply assimilating an event to existing structures signifies that no attempt is made to grasp the peculiar significance of the event, which thus remains a mere expression, or, in psychoanalytic parlance, a projection of that structure. It is therefore clear that both assimilation and accommodation are necessary for an organism to adapt to and 'know' its environment, since the characteristics of both organism and event can be related only when both are present.

It cannot be emphasized too much that the basic unit of analysis provided by the adaptation model is the organism *within* its environment and not the organism *and* its environment or just the organism. Furth (1969) expresses this well when he writes that the term 'adaptation' introduces the fruitful notion that organism and environment are two interlocking systems. Environmental events do not impose their nature upon a passive organism any more than the organism produces whatever results it desires on an indifferent environment. From the start subject and environment are intimately related, for the living organism is at birth provided with certain ways of orientating itself and behaving towards its environment and these characteristic patterns provide a framework for the influence of environmental events. At the same time, the existence of the environment itself in its spatial and temporal organization provides a setting for the activities of the organism. Organism and environment are, therefore, adapted to one another initially in the sense that each provides a framework for the influence of the other. As adults we are accustomed to thinking of subject and object as two separate categories, but this is, as Piaget has demonstrated, the result of a later stage of thinking and the adoption of this distinction to describe the primary relationship between subject and environment only results in a failure to grasp their inherent interrelatedness.

One further implication of the adaptation model may be brought out at this point. In analysing the functions of assimilation and accommodation in the organism-environment interaction, Piaget wishes to convey the idea that this interaction is dynamic and progressive. Pure assimilatory activity and simple accommodation to external events alike involve no genuine intellectual development, because both lack the essential element of confrontation between subject and object. A crucial aspect of adaptive behaviour, on the other hand, is that such a confrontation leads to a change in the subject-object relationship: we can speak loosely of the subject 'knowing' more about his environment, without, of course, assuming that this is necessarily a conscious knowledge. Thus, just as at the biological level the organism grows by the assimilation of foodstuffs, so at the psychological level each adaptive transaction between subject and environment results in a change in the intellectual condition of the subject. Subsequent transactions build upon these acquisitions so that development proceeds in an orderly fashion. To understand the characteristics of this orderly growth and to appreciate that it contains its own dynamic, we must now define two further concepts – the concepts of structure and equilibration.

Structure

The concept of structure refers to the fact that elements are interrelated and organized. This notion is implicit in the description of adaptation as involving two interlocking systems, for to talk of a system is to signify that there are lawful relationships which characterize and, indeed, constitute the system. Piaget has emphasized that assimilation and accommodation cannot occur without some form of organization:

> Organization is inseparable from adaptation. They are two complementary processes of a single mechanism, the first being the internal aspect of the cycle of which adaptation constitutes the external aspect. . . . The 'accord of thought with things' and the 'accord of thought with itself' express this dual functional invariant of adaptation and organization. These two aspects of thought are indissociable: it is by adapting to things that thought organizes itself and it is by organizing itself that it structures things.
>
> (Piaget, 1952a, p. 8)

It can be seen that 'structuring' and organization are, for Piaget, at the very heart of behaviour: all intelligent behaviour involves a structuring or restructuring of the environment, some sort of organization within which it proceeds.

What does Piaget mean by a cognitive as distinct from a physiological structure? In the case of organic adaptation, the interaction is of a material nature and it involves a physical transaction between a part of the body and a part of the external environment. Psychological or cognitive transactions are, however, functional in nature; in these instances, although we still speak of an assimilation of objects, the objects themselves are not altered but are subsumed under the particular activities of the organism. For example, a child confronted with a novel object will act towards that object in certain characteristic ways, striking out at it, grasping, and so on. The object itself undergoes no change, but it is incorporated into existing structures. Similarly, in this example the child's actions may be modified by the particular features of the object, for, in so far as the object is novel, new and possibly finer co-ordinations of actions will be necessary. Thus cognitive structures are, in the first instance, organizations of actions developed through adaptation. This is what Piaget means by the complementariness of the 'accord of thought with itself' and the 'accord of thought with things', since in the process of adapting to objects and events our actions become interco-ordinated. But, although assimilation and accommodation invariably occur in all behaviour, cognitive structures themselves undergo transformations as development proceeds. The structures of the infant are different from those of the child or the adolescent. Piaget aims to describe the essential features of the structures which typify different levels of intellectual development and the process by which such structures develop from one another.

In describing the way in which external reality is assimilated and accommodated to, Piaget makes use of the concept of *scheme*.* A scheme may be defined as the organization of an adaptive action, in short, as a particular cognitive structure. Following Flavell (1963), instead of giving an exhaustive, formal definition of a scheme, it may be helpful to list certain of its attributes to illustrate the manner in which Piaget uses the concept. In the first place, a scheme is defined by the behaviour sequence to which it refers. Thus, in talking about early, sensori-motor development, Piaget speaks of the scheme of sucking, grasping, sight, and so on. This use signifies that a scheme is a particular organization of an activity. With respect to later developments, Piaget refers to the utilization of logical rules, such as relation or classification ,as operational schemes: these too are organizations of actions, but, whereas the former are overt actions, these are 'internalized actions', covertly performed. But, secondly, if Piaget does define schemes of action by the type of action they represent, he does not mean that they are those sequences and nothing else. In talking of

* In most English translations of Piaget's work the term 'schema' is used. However, Piaget and Inhelder (1966) have made a distinction between a scheme and a schema (see below) and, in order to give an accurate account of the theory, it is desirable to adhere to the Geneva convention.

a scheme he wishes to imply that assimilatory functioning has generated a specific cognitive structure. For example, in the case of the scheme of grasping, he intends to convey, not just that the infant shows grasping behaviour, but that he has an organized disposition to grasp objects on repeated occasions. Similarly, once in possession of a logical scheme, the child will apply this course of action to the problems he meets. The final consequence of this usage is the implication that a psychological 'organ' has been created, functionally equivalent to the physiological digestive organ in that it constitutes an instrument for incorporating aspects of reality. Piaget has elaborated this latter notion in a work (Piaget, 1967), in which he makes fully explicit the biological basis of his theory and, in particular, the assumptions that cognitive functions extend organic regulations and that they are a differentiated organ which regulates exchanges with the external environment. Intellectual development entails an increasing differentiation of this organ with the complementary increase in the power to differentiate aspects of the external environment. It must be emphasized that in using such terminology Piaget is not merely resorting to a figure of speech. On the contrary, he wishes to place his theory firmly within a biological perspective in order to carry out his programme of tracing the emergence of thinking from the biological facts of adaptation.

Schemes range from the simple reflex activities of the infant to the complex problem-solving strategies of the adult. However, all schemes possess the quality of being organized wholes and of having component actions which are closely related. There are, moreover, three functions common to all schemes. All schemes, once constituted, apply themselves again and again to assimilable aspects of the environment. Piaget speaks of reproductive or functional assimilation in referring to this tendency of schemes to repetition. Secondly, in the course of their repeated use, schemes extend their field of application to assimilate new and different objects. This is called generalizing assimilation. Thirdly, schemes are said to undergo internal differentiation. In the course of his repeated contact with objects the subject is able to make increasingly finer discriminations between them; the result of this is a 'recognition' of the different properties of objects, so that Piaget refers to this function of the operation of schemes as recognitory assimilation.

Equilibration

The concepts of adaptation and structure describe the organism functioning within its environment but they leave open the question of the development of the organism. To account for the development of structures Piaget introduces the concept of equilibration. This is one of the most important ideas in Piaget's theory and it needs, therefore, to be defined as clearly as possible; probably the best introduction to the concept is the volume reporting the deliberations of a symposium, sponsored by the World Health Organization (Tanner and Inhelder, 1956b), in which a discussion of this concept figures largely.

One way of approaching the concept is through the analysis of certain skilled activities which show particularly clearly how the individual learns to balance one activity against another. The paradigm for such performance would, perhaps, be a man learning to walk a tightrope. Piaget himself, in the same volume, gives the more mundane example of a man driving a car along an icy road. Suppose that he initially tends to slide to the left; he will make a correction to the right, which will tend to make him slide back to the right; he corrects this with a movement to the left and he slides to the left, and so on. At first the corrections the man makes will be too gross, but, as he becomes more skilled, he reduces his corrective movements and eventually is able to make 'corrections in advance' by anticipating the movement of the vehicle. But note that even when a man has acquired the skill, the result is best described, not as a final state of equilibrium, but as an on-going process which maintains equilibrium. In short, equilibrium is not final, but is in the process of being attained. This is because the skilled performance involves a series of compensatory activities in which the results of one action are balanced by the effects of a reverse action. This is why Piaget prefers to speak of equilibration or 'mobile equilibrium'.

This example is but a particular case of the mechanism which Piaget sees as being fundamental to development at all levels. Equilibration is the internal dynamic, not only of actions, but also of perception and thinking. Several authors (e.g. Dewey, 1910) have hinted at the same idea in their assertion that the search for the solution of a problem follows upon the experience of some stress or lack of equilibrium in the person's situation. Piaget would no doubt agree with this idea, but his formulation of the matter is more radical for two main reasons. In the first place, for him, lack of equilibrium would not be just a condition that the organism happens to get itself into; rather, equilibration refers to an intrinsic drive on the part of the organism and it is an essential function of all living systems. Secondly, and following from the first consideration, this tendency towards equilibrium is applicable to all types of structures which can be regarded as 'forming different levels . . . succeeding one another according to a law of development, such that each one brings about a more inclusive and stable equilibrium for the processes that emerge from the preceding level' (Piaget, 1950, p. 7). On this view, therefore, the development of thinking is the emergence of more and more stable cognitive structures as the action-structures of the infant give way to the perception-linked structures of the young child, which, in turn, are superseded by the operational structures of older children. Thus, with respect to the sensori-motor actions of the infant, there is a development in the direction of co-ordinating structures of action-sequences. The infant learns to bring his assimilatory and accommodatory activities into a balanced relationship, as, for instance, when he acquires the ability to grasp an object placed in front of him, he simultaneously accommodates to the properties of the object and assimilates that object to the co-ordinated schemes of sight and grasping. Piaget speaks, therefore, of adaptation as an equilibrium of assimilation and accommodation. Similarly, in studying the development of perception (Piaget, 1969), he stresses the regulating activity of equilibration in compensating for the deforming effects of single acts of fixation. Perceptual adaptation requires that the subject scan the perceptual field and maximize his encounters with it, so that his attention is not centred unduly upon one aspect of it. Perception may, accordingly, be described as the maintenance of a mobile equilibrium between successive centrations and decentrations. But the equilibrium of perception and of action is never complete, since it must be achieved anew at every encounter with the environment. On the other hand, at the next level of development, with the appearance of logico-mathematical structures, there is a sense in which we can, for the first time, speak about equilibrium being final. For example, when a child has managed to construct a series of whole numbers, then this structure will remain in equilibrium until death, unless the individual becomes insane. Piaget wishes to assert that once such an operational structure has been formed, it exists in a stable and permanent form, although, of course, it will be integrated into other systems as the individual's intellectual development progresses. More-over, this equilibrium is not a state of rest, since the individual will continue to make use of this structure in his encounters with objects and with other people. It is, therefore, an equilibrium which is character-ized by mobility and activity.

Since operational equilibrium is characterized in this way, it is continuous with the preceding structures of sensori-motor activity and perception. Indeed, it is Piaget's purpose to explain how thinking develops from these elementary activities. The equilibrium attained by thinking can, therefore, be represented as a progressive extension of the mechanism responsible for equilibration at these earlier levels. Just as the car-driver on the icy road maintained a course by a series of compensatory activities, so the development of logical thinking can be described as an increase in the ability to balance intellectual operations by a number of internal compensations. These compensations take different forms, which can be defined in the language of logic, but the essential feature of thinking is reversibility. An action or a perceptual centration can be regulated by compensatory actions or decentrations, but the equilibrium is always less than complete. Operational structures, on the other hand, are completely reversible: addition can be reversed by subtraction, the act of seriating objects, say, according to size, can be reversed, so that $A > B > C$ becomes $C < B < A$, etc. Consequently, Piaget regards reversibility as the necessary result of the equilibration process, for an equilibrated system entails the compensatory functions of negation and reciprocal operations.

Stages of Intellectual Development

One other essential concept is that of a stage. The development of thinking is essentially a development from simple to more complex ways of organizing or structuring. This point of view implies that it is profitable to consider intellectual development as falling into a number of qualitative stages, each with its distinct structural characteristics. It is important to realize that these stages are not discrete in the sense that the child 'steps out' of one stage into another. The whole process is a continuous one and Piaget goes to great pains in his work to demonstrate the existence of substages, in which patterns of behaviour are of a type intermediate between two major stages. But, although development is continuous, there seem to be certain decisive periods, in which accelerations in intellectual development occur. As Inhelder (in Tanner and Inhelder, 1956a) has put it, it happens as if a slow preparation culminated in an achievement.

Piaget (1956) has listed five criteria for the existence of stages. He points out that the criteria are degrees of the possible structuration of stages and that one criterion alone may be sufficient to define a stage in other fields. However, with respect to the development of thinking, all five criteria can be found in operation. The criteria are:

(1) There should be a constant order of succession, that is, behaviour typifying the first stage must always precede behaviour characterizing the second, and so on.

(2) There should be an integration of the acquisition of one stage into the following stages. Pinard and Laurendeau (1969) suggest that this may be interpreted to mean that the actions or operations which existed in one form or perhaps independently of one another at an earlier stage may be restructured or co-ordinated and this integration marks a new level of development.

(3) Consequently, one stage may be regarded as a preparation for the next, which, conversely, represents an achievement with respect to the preceding level.

(4) There should be a 'whole structure', or '*structure d'ensemble*', characterizing the total aspects of the stage. This refers to the theoretical assumption that actions or operations are closely interconnected to form a unity or structure. In view of the importance that Piaget attaches to the concept of structure, this is one of the most fundamental of the criteria and its application presents a very strict test of the stage concept, since it implies that if, say, operations x, y and z are assumed to form a structure, and if the subject is capable of x, then, other things being equal, he ought to be capable of operations y and z.

(5) The stage should signify the attainment of a level of equilibrium. From the equilibrium model we can infer that there are all kinds of intermediate structures, but these are difficult to define because of their instability, whereas the equilibrium levels marking stages attain the stability of reversible structures.

Of these criteria, (1), (2) and (4) seem to be most amenable to operational formulation, so that the experimental testing of the stage concept has centred around these. One qualification must, however, be made with reference to the fourth criterion. Given that a child possesses a cognitive structure characteristic of a certain stage, this does not mean that he can then apply this technique equally effectively to all the problems which confront him. For example, Piaget has shown that, whilst the child may recognize that the total mass or quantity of an object remains the same when the shape of the object changes, he will not recognize until some time later that the weight of the object also remains unchanged, even though the same operational structures are involved in the two cases. Conservation of mass is typically achieved a year or two earlier than conservation of weight. Piaget calls the phenomenon a *décalage*, which means literally an 'uncoupling'. The existence of these displacements cannot, of course, be used in argument against the stage concept, invoking criterion 4, since it is evident that task materials themselves involve degrees of difficulty which influence the readiness with which the child will apply logical operations to them. The fourth criterion is thus concerned with the theoretically assumed interdependence of the operations themselves.

The above type of *décalage* is called a horizontal *décalage*, because it takes place within one period of development. It is thus distinguished from a vertical *décalage* where there is a formal similarity between structures at two different stages. The crucial difference in a vertical *décalage* concerns the level of functioning: different kinds of operations are involved in the two cases. This is most clearly seen in the contrast between sensori-motor activity and the operational thinking of the older child: the two performances are on different planes, but the same system of logic can be used to describe both types of performance – operations on things and operations on symbols.

To summarize these basic theoretical concepts. Piaget asserts that every cognitive act involves adaptation which, in turn, involves the twin processes of assimilation and accommodation. These cannot occur without the existence of some form of organization or structure. The development of thinking entails an increasing differentiation and co-ordination of cognitive structures which occurs as the result of an intrinsic drive towards more and more stable forms of equilibrium. Although the equilibration process is continuous with development, certain general structures are more stable than others and these mark the stages of development. Having now stated, all too briefly, these concepts, which really require whole books to themselves, we can turn to examine Piaget's major findings.

THE RESEARCH FINDINGS

Piaget describes four main stages of development: there is the sensori-motor period, extending from birth to about 2 years of age, the period of pre-operational thought, from 2 to 7 years, the stage of concrete operations, lasting until 11 or 12 years, and, finally, the period of formal operational thinking, developing from adolescence into adulthood. The sequence of Piaget's research publications itself is divisible into a number of stages (by the application of the five criteria, of course!). In his earliest studies, he employed mainly verbal techniques of investigation to explore the reasoning and concepts of young children (Piaget, 1926, 1928, 1932). Because of this reliance upon purely verbal data, these studies are the least satisfactory of Piaget's experiments. His subsequent longitudinal observations of the sensori-motor development of his own three children, however (Piaget, 1951, 1952a, 1954b), enabled him to clarify his fundamental theoretical conceptions and provided a firm foundation for the next phase of his work on the development of logical thinking in children (e.g. Piaget, 1952b; Piaget and Inhelder, 1956) and in adolescents (Inhelder and Piaget, 1958). More recently, Piaget seems to have entered a fourth stage, in which his theory is given the widest possible scope and relevance, with the appearance of books on perception (Piaget, 1969), memory (Piaget, Inhelder and Sinclair, 1968), biology (Piaget, 1967), and mathematical epistemology (Beth and Piaget, 1966; Piaget, 1970b).

The Sensori-Motor Period (0-2 years)

The starting point of the system is that higher psychological functions grow out of biological mechanisms. Consequently, Piaget looks first at the innate mechanisms present in the newborn infant – the reflexes. He postulates six substages in the sensori-motor period.

Substage 1 – the use of reflexes (0-1 month). Reflexes do not function in fixed and perfectly efficient ways from birth. Piaget points out that even this innate response needs to be used in order to become adapted to its environment. This adaptation consists at the first substage of a gradual accommodation to reality. Perhaps the clearest examples concern the sucking reflex, which can be seen to undergo a primitive kind of accommodation as a result of contact with the environment. For example, an infant during this stage shows some slight but definite progress in distinguishing and localizing his mother's nipple as opposed to surrounding skin areas. But it is important to note that this improvement in performance is not brought about by a change in the action-sequence of sucking; the scheme itself does not change – it simply accommodates more precisely to the demands of the environment. In the same fashion, Piaget observes that more and more objects come to be subsumed under the scheme, for instance, the mother's finger or any object he might encounter: this is generalizing assimilation. Recognitory assimilation also occurs, for it appears that the infant soon manages to discriminate objects that are suckable and nourishing, such as the nipple or bottle, from those that are suckable and non-nourishing, like his mother's finger; witness his abrupt rejection of the latter when hungry. Thus it is possible to speak of a kind of adaptation occurring at this substage, both in the accommodation of schemes to reality and in the assimilation of that reality to them. But these achievements are very limited. Since schemes themselves are merely applied in an unchanging way to things, the assimilation that occurs is essentially only a utilization of the external environment to maintain the schemes in their present form. At the same time, the accommodations made result in no pronounced changes in the scheme which would, in turn, be reflected in subsequent assimilations. Piaget expresses this state of affairs by saying that assimilation and accommodation are as yet undifferentiated; a progressive adaptation to reality can commence only when accommodatory activity is sufficiently dissociated from the assimilatory functioning of the child to permit a reciprocal relationship to exist between them. This process of differentiation begins at the next substage.

Substage 2 – the first acquired adaptations and the primary circular reaction (1-4 months). From about one month onwards the neo-natal reflexes start to alter their form as a function of experience. For example, when the infant is able to bring his thumb to his mouth in order to suck it, this achievement is not due to innate reflexes but, rather, represents a co-ordination due to experience. The ability to suck one's thumb is one of the first of the many interco-ordinations of schemes which develop in the sensori-motor period. Other co-ordinations which begin in this substage are between sight and hearing, between hearing and vocalization, and, most important of all for future development, between sight and grasping. Piaget calls these co-ordinations reciprocal assimilations to indicate that there is not just an association of one scheme to the other but an assimilation by each of the activity of the other. How do these interco-ordinations occur? If we follow the development of thumb-sucking ability, a typical sequence of behaviour is observable. At first the child may suck his hand for a brief moment if it accidentally touches his mouth, but he will soon lose it. Subsequently, he is able to retain the hand for increasingly longer periods, once it is placed in his mouth, and he begins to move his arms and hands about in what appear to be deliberate attempts to effect the co-ordination. Finally, by the third or fourth month, he succeeds in bringing his thumb directly towards and into a mouth already open to receive it. Piaget uses the concept of circular reaction to refer to this type of adaptation. The sequence consists, essentially, of the infant stumbling upon a new experience as a consequence of some action, and of trying to repeat the experience by a re-enactment of the original movement. Here we see the beginnings of the differentiation of assimilation and accommodation, since coming into contact with new objects like his own thumb alters the form of the schemes. The circular reactions of this period are called primary circular reactions, in distinction to the secondary circular reactions of the third substage and tertiary circular reactions of later substages. Primary circular reactions differ from secondary circular reactions in that they are more centred on and around the infant's body, whilst the latter are more directed towards the manipulation of surrounding objects.

Substage 3 – the secondary circular reaction (5-7 months). The distinction is by no means clear-cut, but, whereas the substage 2 infant is primarily concerned with his own bodily activities – sucking for the sake of sucking, grasping, etc. – the infant at this stage is more interested in the environmental consequences of actions. The secondary circular reaction is an attempt to maintain, again by a kind of rhythmic cycle, an interesting change in the environment accidentally produced. The secondary circular reaction is possible because of the co-ordinations achieved at the second substage, especially the co-ordinations of visual and manual schemes, which allow the infant to produce alterations in his environment. Thus, in the course of grasping or striking at things, he eventually notices that the rattle he grasps makes a noise or the wicker-work of his cot produces a particular tactile sensation. Through the function of reproductive assimilation the child tries to recapture the experience. Secondary circular reactions, therefore, signify the beginning of the infant's exploration of the environment. Here is an example of Piaget's observations of his own children:

> At 0;3 (29) Laurent grasps a paper-knife which he sees for the first time; he looks at it a moment and then swings it while holding it in his right hand. During these movements the object happens to rub against the wicker of the bassinet: Laurent then waves his arm vigorously and obviously tries to reproduce the sound he has heard, but without understanding the necessity of contact between the paper-knife and the wicker and, consequently, without achieving this contact otherwise than by chance.
>
> At 0;4 (3) same reactions, but Laurent looks at the object at the time when it happens to rub against the wicker of the bassinet. The same still occurs at 0;4 (5) but there is a slight progress toward systematization.
>
> Finally, at 0;4 (6) the movement becomes intentional: as soon as the child has the object in his hand he rubs it with regularity against the wicker of the bassinet. He does the same, subsequently, with his dolls and rattle (see Obs. 102), etc.
>
> (Piaget, 1952a, pp. 168-9)

As this example makes clear, secondary circular reactions generalize to assimilate new objects, so that the child reacts to the novel object by treating it in a similar way to familiar objects. It happens sometimes that the infant experiences a novel object or event which is not directly

C

manipulable by him, as, for instance, when an unfamiliar sound arouses his curiosity. What occurs in such a situation is that the infant responds by initiating some or all of his secondary circular reactions, as though he were trying to preserve the interesting event by action at a distance. When secondary circular reactions are used in this way Piaget refers to them as 'procedures to make interesting events last'.

Although the formation of secondary circular reactions or secondary schemes represents an advance over the preceding stage, the manner in which they function has certain limitations. Just as there is, initially, in single schemes a lack of differentiation between assimilation and accommodation, secondary circular reactions function at first in an undifferentiated way; for instance, visual and manual schemes form a global unit, into which new objects are incorporated more or less indiscriminately. One consequence of this fusion of object and act is that the child at this substage has no conception of objects as existing permanently in an objective system of relationships. Piaget (1954b) reports a number of observations which demonstrate that infants will abandon interest in an object once it has disappeared behind a screen or cover. He argues that it is only when secondary schemes (i.e. those which are co-ordinations of separate schemes) become differentiated that they can be adjusted to one another; another way of putting this is to say that, when a child discriminates between his own actions and the objects to which these actions are applied, he can observe more closely both the effects of his actions and the properties of the objects themselves. This development is a precondition for the development of the concept of the permanent object.

Substage 4 – the co-ordination of secondary schemes and their application to new situations (8-11 months). From this point onwards, schemes become differentiated and reintegrated into new structures. There are two principal types of stage 4 interco-ordination. The most clear-cut example of the differentiation of schemes is evident in the behaviour sequence of setting aside an obstacle to reach some desired object. At substage 2 the child ignores the object if an obstacle intervenes; later he strikes at the offending obstacle, and from this scheme of striking emerges the successful technique of pushing the object aside to gain his end. There are two distinct schemes in this pattern of behaviour – an act of pushing aside and an act of grasping the desired object. We can thus distinguish for the first time two independent schemes which are co-ordinated with one another. The second example of such behaviour is that in which the infant tries to use objects as instruments in attaining a goal, for example, pushing an adult's hand to make an object move. Again, this is a case of the child putting schemes into relationship with one another, with the result that it is possible to speak of the differentiation of means and ends.

At the same time, with the differentiation of schemes comes an increasing interest in the properties of the objects themselves. At the third substage, Piaget maintains, the novelty of an object is not of great interest to the child, who almost immediately assimilates it to habitual schemes. The substage 4 infant, on the other hand, looks at novel objects for a longer period of time and attempts to explore them. At this stage too, the child will begin to search for a desired object when it is hidden behind a screen. This is an advance over the preceding substage and signifies that the object is becoming dissociated from the child's own activities; but this dissociation is, as yet, only partial, since if the child at this level is allowed to find an object under screen A and the object is subsequently moved to screen B with the child watching, he will search for it where he previously found it, under A, and will not think of looking under B. Thus, it seems that the object is still not the same to the child as to the adult. Piaget says that the object remains a practical object and has not yet acquired the status of a substantial thing; it is still, in short, dependent upon the action-sequence, of which it happens to be a part.

Substage 5 – the tertiary circular reaction and the discovery of new means through active experimentation (12–18 months). The secondary circular reactions are characterized by the fact that they involve the child taking into account the properties of external events and objects. The tertiary circular reaction develops out of the secondary ones as a more effective way of exploring the properties of new objects. There is no precise border-line between them, but, whereas the secondary reaction is the repetition of an act which led to an interesting result, the tertiary reaction is a repetition with *variation*. The infant varies his action apparently in order to see how this variation affects the object. Thus, having discovered the ability to drop objects from heights to observe their trajectory, the child will drop them in different ways or from different positions. A second acquisition is the ability to solve problems which demand new and unfamiliar means. The substage 4 child is only able to solve a problem requiring a differentiation of means and ends, that is, the differentiation and interco-ordination of two schemes into a totality in which one serves as the means, if the scheme which served as the means to the end was already in his repertoire. The child at the fifth substage, however, is able, through the trial-and-error behaviour of the tertiary circular reaction, to discover new means. Thus, he succeeds in finding a way of drawing a desired object towards him by means of the base on which it rests or perhaps by using a stick as an instrument, in the same way that Köhler's (1925) ape was able to retrieve a banana lying outside its cage. The tertiary circular reaction must not, though, be equated with trial-and-error in the sense that Thorndike used the term: in Piaget's theory the trials are guided by schemes which are capable of giving a meaning to fortuitous events, so that trial-and-error is essentially the process of bringing accommodatory activities into relationship with assimilatory co-ordinations.

The limitation of the previous substage with respect to the concept of the permanent object is overcome now: the child will search for an object at the place where he has seen it disappear. This achievement, and the characteristic limitation of this level of development, are apparent in the following observation:

At 1;7 (11) Jacqueline is seated on a bed.
1. I place a pebble on my hand, put my hand under quilt A and withdraw it closed. Jacqueline opens my hand, then searches under A and finds the pebble.
2. Same experiment under my vest B. Jacqueline opens my hand and goes under vest B at the first try. Consequently, success ensues.
3. I place the pebble in my hand and press this hand against the other one in C, leaving the pebble there. Jacqueline searches in my first hand, then under vest B, then finally under the quilt A. She takes no account of position C, although she has watched each of my movements.
4. I repeat the experiment (3). This time Jacqueline looks in my first hand, then under quilt A, then at last under vest B, but still takes no account of my other hand. (Piaget, 1954b, p. 76)

From this and similar observations, Piaget concludes that the child will search and find a disappearing object only when he can actually observe all the successive displacements of the object. When an invisible displacement intervenes, the child relapses into the same difficulties which he has already overcome when visible displacements were involved. Success with invisible displacements involves the child being able to imagine or represent to himself changes in the position of the object. This comes about at the final substage of sensori-motor development.

Substage 6 – the invention of new means through mental combinations (18 months+). This stage can be summarized as follows. The child wishes to achieve some end but has no scheme which could serve as a means. This is similar to the substage 5 pattern, but now the child is able to solve the problem by an internal experimentation. Thus, for example, the child will be able to anticipate that an object is in the way of a door closing or that a ball rolled under the furniture will reappear at a certain position because he can represent the movements of these objects without having to observe them directly. The co-ordination of schemes, then, is no longer confined to the realm of action, but takes place internally. Consequently, since the child can represent the object, it is finally freed from perception and action and is seen as obeying autonomous laws of displacement. With the advent of this capacity, the sensori-motor period draws to a close and subsequently intellectual development occurs in the use of symbols and the internalization of actions.

'Intelligence organizes the world by organizing itself.' Two related themes are apparent in Piaget's work on sensori-motor development, namely, that development consists of an increasing differentiation and co-ordination of assimilatory and accommodatory activities, and that these advances in internal organization parallel the organization and construction of external reality. Initially, assimilation and accommodation are undifferentiated in the sense that there are no specialized operations of accommodation. But development sees the co-ordination of schemes and an increasing accommodation to reality. That these are two complementary aspects of behaviour is evident from the consideration that the more schemes differentiate and relate to one another through reciprocal assimilation, the more ability the child has to explore and accommodate to the properties of the external environment. Thus, because all knowledge is simultaneously accommodation to the object and assimilation to the subject, the progress of intelligence works in the dual direction of externalization and internalization, so that if 'intelligence organizes the world by organizing itself' (Piaget, 1954b, p. 355), we can just as validly assert that 'intelligence organizes itself by organizing the world'. In other words, no priority is accorded either to the activity of the subject or to the constraints of the environment, for the development of thinking can only be understood as a process which occurs between these two poles. It is in this sense that it may be said that adaptation to the environment and the development of organized thinking are complementary.

But at the end of the sensori-motor period we are only at the beginning of the development of thinking. Sensori-motor development is essentially intelligence in action, the first five substages preparing the way for the achievement of substage 6, by which the child can solve a problem for the first time by internal experimentation, not by the manipulation of objects in the environment. That the child reaches the end of the sensori-motor stage does not, of course, imply that no further sensori-motor development takes place. It means only that from this point on the most advanced adaptations take place on a conceptual rather than on a sensori-motor level.

The Pre-operational Stage (2-7 years)

The characterization of the advances made in sensori-motor development as reflecting the increasing differentiation and co-ordination of assimilation and accommodation provides a means of understanding how the achievement of representation both arises from sensori-motor activities and yet comes to signify a qualitatively different level of functioning. The ability to represent or evoke non-perceptible objects has its roots in the increasing differentiation of assimilation and accommodation which allows the child to accommodate to objects in acts of imitation. Imitation, for Piaget, is the primacy of accommodation over assimilation and occurs when behaviour is primarily determined by the properties of the object. This type of behaviour is evident as early as substage 3, in which, for example, an infant will clench and unclench his hands in imitation of an adult. But it is only at the sixth substage that the imitation becomes representative. Piaget (1951) cites the case of one of his children who, in her efforts to get at the contents of a matchbox, repeatedly opened and closed her mouth; she was, he says, representing the enlargement she wanted in the visible opening of the box. In this example, the child imitates the behaviour of the object. What happens subsequently, Piaget believes, is that these exterior imitations on the part of the child become internalized as *images*, an image being a covert reproduction of an initially overt accommodation. Eventually, images cease to be just pale copies of objects and begin to serve as anticipations of events and as plans of action. This can be seen in deferred imitation, in which the child observes a certain behaviour sequence or happening but reproduces it at a later occasion. Thus, one of Piaget's children observed a child in a fit of temper and, once inside its playpen, repeated the behaviour, in a more detached fashion, to observe its effects. In this case, an attempt is made to reproduce the observed behaviour in its entirety, or almost, but in other forms of imitation the act is only a foreshortened version of the original, overt accommodation to the properties of the object. For instance, a visual image is formed, first, through eye-movements tracing the contours of the original object, and secondly, through

these movements becoming reduced in range but none the less repro-
ducing the particular outline and preserving this as a cognitive structure.
Piaget and Inhelder (1966) wish to reserve the term *schema* for the
imitative accommodation that is focused on the outline properties of
an object.

If imitation is the primacy of accommodation, play is the primacy
of assimilation over accommodation. Again, the roots of play can be
traced back to the sensori-motor period. For example, at the fourth
substage a child moves an obstacle out of the way to gain an object.
The execution of this scheme may arouse pleasure and the infant will
re-enact it, regardless of any practical aim. Thus, what was originally
an adaptive action becomes play. By the sixth substage symbolic
play appears in which the child 'makes believe' that an object is something else, as when one of Piaget's children uses a cloth, and subsequently
the tail of her rubber donkey, as a pillow. Both these examples show,
not adaptive behaviour in the sense of an equilibrium between assimilation and accommodation, but primacy of assimilation, since
objects are simply incorporated into existing schemes.

Piaget (1951) makes a distinction between 'signifiers' and 'signified'.
A signifier is something, for instance, an image or word, which
symbolizes or 'stands for' an object or event, whereas the signified is the
event to which the signifier refers. Together, these constitute the
symbolic or representative function. Now, Piaget's views may be
summarized in the statement that accommodation provides the
signifiers and assimilation provides the signified. The symbolic function
can be seen in operation in deferred imitation, in symbolic play, and in
adaptive intelligence. In the first two, there is a lack of equilibrium
between assimilation and accommodation. Where imitative accommodation is the aim, there is a subordination of assimilatory schemes
to the properties of the object; in symbolic play, on the other hand,
assimilation dominates accommodation, the latter merely providing
images which are immediately incorporated into existing schemes.
However, for behaviour to qualify as adaptive intelligence, the images
formed through imitation must be synchronized and equilibrated
with assimilatory schemes, just as it was necessary at the previous
level to effect the co-ordination of assimilatory and accommodatory
actions. The attainment of signifiers and significates at the close of the
sensori-motor period means, therefore, that the child is about to
embark upon a process of development, functionally similar to the
one which he has just accomplished on the level of direct action;
but this new stage is qualitatively distinct from the preceding one,

since the highest achievements of which the child is capable are of a symbolic nature. The attainment of equilibrium between signifiers and significates is not immediate, since play and imitation are the two extreme forms of symbolic functioning, which are only gradually combined in genuine, adaptive intelligence.

One consequence of these views on the development of representation is that language is regarded as one of the manifestations of the symbolic function. Piaget is quite willing to admit that the development of thinking is aided considerably by the development of language (e.g. Piaget, 1951, p. 221) for language makes possible the evocation of events by means of differentiated signifiers. But since language itself is an expression of the more general symbolic function, then it develops along with the symbolic function and cannot, therefore, be regarded as an independent determinant of the development of thinking. As Furth (1968, 1969) emphasized, there is a clear distinction in Piagetian psychology between symbols (images, words, gestures) and the actions or operations performed with these symbols, with the result that Piaget's views are distorted if one derives operations from symbols. It is, rather, the development of operations through the internalization of actions which constitutes the basic aspect of the development of thinking, so that the child's use of symbols, including words, is primarily determined by the extent of his progress in the development of operational structures. In the pre-operational period, as the name implies, the internalization of actions has not yet reached the stage in which the child can make use of a system of operations. But developments in this period can be conceived as preparing the way for this achievement through the increasing co-ordination of assimilation and accommodation in the child's symbolic activities.

In general terms, three phases can be distinguished in the development towards operational thought which occurs during the pre-operational period: the appearance of the first verbal schemes, the use of 'pre-concepts', and the phase of pre-operational reasoning.

1. The first verbal schemes. The first words that the child uses represent schemes of action, either related to the subject or partly objective. Thus the sound 'bow-wow' may be applied, not only to dogs and similar animals, but also to anything that moves; 'mummy' and 'daddy' may, similarly, be generalized to include all women and all men, or they may be used as requests or commands. Piaget says that these first verbal schemes are sensori-motor schemes in the process of becoming concepts: they are sensori-motor in that they are modes of

action capable of generalization, but they are the first approximations to concepts in that the use of a particular symbol implies a partial dissociation from the child's own activity. A concept may be said to exist when a verbal label is consistently applied to the same set of objects or relations. This stability of usage is due to the fact that society defines and stabilizes the use of words, but it is absent in the child's first use of words, for example, in the case of the child who uses the word 'bow-wow' to refer, within the space of a few days, to dogs, cars and men.

2. Pre-concepts. As he grows older, of course, the child makes finer distinctions, but up to about 4 years of age the child's notions predominantly take the form of pre-concepts, which Piaget characterizes as being neither truly individual nor truly general concepts. An example of a pre-concept is given in the following protocol:

> But also at about 2;6 she used the term 'the slug' for the slugs we went to see every morning along a certain road. At 2;7 (2) she cried: 'There it is!' on seeing one, and when we saw another ten yards further on she said: 'There's the slug again.' I answered: 'But isn't it another one?' J. then went back to the first one. 'Is it the same one?' – Yes – 'Another slug?' – Yes – 'Another or the same?' . . . The question obviously had no meaning for J.
>
> (Piaget, 1951, p. 225)

It is apparent that the child has not yet developed the idea of a class of creatures called slugs, so that she can conceptualize neither 'all slugs' nor an individual slug. This exemplifies the essential characteristic of the pre-concept, namely absence of individual identity and of the general class concept. In fact, says Piaget, these two features are synonymous, since the absence of a general class means that the individual elements cannot be assembled within it, and the lack of individuality of the parts prevents the construction of an inclusive class.

3. Pre-operational reasoning. The child's reasoning exhibits the same typical absence of generality. One type of reasoning Piaget calls 'transduction', which may be defined as an assimilation of the particular to the particular. For example, one child seemed to accept the argument that she could not have an orange since they were still green and not yet a nice, yellow colour, until she noticed that her camomile tea was yellow; if the camomile is already yellow, then the oranges can also be yellow . . . and the demand was resumed. Such reasoning, Piaget maintains, is due to the child centring her attention upon one particular

C*

aspect of the situation and assimilating other aspects of the situation to this one.

The centring of attention upon one aspect of the situation, or *centration*, to use Piaget's term, also explains the sort of reasoning shown by the pre-operational child in many of the other problems which Piaget has devised. In his early studies on judgement and reasoning in the child (Piaget, 1928), he demonstrated that the thought of the pre-operational child is largely determined by the child's own point of view. Thus, in one investigation, which was concerned with the child's notion of 'foreigners', Piaget found that although Swiss children at this period of development could grasp that the French are foreigners, they would not admit that the Swiss are foreigners to the French. Another experiment investigated the child's understanding of 'left' and 'right' and found that, whilst the pre-operational child can correctly identify his own right and left hand, he is unable to identify correctly the hands of someone facing him. Both studies signify that the young child is unable to place himself at the point of view of others and it is in this sense that Piaget describes this thinking as *egocentric*. This conclusion was later verified by non-verbal methods, for example, by having the child draw the perspectives of observers at various points around a three-dimensional model (Piaget and Inhelder, 1956).

Another well-known series of experiments concerned the child's understanding of the relationship of the parts to the whole in grouping (Piaget, 1952b). For example, the child may be asked to draw three tulips; having done this he is encouraged to draw a larger number of some other flower, say, daisies, so that he may finish with three tulips and five daisies. It is found that the pre-operational child is quite willing to agree that both tulips and daisies are flowers, but when asked: 'Are there more flowers or more daisies?', he replies that there are more daisies. Here we have a failure to understand the relation of parts to the whole which contains them and the child's failure may be interpreted, once again, as due to his centring upon one element in the situation (more daisies) and assimilating others to it.

The limitations of pre-operational thinking are seen, also, in the experiments on different kinds of *conservation*. This is the term used to refer to the recognition that certain properties of a display are invariant despite changes in other properties in the display. The recognition that objects have an autonomous existence independent of the subject, which occurs at the sixth substage of the sensori-motor period, represents the first major conservation. But, for Piaget, this is only a necessary first step in the construction of reality. Having learned to endow the object with a permanent existence, the child must learn to recognize the invariance of its other attributes. The now classic experiment with different shaped beakers illustrates the conservation of quantity. The child is given two glasses of equal dimensions (A1 and A2), which contain the same quantity of liquid. He is asked whether there is the same amount of liquid in each. Then, the liquid in A2 is poured into two small glasses of equal dimensions (B1 and B2) and the subject is asked whether the quantity of liquid in B1 and B2 is the same as that in A1, which thus operates as a standard. If the child believes that there is the same amount, the experiment may be taken a step further, B1 being poured into two smaller containers (C1 and C2) and B2 into C3 and C4. He is then asked about the equality or inequality of the liquid in the four very small glasses as compared with that in the standard,

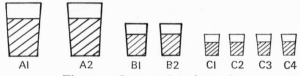

Figure 1. *Conservation of quantity*

A1. The pre-operational child will merely point to the level of the liquid in B1 and B2 and assert that there is less liquid in them because the level is lower, or, alternatively, he may observe that the width of B1 and B2 combined is greater than that of A1 and conclude that there is more liquid in B1 and B2. At a later age the pre-operational child will say that there is the same amount for this comparison, but, when the discrepancies become large, as with the C glasses, he will revert to non-conservation. In brief, the child at this period focusses upon one aspect of the situation to the exclusion of the other. Similarly, experiments testing conservation of weight require the child to relate together the variations along two dimensions. In such an experiment the child may begin with two identical balls of clay which he sees to be of equal weight by testing them on a balance. Next, the experimenter elongates one of the balls and asks the child to say whether it will now still weigh the same as the other. The pre-operational child does not grasp the invariance of weight during transformations in the shape of an object, since his centration upon one dimension (width or length) induces him to believe that the weight of the object will have changed.

All the major limitations of pre-operational thinking – the misunderstanding of the relationship between parts and the whole which contains them, egocentric thought, and the lack of conservation of quantity and weight – arise from centration upon one aspect of the total situation and, in this sense, it may be said that the child's thinking is dominated by his perception. In the language of the assimilation-accommodation model the stage may be summarized by saying that the signifiers provided by accommodation are still in the form of images and are not therefore completely general, whilst assimilation, which provides the signified, is irreversible since objects are simply incorporated into the scheme which constitutes the initial centre of interest. Hence, assimilation is distorting, accommodation inadequate, and there is no equilibrium between the two. Progress within the stage, as in others, can be viewed as a trend towards greater equilibrium. Piaget (1957) has proposed that this equilibration process can be conceptualized in probabilistic terms and has applied this model to the attainment of conservation. According to Piaget, centration upon one dimension makes it increasingly probable (presumably through satiation and contrast) that the subject will subsequently centre upon the other dimension; this, in turn, is likely to lead to a phase in which the subject alternates between the two dimensions and this alternation becomes more rapid, thus increasing the probability that the subject will encompass both aspects in a single cognitive act. When the child reaches this level, assimilation has become completely reversible, since changes in one dimension can be balanced against changes in the other, and accommodation has become generalized and no longer restricted to particular images, since reversible operations permit the use of symbols which are independent of particular stimulus configurations.

No mention has yet been made of the influence of social factors, but these are important in Piaget's theory for two main reasons. In the first place, it is through social interaction that the child acquires linguistic symbols, which are general and not related to specific stimulus displays; the image, of necessity, remains individual and incapable of being communicated, whereas the fact that the conventional signs of language are derived from social co-operation ensures their generality and communicability. Secondly, through social interaction the child is confronted with points of view other than his own; his egocentrism diminishes through repeated encounters with opposing views and he learns, in G. H. Mead's phrase, 'to take the role of the other' (Mead, 1934). Flavell (1968) has extended the Mead-Piaget thesis in his studies of the development of role-taking ability, but it must not be inferred that Piaget believes socialization to be the prime cause of the development of rational thinking. He has stated quite explicitly (Piaget, 1951, p. 239) that operational thinking and socialization must be regarded as interdependent. A system of operations cannot, of course, be general unless there is agreement about the names that can be used to refer to the operations within the system, but this generality does not derive solely from the linguistic conventions established through social interaction, since the operations themselves develop from the internalization of actions and are not therefore reducible to social conventions. This is a basic point in the understanding of Piaget's theory: that which is 'given', whether it is the physical environment, social structure and relationships or linguistic conventions, does not cause the development of the individual; it exists to be utilized by the individual. The success of this utilization will depend upon the extent to which the person has developed structures capable of dealing with social and linguistic factors as well as upon the characteristics of those factors themselves. There is thus a reciprocal relationship throughout development between individual activity and that which is given to the individual, a dynamic interdependence which makes it inappropriate to talk of independent cause and effect.

The Period of Concrete Operations (7-11 years)

The developments of the pre-operational period culminate at about the age of 7 in a method of thinking characterized by decentration and reversibility. The child at this age knows that there are more flowers than daisies, because he recognizes that daisies and tulips are subclasses of flowers; he appreciates that he is a foreigner to a person of another nationality, since he is able to place himself at the point of view of the other; and eventually he insists upon the invariance of quantity and weight in the face of perceptual transformations, because his thought has become flexible enough to identify and coordinate the dimensional changes involved. The appearance of these and similar achievements at approximately the same time signifies that a new level of intellectual development has been reached. Piaget contends that these performances mark the beginning of a stage since the intellectual operations which make these achievements possible form an equilibrated system of reversible operations. He believes, moreover, that this system can be described by the use of an abstract, logical model, in which the relationships between logical operations are derived deductively. He assumes that there is a close correspondence between the deductive system and the actual cognitive structures of the concrete operational child and, accordingly, that the former describes the latter. At the same time, he recognizes this as an assumption and demands that future empirical studies determine whether the relationships established in a deductive system correspond to those that exist in reality.

In order to understand this logical model, it is necessary to understand the meaning of certain distinctions which Piaget makes. Let us first note the distinction between the *logic of classes* and the *logic of relations*. To carry out the operation of classifying means to designate certain elements as classes which can then be combined in various ways. For example, we consider spaniels and fox terriers to be elements in the class of dogs, cats and dogs to be part of the broader class of animals, and so on. Thus, a given number of elements can be hierarchically arranged so that a class can both include and be included in others. Although classification may be described as one technique of relating elements, Piaget follows the tradition of distinguishing it from the logic of relations, of which he identifies two major divisions, *symmetrical* and *asymmetrical* relations. In a symmetrical relationship A has the same relationship to B that B has to A. A favourite example is that of brothers: if A is B's brother, then B is A's brother. In an asymmetrical relationship, however, this is not the case; it is not applicable, for instance, to such asymmetrical relations as A is taller than B, or C is prettier than D, etc.

A further distinction that Piaget makes is between logical *groups* and what he calls logical *'groupings'*. Remember that his intention is to characterize cognitive structures by means of logical models and that these structures represent different levels of equilibrium. For a system to be in equilibrium it must contain the means of compensating for changes that threaten stability, and this is effected, in general, through the existence of reversible operations. Now this state of affairs in a physical-psychological system corresponds closely to the properties of mathematical groups, which have the essential characteristic that the laws of operation, by which the elements in the group are combined, are such as to allow the system to remain stable during its operation. Piaget (1949) gives as an example of a group the system of positive and negative numbers characterized by the operation $+n$ (i.e. addition of an integer). This constitutes a group because it obeys four conditions:

1. Combinativity. Two operations of the system, when combined, result in a new operation, e.g. $+1+1 = +2$.

2. Inversion. Every operation of the system can be annulled by an inverse operation, e.g. $+2-2 = 0$.

3. Identity. There exists a single identity operator, defined as the operation, which, when applied to any assertion, leaves it unchanged. With this group, the identity operator is the resultant of any operation and its inverse and is ±0, since $+1-1 = 0$, and $1\pm0 = 1$.

4. Associativity. The operations are associative and thus the product is the same with different orders of combinations. Thus, $(4+2)-3 = 4+(2-3)$. The group is in equilibrium because any element may be combined with any other and because each operation, which produces a change in the system, is capable of being reversed by its inverse operation. It is thus a closed and stable system.

A 'grouping' is the name that Piaget gives to logical systems which have certain of the properties of groups but which do not form groups as such. For example, Piaget maintains that the logic of classes and of relations together form eight groupings in the period of concrete operations and that both these logics show some of the properties of a group. They show combinativity, for two classes may be combined to form a comprehensive class which embraces them both (all boys and all girls = all children) and two asymmetrical relations (A is taller than B; B is taller than C) may be joined into one relation which contains them (A is taller than C). Reversibility exists also; when reversibility is applied to classes it is called *negation* and it is called *reciprocity* when applied to relations. Thus, the operation of classifying can be reversed by an opposite operation which cancels it, e.g. all children except boys = all girls, as can asymmetrical seriation, e.g. A is taller than B becomes B is smaller than A. However, the operations that constitute classification and seriation do not form a group, since only certain elements may be combined: the elements 'false teeth' and 'children' are not in the normal course of events capable of being subsumed under a comprehensive category which contains both of them, nor can one meaningfully relate 'A is taller than B' to 'C is prettier than D'. The distinguishing feature of groupings is, therefore, that they derive their form from various types of concrete situations and are thus relative to those situations. Piaget calls them concrete operations to draw our attention to the fact that the child's thinking is successful only in so far as it is concerned with a particular concrete situation and that logical operations in this period are still not independent of concrete content. One consequence of the concreteness of early operational reasoning is that the stage is characterized by a number of horizontal *décalages*. Conservation of quantity, for instance, is attained some two years before conservation of weight, although the same logical operations are involved. This is due, Piaget thinks, to the concrete operational child having to observe the results of his operations in different concrete situations, and to his inability to detach his thinking sufficiently from concrete reality so as to achieve a structuring which would be capable of embracing its different aspects.

As examples of the concrete operational groupings we may take that dealing with the primary addition of classes and that dealing with the addition of asymmetrical relations. The first describes the organization among classes, where each one is included in the next larger one. A number of examples of such classification have already been given: cats and dogs are included in the class of animals, and daisies and tulips are subclasses of the class of flowers. This grouping, then, describes the operational performance of the child who is able to solve problems based upon the inclusion of parts in a whole. Similarly, the grouping of the addition of asymmetrical relations describes the performance of the child when solving problems of serial ordering, for instance, arranging a number of sticks in order of size and inserting others between them. Other groupings refer to more difficult tasks; for example, one grouping describes the kinds of relationships that can exist when objects are ordered asymmetrically along two dimensions at the same time, for instance, width and height. This kind of ordering can be represented by a matrix, in which objects are arranged according to their place on one dimension from left to right and by their place on the other from top to bottom. Piaget maintains that the child must understand the ways in which two asymmetrical series combine in order to grasp the conservation problem: the understanding of these logical relationships enables the child to see that although the glass may be taller, it is also narrower, etc.

Thus, just as the behaviour of the sensori-motor child showed an increasing independence from the 'here-and-now' – from perception and the immediate consequences of actions – so the transition from pre-operational to concrete-operational thinking represents an increasing independence of thought from perception. Thought, as behaviour, becomes more intelligent the more it 'detaches itself' from immediate stimulation and it accomplishes this by becoming operational. But if concrete operations have succeeded in taking this progressive liberation a step further, they are not the end-point of intellectual development. The achievements characteristic of concrete operations involve the manipulation of things. It is because of this that they are called 'concrete': their starting-point is always the real and the given, rather than the potential. When the child has to operate with relationships which are not directly given to him in perception, he is unable to follow through his reasoning to its logical outcome. He cannot, therefore, solve a simple problem, such as: 'Edith is fairer than Susan; Edith is darker than Lily; who is the darkest of the three?' The solution of problems like this depends upon the emergence of a new orientation to reality which occurs with the onset of adolescence.

The Period of Formal Operations (from about 12 years)

This reorientation to reality constitutes the major advance of formal over concrete thinking. It has three major characteristics:

1. When the child begins to think in terms of possibilities and to determine 'what is' in the context of 'what might be', we can say that his thought is hypothetico-deductive in character. This means that the child can regard the various possibilities in a given situation as a number of hypotheses which may be confirmed or not.

2. Formal thinking is propositional thinking. The concrete operational child succeeds in classifying and relating objects and events; the adolescent can do this, but he can also take the results of these concrete operations, cast them into the form of propositions, and then proceed to operate upon them by various kinds of logical connections. Formal operations are, therefore, operations performed upon the results of prior concrete operations.

3. When confronted with a problem and the test of considering as many possibilities as he can, the adolescent must isolate systematically all the individual variables together with all the possible combinations of these variables. In other words, he submits the problem to a combinatorial analysis.

An experiment which demonstrates these properties of adolescent thought and serves as an introduction to the logical model used by Piaget to describe this thinking is one reported by Inhelder and Piaget (1958) on the problems raised in the oscillation of a pendulum. This experiment used a simple apparatus, which consisted of a string, which could be shortened or lengthened, and a set of varying weights. The subject's task is to explain what determines the frequency of the oscillations of a weight suspended by the string from a pole. The variables which one might think to be relevant are: the length of the string, the weight of the object, the height of the dropping point, and the force of the push given by the subject. Only the first of these variables is actually relevant, so that the problem is to isolate it from the other three and to exclude them.

The results are easily summarized. The pre-operational child tends to believe that the impetus he gives to the suspended weight is the real cause of the variations in the frequency of the oscillations, but he is incapable of giving a consistent explanation: at one moment he refers to the amount of impetus, at the next to the weight, and so on. The concrete operational child, on the other hand, is able to order the lengths, elevations, etc., serially and to judge the differences between the observed frequencies of oscillation. He can, then, observe that the shorter the string the greater the frequency of oscillation. But he is incapable of isolating this variable from the others and, consequently, does not arrive at the correct conclusion. This is finally achieved in the formal operational period:

> EGG (15;9) at first believes that each of the four factors is influential. She studies different weights with the same string length and does not notice any appreciable change: 'That doesn't change the rhythm'. Then she varies the length of the string with the same 200 gram weight and finds that 'when the string is small, the swing is faster'. Finally, she varies the dropping point and the impetus (successively) with the same medium length string and the same 200 gram weight, concluding for each one of these two factors: 'Nothing has changed'.
>
> (Inhelder and Piaget, 1958, pp. 75-6)

There is, Piaget believes, a complex reasoning process behind these simple statements which can be described in the language of propositional logic. This involves the substitution of symbols for the propositions appearing in an argument and the elaboration of a number of rules, also symbolized, that are used as operators on the propositional symbols. In the present case, for example, p can refer to the statement that there is a variation in the length of the string, q to the statement of variation in weight, and r and s to modifications in the height of drop and the impetus. Finally x is used to refer to the proposition stating a modification of the result, i.e. the frequency of oscillations. The basic operations are implication ($\supset$): $p \supset q$ signifies that *if p occurs then q* does also; disjunction ($\vee$): $p \vee q$ means *either p or q*; the negation of a proposition is indicated by a bar over the symbol for the proposition: thus, not $p = \bar{p}$; lastly, conjunction takes the form $p.q$ (p and q).

Applying this notation to the pendulum problem, we can describe the successive stages in the solution of the problem. For example:

1. When, initially, a subject believes that each of the four variables is influential, he is asserting:

$$p \vee q \vee r \vee s \supset x \quad \text{or} \quad p.q.r.s.x.$$

2. Next, one variable, say weight, is excluded by the subject using different weights with the same length of string and the same weight with varying lengths of string. He finds out by this experimentation that the modification of the length corresponds, with or without modification of the weight, to a modification of the frequency of oscillation, and its absence corresponds to the absence of changes in

frequency. This amounts to stating the truth of the following combinations:

$$(p.q.x) \vee (p.\bar{q}.x) \vee (\bar{p}.q.\bar{x}) \vee (\bar{p}.\bar{q}.\bar{x})$$

3. The reasoning process is the same for the exclusion of height of drop. But, to exclude this third variable, the subject must take the previous two, length of string and weight, into account, and consequently the successful exclusion of two variables from three involves eight true combinations:

$$(p.q.r.x) \vee (p.q.\bar{r}.x) \vee (p.\bar{q}.r.x) \vee (p.\bar{q}.\bar{r}.x) \vee (\bar{p}.q.r.\bar{x})$$
$$(\bar{p}.q.\bar{r}.\bar{x}) \vee (\bar{p}.\bar{q}.r.\bar{x}) \vee (\bar{p}.\bar{q}.\bar{r}.\bar{x})$$

4. Finally, when the subject isolates the variable of impetus, he takes into account the other three variables. There are, then, sixteen true combinations:

$$(p.q.r.s.x) \vee (p.q.r.\bar{s}.x) \vee (p.q.\bar{r}.s.x) \vee (p.q.\bar{r}.\bar{s}.x)$$
$$\vee (p.\bar{q}.r.s.x) \vee (p.\bar{q}.r.\bar{s}.x) \vee (p.\bar{q}.\bar{r}.s.x) \vee (p.\bar{q}.\bar{r}.\bar{s}.x)$$
$$\vee (\bar{p}.q.r.s.\bar{x}) \vee (\bar{p}.q.r.\bar{s}.\bar{x}) \vee (\bar{p}.q.\bar{r}.s.\bar{x}) \vee (\bar{p}.q.\bar{r}.\bar{s}.\bar{x})$$
$$\vee (\bar{p}.\bar{q}.r.s.\bar{x}) \vee (\bar{p}.\bar{q}.r.\bar{s}.\bar{x}) \vee (\bar{p}.\bar{q}.\bar{r}.s.\bar{x}) \vee (\bar{p}.\bar{q}.\bar{r}.\bar{s}.\bar{x})$$

The solution of the pendulum problem, therefore, presupposes the understanding of a complicated combinatorial system and the ability to think in a hypothetico-deductive manner. Piaget admits that this understanding may not be fully articulate, so that subjects might reason explicitly with some combinations and have only an 'approximate idea' of the others. But the essential point is that the subject's performance entails a cognitive structure describable in terms of propositional logic.

In addition to operations such as disjunction and implication, there are four, more general transformations, whose function is to transform particular operators into others. The four transformations are inversion or negation (N), reciprocity (R), identity (I) and correlativity (C). The first three of these terms have already been defined with reference to concrete operations; in the period of formal thinking, the three operations are applied to other operations. Thus, in negation the operator, $p \vee q$ is transformed into $\bar{p}.\bar{q}$ (i.e. the negation of p or q is neither p nor q); the reciprocal of $p \vee q$ is $\bar{p} \vee \bar{q}$; the identity operation leaves the operator unchanged, so that $p \vee q$ remains $p \vee q$. The correlate of an expression is defined by replacing the disjunctive with the conjunctive sign, or vice versa; thus the correlate of $p \vee q$ is $p.q$, and the correlate of $\bar{p} \vee \bar{q}$ is $\bar{p}.\bar{q}$. These four transformations together form a group, fulfilling the four criteria for groups – combinativity, inversion, identity and associativity. Any transformation can be combined with any other and whatever sequence of transformations is performed, the final result is always equivalent to one of them. For instance, NRC = I because

$$N (p \vee q) = \bar{p}.\bar{q}$$
$$\text{and R } (\bar{p}.\bar{q}) = p.q$$
$$\text{and C } (p.q) = p \vee q$$
$$\text{but I } (p \vee q) = p \vee q$$
$$\text{hence NRC} = I$$

The structure constituted by these transformations thus forms an equilibrated system. Piaget believes the structure to be of psychological importance, since it enables the subject to co-ordinate operations. When the subject can do this, his thinking is at once flexible and stable.

But Piaget believes that formal thinking has implications beyond a restricted range of intellectual problems; he believes it shapes the adolescent's whole way of looking at life. Logic, he affirms, is not isolated from life, because logic is no more than the expression of the operational co-ordinations essential to action. It is not difficult to see how the adolescent's ability to think of possibilities implies a new orientation to life. The adolescent becomes capable of living in the future as well as in the present. Reality is no longer accepted, for there are now various alternatives to choose between. In the early stages of using this newly acquired ability, the adolescent goes through a phase of egocentrism, in the sense that his hypothetical thinking typically shows a lack of differentiation between private desires and fantasies on the one hand and general theories on the other. The major factors which make adolescents accommodate to reality eventually are social interaction and having to settle down to do a job.

3

Cognitive competence
and performance

In discussing the relationship between logic and psychology, it was concluded that Piaget's operationalism overcame the major limitations of previous points of view but that, nevertheless, an assessment of the theory must await evidence and discussion on a number of outstanding issues. Having examined the theory more closely, we are now in a position to pursue these issues. The first has to do with the orderliness of intellectual development: is there an inevitable order in the sequence of successive achievements, as Piaget's theory holds, or do we find variations in this development among individuals belonging to similar social or cultural groups? Assessment of this aspect of the theory entails an examination of the sequence of development both over the entire range of stages and within each stage. The second issue concerns the influence of social and cultural factors on thinking: on Piaget's theory, logical rules are universal since they are formed by abstraction from actions common to all men; this suggests that there will be a common core to the thinking of men from widely different cultural backgrounds; but, against this, it may be argued that such backgrounds are likely to foster radically different modes of thought. Which is the truer statement? The mechanism of intellectual development is the third point at issue: Piaget's theory appears to make language subsidiary to operational development. For instance, the development of the concept of conservation is attributed to the operations of reversibility and compensation rather than to the development of a linguistic ability independent of operational development. Does research on the attainment of conservation enable us to assess the influence of these factors? Finally, there is the general, theoretical issue of whether the adaptation-equilibration model is an adequate or even a permissible one. In what sense can we say that equilibration 'explains' the simultaneous development of adaptation to the environment and of thinking? Is this a principle applicable to actual cases, or is there here, as Husserl intimated, a confusion of an ideal principle with actual cases?

These issues are by no means separate for they are particular expressions of a yet more general dichotomy of opinion. The whole impetus of Piagetian theory is towards accounting for the existence of rational thought. The major constructs are essentially descriptive of the organized nature of thinking at each stage and of the systematic progression through a mechanism (equilibration) intrinsic to the system from one stage to the next. However, this view is adequate only if the assumption is correct that those factors that might produce diversity of types of thinking at each stage or variability in the sequence of attainment – social norms and linguistic usages, for example – are either subsidiary to or isomorphic with the development of operational structures guided by the equilibration process. The existence of this basic assumption was emphasized in the previous chapter. But if it can be demonstrated that these factors are independent of operational development to the extent that they produce variability not predictable from a knowledge of operational level alone, then it may be concluded that this points to a limitation inherent in the theory. This demonstration would imply, not, of course, that the theory is totally invalid, but that there are events which lie outside its frame of reference. The general purpose of a review of the experimental evidence for Piaget's theory must, then, be to consider the truth of this criticism.

STAGES IN DEVELOPMENT

The theory states that the development of thinking follows a regular course: the sequence of attainments is logically, and hence psychologically, invariant, and there are certain levels of development which mark the formation of co-ordinated systems of schemes, first of actions and later of operations. The hypothesis of invariant sequences may be tested by observing whether children at given levels are able to perform satisfactorily on tests which relate theoretically to earlier levels; Guttman's (1944) scalogram analysis fulfils this function. The hypothesis of co-ordinated schemes is testable by reference to the intercorrelations between theoretically related tests. Further, given these hypotheses and the theory as a whole, it follows that the relationship between stages and chronological age will also be fairly constant, at least in Western cultures.

Sensori-Motor Development

The evidence for these notions is not equally extensive for all phases of development. The sensori-motor period, for example, remains relatively unexplored. Woodward (1959) tested the sequential nature of development in this period by studying a group of severely mentally defective children, whose chronological ages ranged from 7 to 16 years. She found that the order of difficulty of the observed behaviours, as measured by the number of subjects capable of performing them, corresponded to Piaget's description and that, if a subject could perform at a given level, he could, in general, perform at the earlier levels. Woodward also found a correlation between general developmental level and degree of attainment of the object concept. This has been verified by Charlesworth (1966), who found that the active search for a hidden object, as well as other modes of behaviour typical of the fourth substage, appears at 8 months of age, as predicted by Piaget. A necessary qualification to these findings, however, is that the development of the object concept does not proceed at the same rate for all objects. Décarie (1965) and Bell (1970) report that the mother tends to be responded to in this way before other objects, although 27 per cent of the infants in Bell's study showed the concept of object permanence before that of person permanence: these infants differed from the majority in showing little interest in proximity to or contact with the mother.

The existence of this '*décalage*' is not inconsistent with Piagetian theory, but it must be observed that, in order to account for the nature of the '*décalages*' that do occur, we require knowledge of the subject's experience and of the stimulus situation. Now, although the adaptation model allows for the influence of these factors, it does not treat them systematically. Bower (1967) has commented that Piaget's presentation makes no mention of the stimulus aspects of his test situations. Bower's demonstration that the week-old baby 'recognizes' objects when they reappear from behind a screen, as evidenced by changes in sucking responses, has been criticized by Piaget (1968a) on the grounds that these results do not signify that the infant believes that the object continues to exist behind the screen since this presupposes an organization of space and a substantiation of reality. Bower's (1971) other experiments, in which infants were presented with the optical illusion of several images of mother, are perhaps more truly indicative of the stage of development of the object concept, since it was only after the age of 5 months that infants reacted with concern at this illusion. These experiments raise the general question of the relationship between specific experiences and the development of the object concept. The same issue emerges from White's (1969) observations on the co-ordination of sensori-motor schemes. Piaget's general position that development in the first few months is from sequential activation of isolated schemes to their reciprocal co-ordination is supported, but White finds a great many more schemes than Piaget reported and, furthermore, that their development is related to the infant's experiences of being handled.

Pre-operational and Concrete Operational Development

Validation of development within the pre-operational and concrete operational periods has been much more thorough and systematic. Studies by Lovell (1959a, b), Lovell and Ogilvie (1960, 1961a, b), Lovell and Slater (1960), Lovell, Healey and Rowland (1962), Lovell, Kellett and Moorhouse (1962), Lovell, Mitchell and Everett (1962), Elkind (1961a, b, c, d, 1962), Beard (1963), Dodwell (1960, 1961, 1962) and Hood (1962) lend strong support to the major features of Piaget's system, namely (*a*) that qualitatively different modes of response are associated with different age levels to the extent that it is reasonable to talk of pre-operational or concrete operational thinking; (*b*) that development on the developmental tasks is related to age, so that one can talk of a general sequence of development; (*c*) that the ages stated by Piaget for the various achievements are, by and large, representative. These conclusions apply to the different conservations – of quantity (Lovell, 1959a; Elkind, 1961a), weight (Lovell and Ogilvie, 1961a, Elkind, 1961b) and volume (Lovell and Ogilvie, 1961b) – and to other concepts such as number (Dodwell, 1960, 1961; Hood, 1962; Beard, 1963) and classification (Elkind, 1961c). However, a more stringent assessment of the theory requires a closer scrutiny of each of these three conclusions, since, in particular, it is not sufficient that general 'modes of responding' be established or that there should be a 'general' sequence of development; rather, there ought to be evidence of co-ordinated operational schemes – the *'structures d'ensembles'* – and of invariant sequences.

(*a*) Although pre-operational and concrete operational modes are discriminable, a typical conclusion of the validation studies is that there is more variability across logically identical or related tasks than would be predicted from Piaget's writings. For example, Lovell and Ogilvie (1961a) point out that, whilst they obtained results very similar to those of Piaget, it is also evident that children who are conservers of weight on one test are non-conservers on another. Similarly, both Beard (1961) and Dodwell (1960) noted that, although older children gave more concrete operational responses than younger children, a child's type of response varied from one situation to another. Among other investigators who have reported this sort of variation are Mannix (1960), Feigenbaum (1963) and Uzgiris (1964). Research demonstrates, not only that there is variability in performance on tasks which purportedly measure the same concept, but also that the relationship between theoretically related concepts is not as predictable as Piaget would have us believe. Dodwell (1962), for instance, could not confirm the predicted relationship between the child's understanding of number and his understanding of classification: he found that the two kinds of concept develop within the same age range but that there is no clear relationship between them, either in the sense that one is prior to the other or that they develop concomitantly. Or again, Lovell (1961) found, contrary to Piaget, that a high proportion of children who were non-conservers of weight understood transitivity of weight. It is apparent, therefore, that equivalent levels of performance do not follow from the simple fact that tasks have the same logical structure or are related logically.

But perhaps Piaget's theory is ambiguous on this point. On the one hand, the notion of '*structures d'ensembles*' suggests that there ought to be striking relationships between certain concepts; on the other hand, the adaptation-equilibration model attests to the role of experience and, therefore, to the possibility of variations in performance due to the history of the subject's experiences and to the relative difficulty of the tasks. One means of resolving this apparent contradiction is to argue that there will be considerable variations in performance during the transition or formative phases of a stage but that, thereafter, there will be increasing evidence of integrated schemes. This reasoning has been advanced by Pinard and Laurendeau (1969) and by Flavell and Wohlwill (1969).

(*b*) The second, testable criterion for the existence of stages is that there should be a constant order of succession of attainments. This criterion requires evidence beyond that showing significant relations between tasks and age. It may be tested by longitudinal assessment of subjects but the most frequently used method is scalogram analysis (Guttman, 1944, 1950; Green, 1956). This technique assesses how closely each individual's attainment of concepts corresponds with the order of attainment of the group as a whole. If, say, each subject in a group attained the concepts in the same invariant order, the tests would be said to form a perfectly reproducible scale, although, of course, in psychological research we must be satisfied with something less than this. Wallace (1965) provides a critical review of the studies using this technique.

The available evidence is somewhat contradictory. On the one hand, Dodwell (1960, 1961), Smedslund (1964), Kofsky (1966) and Goldschmid and Bentler (1968) report considerable variation in the sequence by which subjects master Piagetian tasks. On the other hand, Laurendeau and Pinard (1962) were able largely to confirm the progression identified by Piaget, and both Siegelman and Block (1969) and Zern (1969) re-analysed Smedslund's (1964) data to find significant indices of reproducibility. Moreover, Siegelman and Block report that the item order is consistent with Piaget's theory, in that conservation of discontinuous quantity precedes conservation of continuous quantity, transitivity of discontinuous quantity precedes transitivity of length, and class-inclusion precedes multiplication of relations. Schwartz and Scholnick (1970) carried out a study in which the logical and perceptual components of tasks assessing conservation of discontinuous quantity were varied systematically; they discovered that the tasks formed a Guttman scale.

A study by Freyberg (1966) is of special interest since the author concerned himself with the criterion of an invariant sequence and with the criterion of intercorrelation between logically related tests. He administered a battery of Piagetian tests to a sample of children, ranging in age from 6 to 8 years, at three-month intervals for two years. Freyberg found that twelve out of the eighteen concepts formed a significantly reproducible scale, but analysis of the longitudinal data for each child revealed a steady and gradual progression rather than a sudden acceleration to a higher level. He concluded that the hypothesis of an invariant sequence may be correct, but that it is not possible to identify a new stage of development at about the age of 7. It may be, however, that Freyberg's tests, which were administered in booklet form to groups of subjects, were too global in nature. In this connection, the study by Nassefat (1963), quoted by Flavell and Wohlwill (1969), demonstrates the desirability of assessing scalability against different age levels and different types of response. Nassefat assessed scalability separately for each age level and for each of three item categories (concrete, intermediate and formal). In general, consistency was found to be highest at the age level at which the discriminative power of each item category is maximal, that is, at age 9 for the concrete operational items, at age 11 for the intermediate items and at age 12 for the formal operational items.

In the assessment of the second criterion, as in the assessment of the first, it is necessary to distinguish phases of transition and phases of consolidation. On balance, research carried out to date suggests that the search for invariant sequences is not without foundation. Future work must, however, be sensitive to the existence of transitional phases; the optimal strategy would seem to be the longitudinal one.

(c) Although the validation studies confirmed the age at which the child can perform concrete operational tasks as between 5 and 7 years, there has for a long time been a body of opinion which claims that Piaget tends to underestimate the capabilities of the child, largely, it is thought, because of an excessive reliance upon verbal methods of assessment. The early work on reasoning in the child (Piaget, 1926, 1928) was criticized by a number of workers. Isaacs (1930) presented examples of logical thinking in very young children and McCarthy's (1954) review of research into childhood egocentrism yielded the conclusion that pre-operational children were much more socialized in their speech than Piaget allowed. Piaget (1962) has since admitted that these early studies relied too much upon verbal exchanges between subject and experimenter and he maintains that the subsequent, more behavioural studies demonstrate the theoretical argument more effectively.

However, there are those who believe that these later studies do not escape the censure directed at the earlier ones. Berko and Brown (1960), with specific reference to conservation, suggest that the child may equate the words 'more' and 'less' with dimensions of height or width, so that their failure to conserve may be the result of a lack of verbal sophistication. Braine (1964) and Braine and Shanks (1965) also suggest that younger children use and respond to words like 'big', 'more' and 'same' in terms of phenomenal size rather than actual quantity. A number of studies have demonstrated these verbal difficulties. Griffiths, Schantz and Sigel (1967) found that children had most difficulty in using the term 'same' correctly. Lumsden and Poteat (1968) reported that young children tend to interpret 'bigger' in experiments on size conservation in terms of the vertical dimension and Lumsden and Kling (1969) found that training directed towards teaching the child a multi-dimensional concept of bigger produced significant gains in conservation behaviour. Nummedal and Murray (1969) found that subjects who can make correct denotative discriminations perform significantly better on conservation of weight problems than subjects who are unable to discriminate connotative from denotative meaning. One implication of these studies is that the child may have an understanding of conservation prior to his being able to express that understanding in words. Consequently, if verbal factors are eliminated from conservation tests, as far as this is possible, we should find an earlier age of attainment than that reported by Piaget. Cohen (1967) tested this reasoning in an experiment in which 'size' words like 'more' and 'bigger' were omitted from the instructions and from the responses, the child being asked to perform a task bringing about a new state of affairs rather than passing judgement on an existing state of affairs. Cohen found that conservation of quantity could be elicited by these means in children as young as $4\frac{1}{2}$ years. Also pertinent is the study by Goldschmid and Bentler (1968) which utilized both behavioural and verbal criteria for the measurement of conservation: it was found that the two sets of scores were significantly correlated, but that, in general, all the behaviour items were easier than the easiest verbal explanation item. The two indices, therefore, reflect different levels of understanding of the same concept.

This research does suggest that the age at which the child attains conservation is partly dependent upon the degree of verbalization present in the instructions and in the response. But it cannot be suggested that the results of these experiments contradict Piagetian theory. The findings that children experience difficulty with certain words and that their understanding of conservation is expressible through behaviour prior to its verbal expression are compatible with the view that the linguistic difficulties of the young child reflect his inability to handle operations, but once conservation has been achieved through the development of these operations, the correct verbalization will appear, given a facilitating environment. It cannot be decided, on the basis of these results, whether language plays a part in the formation of operations or whether it merely provides the expression of an understanding already attained. One might argue that the demonstration of the priority of a behavioural to a linguistic solution of the conservation problem implies that the latter is secondary, but this raises the question of whether the child who understands 'in his behaviour' has the same concept as the child who expresses his understanding linguistically. We must return to this problem in a while.

Further instances of the influence of methods of assessment on the identification of the ages at which concepts are attained are the controversies over the presence of conservation in very young children and over the occurrence of transitivity judgements. Mehler and Bever (1967) claimed to have discovered conservation in children as young as $2\frac{1}{2}$ years. However, the upshot of the resulting controversy (Beilin, 1968a, b;

Bever, Mehler and Epstein, 1968; Piaget, 1968a; Mehler and Bever, 1968) seems to be that the behaviour observed by Mehler and Bever did not signify a genuine understanding of conservation but, rather, a judgement of stimulus arrays in terms of their topological characteristics, in particular, the extent to which elements are 'heaped together'. Similarly, the controversy, in which Braine (1959, 1964) contested that the child understands transitivity at 5 years of age, while Smedslund (1963a, 1965) confirmed Piaget's finding (Piaget, Inhelder and Szeminska, 1960) of attainment at about the age of 7, appears to have been resolved in favour of the latter by the experiments of Murray and Youniss (1968) and Youniss and Murray (1970). These authors were able to eliminate non-transitive but outwardly correct solutions to transitivity problems, such solutions giving a misleading impression of the ability of the younger child. Briefly, a typical transitivity problem requires the subject to make judgements about three sticks; if, in comparing stick A with stick B, the subject responds that 'A is longer' and, in comparing B with C, says that 'B is longer', when asked to compare A and C (the transitivity problem), he may respond correctly because of the two only A has been labelled as 'longer'.

Formal Operational Development

Piaget's description of the development of formal thinking has been validated by a small number of studies but the applicability of his logical model has been questioned. Lovell (1961) examined 200 subjects, mostly adolescents, on experiments similar to those carried out by Piaget and Inhelder (1958), for example, the problems of the oscillation of a pendulum and the combination of colourless liquids. The different tests were found to be associated with one another and the main stages in the development of logical thinking proposed by Piaget and Inhelder were confirmed. Studies by Lodwick (1959) and Case and Collinson (1962), which classified children's responses to questions about various prose passages for intuitive, concrete and formal modes of thinking, supported the general nature of Piaget's formulation, although Stone and Ausubel (1969) found that the ability to comprehend such material developed selectively in each subject-field 'rather than, as Piaget implies, synchronously, in all fields'. Neimark's (1970) results were, however, consistent with the view that formal operational tasks are correlated, and Elkind (1967b) confirmed the emergence of a new form of egocentrism at this level. Shapiro and O'Brien (1970) were able to show that children below the age of 11 do not reason in a hypothetico-deductive manner, and, likewise, Lunzer (1960) confirmed Piaget's main findings on the development of the child's understanding of volume, finding that a proper understanding of this concept does not occur until about the age of 11 or 12.

However, Piaget's contention that the conservation of displacement volume and the ability to multiply three linear dimensions to calculate volume depend upon notions of infinity and continuity was not supported by Lunzer's study. Lunzer's comment that Piaget errs in deducing the psychological relationship of concepts from their logical interdependence has been echoed by others. Parsons (1960) has strongly criticized Piaget's use of logical models; he argues, for example, that Piaget has nowhere shown that subjects actually think in terms of the truth-functional form of the group. Parsons' strictures receive support from studies by Smedslund (1963b) and Jenkins and Ward (1965) which conclude that adults with no training in statistics do not have a cognitive structure corresponding to the concept of correlation. It must be recalled, though, that Piaget's own view is that the correspondence of logical model with actual thought is a matter for experimental confirmation. In this context, the work of Seggie (1969, 1970) is of interest, since it represents an attempt to examine the extent to which subjects use the logical operations identified by Piaget in concept learning. He has found a significant relationship between the difficulty of a concept and the subject's tendency to use hypothetico-deductive reasoning, and that adults are relatively more efficient in the use of logical relationships than adolescents.

COMPETENCE AND PERFORMANCE

Reviewing this research, one cannot but be impressed by the evidence of structure in thinking and in its development; many studies point to the orderly character of development and to the existence of developmental levels, as evidenced by interrelationships among tasks. Equally impressive, on the other hand, is the evidence for variation in performance due, largely, to variations in the characteristics of the environment encountered by the organism: this is true at the sensori-motor level, with the *décalages* in person and object permanence and the effect of 'handling' upon the development of the sensori-motor co-ordinations; at the concrete-operational level, with the existence of variations in concept attainment due to such factors as task complexity or the degree of verbalization required of the child; and at the formal operational level, with the suggestion that the correspondence between Piaget's logical model and the way in which subjects actually think is less than perfect. If the evidence points to both order and variability, what are we to make of the concept of stage?

Note in the first place that Piaget's system contains a logical model, which permits a fairly precise testing of predictions about the structural aspects of development, and the general notion of the adaptation-equilibration mechanism. Many investigators have argued that the demonstration of deviations from the predictions of the logical model, namely, lack of a constant order of succession and no interrelationships between logically related tests, is sufficient to invalidate the concept of stages and the theory underpinning this concept. Stone and Ausubel (1969) reason in this way; and the reasoning is sound enough, in so far as it relates either to predictions made from the logical model alone, or from the assumption that the logical model describes the structure of thinking and the concepts of adaptation and equilibration are introduced merely in order to explain or guarantee this structure. But there is another interpretation of the meaning of these concepts and their relation to the logical model. Adaptation, Piaget tells us, signifies an accommodation of the organism to the characteristics of the environment; therefore, the development of logical thinking will be subject to variation as a result of these characteristics, but, with further experience and because logical thinking is an abstraction from action and not from these characteristics, there will be increasing evidence of integrated structures that will match those described by the logical model. On this interpretation the existence of logical structures may be reconciled with the existence of variations due to task and situation variables and the concept of stage retained as a useful summary of this state of affairs.

However, although the logical model permits the systematic description of operational structures, we are not able, at the moment, to be equally systematic about those variables which produce '*décalages*'. Piaget (1970a) has acknowledged this fact and has suggested that further research will help to clarify the nature of the 'resistances' of things to operational activity. An indication of the direction which this research must pursue is given by Flavell and Wohlwill (1969), who have proposed that, as well as the logical, competence model, which represents what the subject knows or could do in an environment which offers no resistance to his activity, we need a 'performance' model, which represents the psychological processes by which the information embodied in competence actually gets utilized in real situations. There are, therefore, two main determinants of the child's performance in a cognitive task; the rules, upon whose application the solution of the task depends, and a set of variables related to task-difficulty, such as familiarity and complexity of the stimulus material, the role played by memory and the amount of irrelevant information. In other words, we need to know Pa, the probability that a given operation is functional for the subject, and Pb, a coefficient applying to a given task and reflecting the influence of the performance variables. Applying this analysis to the stage concept, Flavell and Wohlwill argue that investigations of the interrelationships between tasks should take into account the existence of four distinct phases: a phase in which competence is absent ($Pa = 0$) and in which correlations will be low for lack of variance, a second phase in which competence becomes established (Pa increases from 0 to an ideal of 1) and in which correlations are still low due to oscillations in competence, a third phase characterized by greater consistency, for items of equivalent Pbs are passed about equally often and items of discrepant Pbs exhibit a Guttman-type pattern, and, finally, a phase in which both Pa and Pb are maximal so that the subject will be successful in most, if not all, tasks.

CROSS-CULTURAL STUDIES

Cross-cultural studies may be regarded as a means of exploring those factors which produce variability in thinking. Piaget's view that logical thinking is the result of a process of abstraction from actions common to all men (a process which he terms logico-mathematical experience) implies the generality of operational structures across cultural variations. An alternative position is to argue that these cultural variations are sufficiently important to produce radically different modes of thought. Bruner, Olver and Greenfield (1966), for example, reason that the development of thinking depends to a great extent upon the supply of 'amplifiers' that a culture has in stock, that is, what images, skills and symbolic representations the culture has developed and transmits to its members. Perhaps the essential difference between these two positions is that, whereas Bruner regards the cultural 'givens' as amplifiers or instruments that shape thought into certain moulds, Piaget might regard them more as 'resistances' necessary for the development of operational thought in the sense that they are *particular* manifestations, to which the individual must accommodate in order that he develop *general* operational co-ordinations. Stated in this way, the difference between the two is not that one emphasizes cultural factors and the other does not. For Piagetian theory, far from denying the influence of cultural variables, would actually predict that attainments within any one major period of development would vary according to cultural preoccupations, since these are part-and-parcel of that to which the subject accommodates. But these variations would be variations within the general developmental process, because the equilibration mechanism and the transition from sensori-motor through perceptual to operational modes are assumed to be general developmental phenomena. Bruner, on the other hand, goes beyond this position when he maintains that cultural preoccupations influence not only the rate of progress but also the mechanism of thinking: he argues that Western culture favours the development of the linguistic-symbolic mode of representation whereas other cultures represent reality in terms of actions or images. Thus, to borrow a phrase from another of Bruner's works (Bruner, Goodnow and Austin, 1956), he believes that one should talk of culturally determined strategies of thinking rather than a general sequence cutting across cultural differences.

Bruner refers to the experiment by Greenfield (Bruner, Olver and Greenfield, 1966) on conservation of quantity in Wolof children of Senegal as support for this view. Greenfield found that both rural and urban children who were attending school showed the familiar developmental sequence with conservation attained in all cases by 12 years of age. In contrast, half of the unschooled rural children had not attained conservation at this age. Bruner's comment upon this experiment is that these children do not achieve verbal conservation but they are quite capable of handling liquids and objects in the course of their life. He concludes from this and other studies, therefore, that, since technological societies emphasize linguistic representation rather than action or imagery, tests based upon this cultural emphasis will underestimate the understanding of children from other kinds of society. The unschooled Wolof child, like the 4-year-old European child, possesses the concept of conservation pragmatically; his deficiency lies in the linguistic expression of this understanding.

Several studies indicate considerable cross-cultural variations in Piagetian tasks. Goodnow and Bethon (1966) report a significant difference between American and unschooled Chinese children on a task of combinatorial reasoning; Peluffo's (1964) study of deprived Italian children confirms the vulnerability of combinatorial reasoning. Pascal-Leone and Bovet (1966) found that the conservation of time is particularly variable across cultures, and Vernon (1969) reports poor conservation performance in Ugandan and Eskimo children. Mermelstein and Shulman (1967), after comparing groups of Negro children

D

with varying amounts of formal schooling, suggest that significant differences between verbal and non-verbal tasks point to the importance of language in the development and assessment of conservation.

At the same time, cross-cultural stability of certain Piagetian tasks has been demonstrated in a number of studies. The evidence points to greatest stability for conservation of quantity, weight and volume (Goodnow, 1969a, b). Hyde (1959) confirmed Piaget's findings on a multiracial group in Aden with respect to numerical understanding and conservation of quantity. Price-Williams (1962) studied the occurrence of abstract and concrete modes of classification in children of the Nigerian Tiv tribe. Using material with which the children were familiar, he found that literate and illiterate groups did not differ significantly and that the formation of class concepts proceeded in a fashion similar to that observed in Western children. Goodnow and Bethon (1966) reported that the performance of unschooled Chinese children on conservation of weight, surface and volume did not differ significantly from that of an American sample. Similarly, Vernon (1969) observed a close correspondence between the performance of English and West Indian schoolboys on tasks assessing conservation of surface, quantity and volume.

Goodnow (1969b) proposes that these findings may be reconciled if two principal hypotheses are, tentatively, adopted. The first is that the tasks less vulnerable to cross-cultural variation are those for which the child has an action model. She points out that the studies by Goodnow and Bethon (1966), Peluffo (1964) and Price-Williams (1962) support the view that children with little formal schooling may depend in particular on action and manipulation. Greenfield's unschooled Wolof children demonstrate this feature well. A relevant investigation in this connection is that of Price-Williams, Gordon and Ramirez (1969) relating skill in pottery-making to conservation of liquid, substance, weight and volume in Mexican children. The second hypothesis states that the more vulnerable tasks may be those requiring some kind of non-motor representation – words, drawings or visual imagery. This would account for the poorer performance of some of Vernon's groups on imaging tests and the poorer performance for combinatorial tasks by Goodnow and Bethon and Peluffo on the assumption that combinatorial reasoning requires the manipulation of symbols.

Much more cross-cultural research is necessary before firm conclusions can be reached, but these findings and hypotheses are of interest in suggesting that the opposing conceptions of Piaget and Bruner may be reconciled up to a point. On Piaget's theory, it may be anticipated that action provides the means for cross-cultural generality and that such generality would be particularly evident for those conservations attained through concrete operations. Equally, Bruner's insistence on the importance of language in the thinking of people in technological societies is vindicated by the inability of people in non-technological societies to manipulate symbols in conventional formal reasoning tasks. There may, then, be a general developmental sequence, but the occurrence of the later phases of this sequence is contingent upon the presence of a language adapted to the needs of hypothetical-deductive thinking.

However, Bruner would quarrel with this formulation since he denies that internalized operations are the fundamental factors in conservation or in intellectual development as a whole. He believes that the primary mechanism responsible for conservation is a primitive sense of the identity of an object; for example, if a single quantity of liquid, first contained in a standard beaker, is poured into another that is taller and thinner, the only 'similarity' between the two is achieved through maintenance of their identity – it is the same liquid. Bruner assumes that this sense of identity is either innate or develops well before the child is active in the manipulation of objects. This view of conservation may be related to those studies which have shown conservation responses in young children when language is reduced to a minimum (e.g. Cohen, 1967). On Bruner's view, it is not a question of an operational understanding preceding its verbal expression, but of an understanding based upon an identity argument being obscured by the verbal nature of the conventional conservation tests. This issue of the mechanism of conservation attainment must now, therefore, be considered more fully.

THE ATTAINMENT OF CONSERVATION

The concept of conservation has been the focus of research inspired by Piaget's theory into the mechanism of intellectual development. The strategy of this research is to train children who exhibit non-conservation responses on the assumption that the training technique which is most effective in the laboratory is probably the most important influence in the normal course of development of the concept. The majority of these studies appear to be guided by one of three general theories about the nature of intellectual development. There are, in the first place, studies within the traditional Piagetian framework; on the view that the child attains conservation when he has mastered the appropriate operations, these studies attempt to teach understanding of reversibility or compensation, or instruct the child in the rules according to which we say that a property is conserved, or attempt to induce him to understand the logical necessity of conservation by equilibration training. A second view, which we have encountered in Bruner's work and in studies showing the influence of language on the age of attainment of the concept, is that the young child who fails on a conventional measure of conservation really possesses the concept but is unable to express it, either because he lacks linguistic ability or because he is temporarily misled by perceptual cues. On the third view, it is argued that the concept is acquired as a result of experience; however, this experience is not logico-mathematical (the internalization and co-ordination of actions) but refers to practice, reinforcement and exposure to adult models. This viewpoint, therefore, agrees with the first, rather than the second, in assuming that the young child does not possess the concept, but agrees with the second, rather than the first, in the importance it attaches to factors other than operational ones. Piaget would, no doubt, characterize these alternatives to operationalism as a 'structuralism without genesis' or a 'geneticism without structure' (Piaget, 1969).

Training in Operations and Rules

The evidence suggests that operational or rule-learning training procedures are often effective in fostering conservation responses but it is by no means clear how and why these procedures are effective. For example, Wallach and Sprott (1964) trained children to understand the operation of reversibility by having them reverse the experimenter's action; the success of this technique led the investigators to believe that reversibility was the key to conservation attainment. However, they and other authors (e.g. Bruner, Olver and Greenfield, 1966) reported many cases of children understanding reversibility without admitting conservation. In a later experiment (Wallach, Wall and Anderson, 1967) they confirmed the role of reversibility training but argued that the effect of this training was to stop subjects using a misleading perceptual cue, namely the appearance of one object being left over after the others in the two rows had been paired. But the authors affirmed that recognizing a misleading cue is not sufficient to account for a property being regarded the same after certain transformations and that, therefore, the child must both recognize reversibility *and* not rely on inappropriate cues in order to conserve. Roll (1970) also found reversibility training to be effective.

The evidence on the role of compensation (or addition-subtraction) is equivocal. Wohlwill (1960), Wohlwill and Lowe (1962) and Smedslund (1961a) report data suggesting that training children in adding an element to a collection or subtracting one from it can lead to the child inferring conservation as a result of change involving neither addition nor subtraction. Winer (1968) reports some success with this technique, but Wallach, Wall and Anderson (1967) and Smith (1968) found this type of training to be ineffective. However, Bruner, Olver and Greenfield (1966) found that a training technique which provided children with verbal labels for compensating attributes was effective in inducing conservation when children were allowed to manipulate the stimulus material.

Smedslund (1961a, b, c, d, e) developed the hypothesis that conservation originates from a conflict between the addition-subtraction scheme and the child's perception of the deformation of objects. Studying the conservation of weight, Smedslund's procedure was to deform one ball of plasticine into a sausage-shape while, at the same time, subtracting a piece from the other ball. Theoretically, if the child saw the deformation as making the one ball lighter and the subtraction as making the other ball lighter, there should be a cognitive conflict which might well produce a resolution in the form of a conservation judgement. In Smedslund's earlier studies, only five out of a hundred subjects had changed to conservation as a result of other training procedures; since the conflict training induced conservation in four out of thirteen subjects, Smedslund maintained that this was quite an encouraging result. Gruen (1965) found some support for the conflict hypothesis, but Winer (1968) did not.

In addition, several studies have reported success with training procedures which have combined two or more operations in a training programme. Successful training has been reported for a programme which included classification, compensation and reversibility training (Sigel, Roeper and Hooper, 1966), for compensation and identity (Lefrançois, 1968), for a reversibility and cognitive conflict procedure (Murray, 1968) and for reversibility, identity and compensation (Sullivan, 1967, 1969; Rothenberg and Orost, 1969). Beilin's (1965) subjects were successfully trained on verbal rules, which embodied either compensation for length conservation or reversibility for number conservation, and Smith (1968) has confirmed the efficacy of such training. However, Beilin (1969) has argued that his subjects learn a model or algorithm for solving a specific type of problem rather than the principles of reversibility or compensation themselves.

Identity and Conservation

But Bruner believes that Piaget 'has missed the heart of conservation' (Bruner, Olver and Greenfield, 1966, p. 185) which, he holds, is the product of a primitive sense of identity rather than the application of logical operations. The young child is a 'non-conserver', not, therefore, because he is in a pre-operational period of development, but because his understanding of identity is obscured by perceptual cues or because of his inability to use words like 'more' and 'same' as adults do.

A number of studies have attempted to demonstrate the nature of the young child's perceptual difficulties. After showing the child a half-full standard beaker and an empty comparison beaker, Frank (reported in Bruner, Olver and Greenfield, 1966) placed the two behind a screen before pouring the liquid from one to the other. She then asked the child whether there was still the same amount of water. It was found that this screening procedure led, in all subjects except the 4-year-olds, to a conservation judgement. This was interpreted as supporting the view that the 5-year-old child has to learn not to be distracted by irrelevant cues and that screening derives its effectiveness from forcing the child to rely upon an identity argument. Feigenbaum and Sulkin (1964) corroborated this finding, but Strauss and Langer (1970) could not do so. Gelman's (1969) analyses support the view that the young child does not have to learn to define quantity and invariance *de novo* but has to learn to avoid reliance upon misleading perceptual cues. Minichiello and Goodnow (1969) allowed children to observe the experimenter pour water simultaneously from two cups into two differently shaped beakers and attributed the successful outcome of this training to its drawing the child's attention away from perceptual cues. Halford (1968) found conservers to be superior to non-conservers in the recognition of equal and unequal quantities in different shaped containers in the absence of a known standard: this performance seems, therefore, to reflect an intuitive or perceptual estimation.

Studies which appear to support a semantic interpretation of conservation have been referred to in an earlier section (e.g. Braine and Shanks, 1965; Cohen, 1967; Lumsden and Poteat, 1968). Against these, it has been pointed out that there are examples of non-conservers who do know the relevant words (Inhelder *et al.*, 1966) and that the semantic interpretation does not provide an adequate explanation of the behaviour of children in the transitional stage who assert conservation in some instances but not in others (Flavell, 1963). Moreover, Oléron (1961) and Furth (1966) have shown that deaf children do not

differ greatly from hearing children with respect to the age of conservation attainment, although the interpretation that this result signifies
the prime importance of operations rather than language *per se* has been
challenged by Ausubel (1968), who has argued that deaf children are
by no means isolated from socialized verbal language. Peters (1970) has
found verbal training for conservation to be effective.

Piaget (1968b) has replied to Bruner by distinguishing between pre-
operative and operative identity. The former relates to single, qualitative
invariants and it is this sense of identity which Frank's subjects rely
upon in the screening condition when they say that the water remains
the same (that is, it is the same water). But for Piaget this is a pseudo-
conservation since this sense of identity alone does not enable the child
to recognize that the quantity is unchanged. This achievement requires
the co-ordination of physical dimensions and can only occur when
operative identity, dealing with quantitative invariants, is established
and co-ordinated with the operations of reversibility and compensation.
Thus, true conservation depends upon operational competence.

Reinforcement and Social Learning

Conventional reinforcement procedures seem to be ineffective in
inducing conservation. Wohlwill (1959, 1960), Wohlwill and Lowe
(1962) and Smedslund (1961a, b, d) attempted, without success, to
train children in this way. Smedslund (1961b) demonstrated that
children who had acquired the conservation of weight by control on a
balance reverted to non-conservation response when confronted with
instances of apparent non-conservation (Smedslund surreptitiously
removed a piece of plasticine from one of the balls), whereas half of
the subjects who had acquired the concept 'normally' resisted the
attempt at extinction and interpreted the apparent non-conservation
as meaning that something has been added or taken away. These
experiments are, of course, open to the criticism that insufficient
reinforcement experience was provided. Success has been reported,
however, for techniques involving the child's exposure to a model.
Sullivan (1967, 1969) and Waghorn and Sullivan (1970) managed to
induce conservation judgements by exposing subjects to filmed models
who verbalized the principles (reversibility, compensation, etc.)
underlying conservation. Whilst it is not immediately clear just how
Sullivan's subjects learned conservation, these experiments do raise the
question of how much adult intervention is necessary for understanding
the concept. There are opposing views on this matter. Beilin (1969)
contends that the likelihood of the child achieving this insight solely

through his own actions is slight. On the other hand, as Wallach (1969) points out, the social learning hypothesis leaves unexplained how anyone ever began to believe in the principle or how it is possible for people from widely different cultures to possess essentially the same concept.

These opposing views bring us to perhaps the most general issue underlying research on the attainment of conservation. This research has succeeded in demonstrating that a number of variables may be influential but it does not enable us to state that one is more fundamental than another. The Piagetian view that conservation is attained when competence in the operations of reversibility and compensation is attained receives some support, but the existence of such operational competence alongside non-conservation responses suggests that this cannot be a sufficient condition. Pre-operative identity may be a precursor of genuine conservation, but the understanding of quantitative invariances seems to call for the understanding of operational coordinations. Similarly, language, the overcoming of perceptual errors and exposure to adult models may be important influences but it is difficult to imagine how they can be constituted as sufficient causes of conservation. Does this not all suggest that we should move away from 'nothing-but-arguments' to a study of the interaction of the relevant variables?

For it seems fair to say that this state of affairs has come about because, on the one hand, workers within the traditional Piagetian framework have tended to focus upon competence and training in operations to the neglect of task variables, language and social learning, while, on the other hand, those who have wished to oppose operationalism have either tended to point to these variables, as if their mere existence were enough to discredit the theory, or to resort to the concept of a primitive sense of identity, as though this dispensed with the necessity of explaining the development of operational competence and its role in problem-solving. But, granted that the outcome of a conservation task is a function of the subject's ability to use certain operations, of the nature of the task and of the extent to which the subject can draw upon a facilitating language and cultural background, then the basic problem is to find the right measure for each of them. In general terms, this implies the study of what Hunt (1961) called the 'match' between environmental circumstances and the operational schemes of the subject. These schemes develop and are effective only in an environment which facilitates them; conversely, the environmental circumstances are effective in so far as they provide opportunities for the subject to use his operational schemes. This view is implicit in the adaptation model, on which the only possible relationship between environment and operativity is one of reciprocity. Most of the research on conservation would appear not to have been informed by this model, since this would entail that the testing of the logical model and the systematic manipulation of stimulus events are regarded as necessarily parallel activities.

THE ADAPTATION MODEL

The significance of these ideas can, perhaps, best be understood through considering some of the criticisms directed towards Piaget's theory. I believe that many of these criticisms can be refuted but that, nevertheless, they indicate important shortcomings in the manner in which the theory has been applied.

Consider, for example, how the often-repeated criticism (e.g. Fowler, 1962; Bandura and Walters, 1965) that the theory is essentially a maturational perspective which regards behaviour as being determined largely by factors intrinsic to the organism is contradicted by the idea that development in thought occurs because of adaptation to the environment, an idea which certainly gives experience its due. Now, although this refutation is clear-cut, the manner in which Piaget has used logical models to describe the structure of thought together with the concept of equilibration, which appears to guarantee the development of a mode of thinking that is both logical and adapted to its environment, lends some justification to the complaint that the role of environmental circumstances has been neglected. As Lunzer (1968) says, it is generally felt that Piaget attributes too much order and structure to thinking. Thus, Bruner (1959) criticizes the concept of equilibration on the grounds that it is not precise enough to specify how different modes of thought arise in response to the demands which the environment makes upon the subject. Thus, Boyle (1969) characterizes Piaget's theory as a closed system in which all internal forces are accounted for rather than one which specifies the various interactions of subject and environment. In a sense, therefore, it is true to say that the concept of adaptation is an ideal principle rather than a useful description of what actually happens. But it would be misleading to allow these comments to stand as the verdict upon the theory, since the concept of adaptation also contains an insight into the nature of thought and behaviour which allows us to supersede the immediate limitations of research inspired by the theory and the partial truths of these criticisms.

D*

This insight is that environmental events do not impose their nature upon a passive organism any more than the organism produces whatever results it desires on an indifferent environment because all knowledge is simultaneously accommodation to the object and assimilation to the subject. The progress of intelligence works in the dual direction of externalization and internalization and the development of operational structures parallels the construction of reality. This idea is most evident in the work on sensori-motor development where it is plain that adaptation signifies the development of schemes and, simultaneously, the development of stimulus discrimination and generalization, but it surely has general application. The principle has a number of implications. Operational competence is not reducible to environmental circumstances (the error of empiricism), nor is performance merely a distorting influence (the error of idealism). To say that a subject has a certain level of operational competence is to say that his competence is manifest under certain stimulus conditions; to say that these stimulus conditions control the subject's performance is to say that they act in conjunction with the subject's operational competence; and moreover, these two statements are equivalent. Competence may be defined as the subject's understanding of operations or rules but it can only be measured by observing the extent to which the subject makes use of this understanding in a range of tasks; because of this, Flavell and Wohlwill's (1969) mathematical model, in which operational competence increases to a maximum at substage two independently of task variations, is not true to the central insight of the adaptation concept. Equally, it is impossible to assess stimulus control independently of the subject's operational competence. This entails that the testing of the logical model, which is to describe the structure of the subject's thought, and the manipulation of stimulus events, which is to result in a description of the conditions which facilitate or impede this thought, are necessarily parallel activities.

This confrontation of logic and psychology is, after all, one of the reasons why we can expect that Piaget's work will continue to exert a considerable influence upon theory and research.

PART TWO

Concept Formation

4

The theory of abstraction

The theory of abstraction can be traced back to Aristotle, who opposed the doctrine that there are innate ideas in favour of the view that all our knowledge is derived from particular things: thinking, he maintained, is a matter of proceeding from the particular to the general and then, by analysis of the general, back to the particular. Aristotle's theory of knowledge was elaborated by medieval scholastic philosophers, but it was also taken up by British empiricist philosophers such as Hobbes and, more notably, John Locke.

Locke, in his *Essay Concerning Human Understanding* (1690), identified two sources of ideas which he termed sensation and reflection. The senses convey into the mind distinct perceptions of things, for instance, their colour or shape, while he defines reflection as the perception of the operations of our own minds, as when we perceive ourselves to be thinking or believing or doubting. Locke held that sensation and reflection provide us with 'simple ideas' and he emphasized that, since we cannot help but receive these impressions, the mind is passive in their reception. In contrast, the mind is active in forming 'complex ideas' from the simple ones. When simple ideas are combined into complex ones, Locke calls them 'mixed modes'; for example, the idea of beauty is constituted by the combination of colour and figure. In a crucial passage Locke states that 'ideas become general by separating from them the circumstances of time, and place, and any other ideas that may determine them to this or that particular existence. By this way of abstraction they are made capable of representing more individuals than one; each of which, having in it a conformity to that abstract idea, is (as we call it) of that sort' (Book III, Ch. 3, 6). Thus, children begin by using names which refer to particular individuals, such as mummy and daddy, but notice, as they grow older, that there are a great many other things in the world which resemble their mother and father, so that 'they frame an idea' which embraces these similarities, for instance, the name 'man'.

Substituting 'concept' for 'idea', this view asserts that it is by a process of abstraction that concepts are formed; we observe a number of particular objects and abstract (literally, draw away) from them those features that are common to several of them. Concepts are formed when objects are classified. From Locke's account, it is evident that there are two aspects to this process. Not only must we notice similarities to form a general idea, but we must also set aside particular differences, which are not relevant to the concept in question. The former corresponds to what we now call generalization, the latter to discrimination.

In attempting to demonstrate that abstract ideas are not present in children but are acquired only through experience, Locke referred to the general idea of a triangle, which, he maintained, does not indicate any particular type of triangle but which refers to all types and none of them at once. But how can this be so? Berkeley, in his *Treatise Concerning the Principles of Human Knowledge* (1708), argued that it is impossible that an idea should combine inconsistent qualities. If we form the concept of a triangle, it must be a particular triangle; if we form the concept of a man, it must be a man of some particular colour, shape and height. Every idea must have a single determinate set of qualities and, accordingly, Berkeley denied that there are abstract ideas, in Locke's sense of the term. He did not deny that there are general ideas, but he thought that what Locke called a general idea is really a particular idea which is made general by being taken as a sign for other particular ideas, between which there is some resemblance. Thus, whilst Locke's general idea is the representation of the common nature of a number of particular ideas, Berkeley's general idea depends only upon the particular ideas resembling one another in some way.

In spite of this important disagreement, the ideas of Locke and Berkeley lay the foundation for the development of the empiricist tradition with its emphasis upon the primacy of sensation in the acquisition of concepts. The net effect of Berkeley's critique was to transfer the traditional notion of the concept to another dimension. If simple, sensory data are all that we can hope to know without falling into error and illusion, then concepts are derived when we compare, not objects in the environment, but presentations or representations of those objects. The contents of perception, not the things themselves, are the stimuli which serve as the units for abstraction. The theory of abstraction has altered little since this time. If anything, as Reeves (1965) points out, the tradition gave increasing emphasis to the view that thinking consists of the formation of concepts through the association of simple, sensory elements, the doctrine receiving its most radical formulation by John Stuart Mill.

The process of abstracting is still widely regarded as the key to our thought processes. The vitality of the doctrine may be seen in a recent, philosophical exposition of it by Price (1962), who begins by contrasting the two major philosophical approaches to abstraction that we have encountered in the different conceptions of Locke and Berkeley. Price distinguishes between the theory of universals, according to which general ideas are formed by abstraction of the common feature in a number of particular perceptions, and the theory of resemblances, according to which the subject takes a specific perceptual item and groups other items in respect of their resemblance to it. Price favours the latter theory, holding that it provides a more accurate psychological description of the process of abstraction. In outline, his argument takes the following form. In order that the subject can group perceptual data by their resemblances, he must, clearly, be capable of *recognizing* these resemblances. Recognition, for Price, is a type of 'sign cognition', which he defines as the act of responding to a stimulus as a sign of another stimulus, when that other stimulus is not present. For example, we have learned to recognize that an overcast sky signifies rain, or that the notice, 'Warning', signifies the presence of a hazard. One implication of this theory is the belief that the simpler forms of sign cognition are within the capabilities of animals and that the major advance attained in human sign cognition is the relatively greater independence of signs from immediate stimulation. But the main consequence of Price's theory is that a concept may be regarded as a system of recognitional dispositions, rather than an abstracted common feature, a disposition being defined as a readiness to respond in a particular way determined largely by previous learning to particular signs. Such a theory permits a behaviouristic approach to concept formation and we shall see that Price's theory is compatible with contemporary, psychological approaches based upon an *S-R* orientation.

ABSTRACTION THEORY IN PSYCHOLOGY

It is possible to discern three phases in the use of abstraction theory, with corresponding variations in the definition of the concept, in psychological research. Initially, there was the introspectionist period, in which the empiricist doctrine tended to be accepted without any substantial change. This was followed by the behaviourist approach, in which conscious acts of judgement and recognition were replaced by conditioned associations between stimuli and responses. The most recent phase may be characterized as neo-behaviourist in orientation, since the laws of learning formulated in the earlier period are retained, while at the same time processes mediating between external stimulus and response are introduced. This classification is, to be sure, an idealized one, depicting only the main trend of theorizing, but my main purpose at the moment is to show to what extent the essential aspects of abstraction theory itself remain unaltered and unchallenged by these developments.

The introspectionist approach may be seen in Wundt's theorizing and in the experiments performed during the first two decades of this century. Wundt (1894) defined abstraction as 'the procedure by which certain constituent parts are eliminated from a compound idea or from several such ideas and what remains is retained as the elements of a concept' (p. 11). Like Locke, he distinguished between 'singular concepts' and 'general concepts', arguing that the former are transformed into the latter by acts of judgement which organize and relate experiences. The majority of researchers in this period accepted the idea that judgement is chiefly exercised in perceiving common elements. In Fisher's (1916) experiment, for example, the subject had to learn to associate nonsense syllables with figures capable of being classified in a number of ways: his task was to abstract the common features in the figures and ignore the irrelevant differences. Similar experiments were carried out by, among others, Grünbaum (1908), Moore (1910) and Aveling (1912).

Introspectionism was overthrown with the emergence of behaviourism, which denied that we need to resort to consciousness in order to understand concept formation. Hull (1920) used the conditioning paradigm, asserting that a concept is formed through the establishment of associative links between the identical element in a number of stimuli and a particular response. Thus a child learns the concept 'dog' by hearing the word 'dog' in a number of 'somewhat different' situations. Hull's experiments, in which subjects learned to attach nonsense syllables to the common elements in a number of Chinese letters, were designed to demonstrate that concept formation could be explained by invoking the principles used to explain animal learning. If this is correct, it follows that animals can learn simple concepts too. Fields (1932), in a paper entitled 'The development of the concept of triangularity by the white rat', showed that rats can be trained to respond consistently to triangles in a discrimination task when the size and orientation of the triangle is varied during training. Fields thought that the animal learns the concept through stimulus generalization. Thus, if the animal is trained to respond to a large, equilateral triangle by being rewarded when approaching it, the training will generalize to smaller and larger equilateral triangles and also to triangles which depart from the equilateral form. If the rat is also trained to respond to triangles having varying angles and sides of varying length, the generalization gradients will overlap to such an extent that the animal will respond to any stimulus which has the three-pointed characteristic of triangles. We may then attribute to the rat the concept of triangularity. In the same way, it may be argued, the child builds up his concepts. Through being rewarded for responding in an identical manner to objects which initially appear different, the child succeeds in making a generalization about the objects and we refer to this generalization as a concept. This reasoning lies behind a simple experiment by Long (1940) with children from 3 to 6 years of age. A box with two small windows was placed before the child; if he pressed on the correct window, a small piece of candy rolled out to him. At first, he saw a rubber ball through one window and a rectangular block of wood through the other. When the child had learned to choose the ball regularly, he was tested for 'equivalent' stimuli; that is, spherical objects of various sizes, colours and materials were paired with various angular objects. Long found that the spheres were consistently chosen and concluded that this sort of learning is responsible for the development of the concept of a sphere in real life.

Thus, whereas the introspectionists regarded concept formation as a conscious process of identifying common features and, as such, beyond the capacities of infra-human organisms, the behaviourists maintained that the concept was formed through the conditioning of a response to common features and that, consequently, animals, children and human adults could all possess concepts in some form or another. What is common to the two approaches is the assumption of the philosophy of universals about identical elements. The third perspective, that of mediational learning theory, characteristically rejects this assumption, although retaining the conditioning model with additional processes intervening between external stimulus and response – the so-called mediational processes, whose presence or absence carries implications for the comparative development of concepts in animals and humans. Let us examine these three characteristics in turn.

1. Identical stimulus elements. Smoke (1932) had already questioned Hull's theory that abstraction necessarily involved identical elements. What, he asked, are the identical stimulus elements present in, say, the various kinds of dog? Smoke thought that it made more sense to talk of common perceptual relations and substantiated this by successfully training subjects to attach nonsense syllables to figures which varied widely in their physical dimensions but which were classifiable according to certain recurring perceptual relations. Osgood (1953) advanced this reasoning a step further by arguing that common perceptual relations are no more essential to concept formation than identical elements. There is, for example, no common perceptual relation between mittens, hats and neckties, although they are classifiable under the concept of 'clothing', or between crawling, swimming and flying, although these are all types of movement. He concluded that the only essential condition for concept formation is the learning of a common response for a group of objects or situations, not necessarily containing any features in common. Kendler (1961) had Osgood's theory in mind when she defined the concept as 'a common response to dissimilar stimuli'.

2. Mediational processes. According to Osgood, what has to be taken into account in the explanation of human conceptual behaviour is the presence of signs – principally words – which mediate between stimulus and response. Osgood's theory, which is derived from the theory of signs proposed by Morris (1946), is that a word becomes a sign virtually by eliciting some of the same behaviour as the object of which it is the sign; this behaviour is a partial revival of what occurred in the first instance and it acts as an internalized stimulus to an overt response. Thus, for example, the external stimulus (S) of a dog initially produces an overt response (R) of approaching, stroking, etc. The word 'dog' is associated with the presence of various sorts of dog and this sign, because of its repeated association with S, becomes capable of eliciting the kind of behaviour typified in the overt response, for example, anticipatory approach movements. This response (r) then acts as a stimulus (s) to the overt response (R), and can do so in the absence of S. This process may be represented schematically:

1. $S_{(\text{dog})}$ ——— R (behaviour of approaching, stroking, etc.)

2. $S^1_{(\text{'dog'})}$ ——— r_m ——————— s_m ——————— R^1

| (elements of the original response) | (distinctive pattern of self-stimulation) | (anticipatory approach movements) |

This scheme is equivalent to Price's definition of sign cognition as the act of responding to a stimulus as a sign of another stimulus, when the other stimulus is not present. The organism having mediational processes in its repertoire is relatively free from a dependence upon immediate stimulation and it is able to handle new instances of concepts effectively by relating them to its 'store' of signs.

3. Developmental differences in concept formation. Osgood was critical of earlier assumptions that animals and humans possess concepts in much the same form. He pointed out that we cannot say that the rat in the experiment by Fields has acquired the concept of triangularity in the same way that a human adult has the concept. We cannot say that the rat has the abstract concept of the triangle, in that it would not, probably, react positively to three people or to three places on a map as triangles. Kendler and Kendler (1962) have demonstrated important differences in concept formation between animals and humans and have attributed these differences to the existence of mediational responding in humans and its absence in animals. This work will be discussed in the next chapter.

As Pikas (1966) says, the definition of concept formation as the learning of a common response to dissimilar stimuli most faithfully expresses the dominant contemporary orientation. This definition arose from the insight that identical physical elements or common perceptual relations are not essential for concept formation. It would appear, then, that the phrase 'dissimilar stimuli' should be taken to mean 'stimuli not alike physically or from the point of view of perceptual relation', but, of course, as H. H. Kendler (1964) has acknowledged, it is impossible to say that any two objects are entirely dissimilar: all objects, for instance, have weight and substance, and they are all *something*. What this definition of the concept really achieves, therefore, is a broadening of the concept of the concept to include *other* kinds of *classification* besides those based upon the identity or similarity of physical or perceptual-relational elements, for instance, the classification of mittens, hats and neckties by their function as clothing, or the classification of crawling, swimming and flying as instances of the concept of 'movement'. There are, in short, as many types of concept as there are criteria for relating the stimuli which constitute them.

What, then, is the current status of the theory of abstraction in psychology? The idea that a concept does not necessarily entail identical elements or resemblances in the stimuli themselves and that the only

essential feature of a concept is the association of a common response
to a variety of stimuli is directly contrary to the theory. Are we to conclude that abstraction theory has been totally replaced? Unfortunately,
the position is complicated by the fact that two different interpretations have been placed upon the new orientation. One of these merely
assigns a less important role in concept learning to the notion of
abstraction, whereas on the other interpretation it is rejected totally
and replaced by a conditioning model, whose principal explanatory
concept is the mechanism of association.

On the first interpretation it may be argued that there are different
kinds of concepts corresponding to the mechanisms responsible for their
attainment and that abstraction is but one way in which concepts are
formed. Gagné and Jenkins argue in this way. Gagné (1966) reasons
that the concepts which experimenters get subjects to learn in the
laboratory are valid enough, but that there are other concepts which
appear as altogether too complex to be viewed in this light, for example,
physical concepts, such as gravitation, heat and light. Gagné says that
concepts like 'work' are more properly defined as principles and should
not be equated with simple concepts. The problem of fitting principles
into the scheme of learning theory can be solved, he believes, by
interpreting them as being relationships among two or more concepts.
With the principle of work, for instance, a subject must learn that

$$\text{work} = \text{force} \times \text{distance}.$$

The subject who is to understand this principle must identify several
concepts and their proper sequence. He must identify a member of the
class 'force' (a concept), a member of the class 'distance' (another
concept) and an instance of the class 'product' or 'multiply' (a third
concept). Their sequence must also be identified in order to obtain the
product. In short, demonstration of a rule or principle involves the
simpler performances of identifying each concept and the sequence
that relates them. (This reasoning is very reminiscent of Locke's
'mixed modes'.) Very similar reasoning is advanced by Jenkins (1966),
who distinguishes between three kinds of concepts. The first is the
concept that is formed through the isolation of some aspect or aspects
of the stimuli which are instances of the concept – the type of concept
dealt with in the traditional theory of abstraction. The second class
is that of concepts that depend upon agreement of particular responses
to stimuli, the simplest case being that of 'naming' or 'labelling'
responses – this is the sort of concept that Osgood and Kendler had
in mind. The third type is analogous to Gagné's principles, its

distinguishing feature being that it is the expression of the application of a set of rules of relation.

It is evident that the effect of such reasoning is to place the theory of abstraction in a perspective but, at the same time, to leave it un-challenged as a theory. The persistence of the theory can be seen in Underwood's (1966) definition of the concept: 'The crux of concept learning is the abstraction – selection – of a common feature, character-istic or property which is present in a number of stimuli which differ on other characteristics' (p. 57). It is also apparent, strangely enough, in a recent paper by Kendler and Kendler (1970), who say, in discussing the relationship between mediational processes and the stimuli serving as the material for concept learning, that 'each of these symbolic responses refers to a class of events that differ in other features but have a given feature in common' (p. 24).

However, on the second interpretation, abstraction theory is rejected. If a concept is 'a common response to dissimilar stimuli', then it is formed, not through the abstraction of similarities, but through the different stimuli becoming associated with the same response. In short, it is assumed that the first and third 'types' of concept identified by Jenkins (1966) are reducible to the second. This seems to be the most consistent interpretation of the Osgood-Kendler definition. Both Osgood and Kendler inform us that the mediational processes obey the same principles that operate in observable *S-R* relations (Osgood, 1953, p. 411; Kendler and Kendler, 1962) and that it is through conditioning that the common mediational response – probably a word – becomes associated with the stimuli that form a particular class. Staats (1961) puts this case most explicitly when he states that abstraction in the development of concepts depends upon the conditioning of a common mediating response to a variety of stimulus objects exemplary of the concept.

In assessing the validity of these interpretations, therefore, we must ask, in the first place, whether it is justifiable to retain the theory of abstraction at all (even in a relatively minor role), and, if not, whether it is justifiable to replace it with a model which relies upon the principle of association – the conditioning model.

CRITIQUE OF THE THEORY OF ABSTRACTION

Opponents of abstraction theory usually begin by considering those concepts for which the theory is least plausible, namely mathematical and logical concepts, and then continue to demonstrate that the deficiencies of the theory in this respect are also evident in those simpler concepts which are the favourite examples of the abstractionists themselves.

Mathematical Concepts

John Stuart Mill (1874), applying the basic, empiricist assumption that all knowledge derives from experience, believed that mathematical concepts were nothing other than expressions of the relationships we find to apply in our dealing with the environment. Accordingly, all mathematical rules are about relationships in the material world that surrounds us and, consequently, they are accidental and variable in the same sense as all such relationships are. If, therefore, we grew up in a different environment, we would have a different kind of arithmetic and geometry, so that on another planet, say, there would be different numerical laws. For example, 2×2 might equal 5 and not 4. Thus, 'the reverse of the most familiar principles of arithmetic and geometry might have been made conceivable even to our present mental faculties, if those faculties had coexisted with a totally different constitution of external nature' (Mill, 1869, p. 89).

The first mathematician to argue convincingly against Mill was Frege (1884). According to Frege, Mill's fundamental mistake was the assumption that mathematical laws represent abstraction from our experience of things. He maintained that mathematical laws are not laws about objects, since this would deprive them of the objectivity which constitutes their most important feature. For example, one consequence of Mill's reasoning that our understanding of numbers is based upon our sensory impressions is that this understanding would be restricted to whatever capacity of discrimination we had attained in the perception of a given group of objects. The absurdity of this consequence can be seen very easily, however: the number, 753,684 is just as definitely and clearly differentiated from the number that immediately precedes it and that which follows it as 3 is from 2 or 4, but who could point out the 'impression' by which we discriminate between concrete groups of objects of this size? Moreover, Frege argued, if Mill's theory of abstraction were correct, we would not be able to use numbers in respect of non-physical objects, since Mill thought that the operations of counting, etc., are only possible where things themselves can be collected and separated into perceptible, spatial groups. This, however, is contradicted by the fact that we do operate with non-physical properties as readily as we do with actual things, for example, the number of categories or the number of parliamentary laws.

There is a reply to this criticism that will, no doubt, occur to those familiar with psychological learning theory. This is to argue that we begin with comparing and grouping actual objects, but generalize our experiences with these to non-physical events and properties or to larger complexes of objects not actually present. Now, this reasoning may be correct, but, as Cassirer has pointed out, it contains a concealed assumption, whose recognition is quite fatal to the theory of abstraction. For, if it is possible to generalize from the concrete to the non-concrete,

> we must assume that some form of connection and dependence exists between the compared cases, by virtue of which the one can be deduced from the other. We would not have the right to extend any determination, which appears to us in any individual group, to groups of a larger or smaller number of elements, if we did not comprehend them all as similar in 'nature'. This similarity, however, means nothing more than that they are connected by a definite rule, such as permits us to proceed from one manifold to another by continued, identical application of the same fundamental relation.
>
> (Cassirer, 1953a, p. 30)

If we did not hold this assumption, we would have to be prepared to admit that it would be impossible to apply the same mathematical rules to groups whose elements differed in size or in type, for every rule would have to be proved anew with every different group. Therefore, the argument of generalization contains the concealed assumption that number concepts are general, but this is the very notion that abstraction theory begins by denying.

These considerations, Cassirer recognized, provide an insight into the necessary foundations of mathematical concepts. In order to apply the same arithmetical rules to large as well as small groups and to abstract as well as concrete properties, we must, in effect, make a decision that the various kinds of property can be treated as being *alike in principle*. This amounts to saying that what holds the elements together from the mathematical point of view is the fact that they are all capable of being treated by the same *operations*. For, as such philosophers as Frege and Cassirer have indicated, mathematical concepts are concerned with relations and are derived, not from the recognition of similarities in groups of objects, but from the various kinds of operations (e.g. adding, subtracting, etc.) performed, initially at least, upon objects. For Cassirer, this distinction corresponds to that commonly made between the logic of classes, dealing with the classification of objects according to their perceived similarities, and the logic of relations, which deals with the rules applied in the relating of both concrete and abstract elements. Therefore, the concept of number involves the unification of elements of a series by the application of a serial principle, not their agreement in some factual context (Cassirer, 1950). After a certain starting-point has been fixed by an original assumption, i.e. the concept of 1 as the first member of the set and the general relation of ordering are the basic presuppositions, all further elements are generated by the fact that a relation is given, which in continued application creates all the members of the set. Thus, the system of numbers arises without it being necessary that one element be connected with another by any sort of factual similarity. Once this essential characteristic of number is grasped, it is possible to see that development in mathematics consists of advancing from a system of relatively simple relationships to more complex systems of relations and of creating for them appropriate symbolic expressions.

Geach (1957) makes a similar point when he remarks that the child learning to do arithmetic needs to master a way of talking about number which has nothing to do with groups of concrete units, for instance, expressions of the form 'doing a thing *n* times over'. Adding 5 to 7 can be explained as performing 5 times over upon the number 7 the operation of going on to the next number – (7) 8, 9, 10, 11, 12. Subtraction is similarly explicable in terms of counting backwards. This ability cannot be derived from any number of trials in which the child attaches a number label to groups of apples varying in number.

Logical Concepts

Geach points out that abstractionists rarely attempt to give an account of logical concepts, like those of 'some', 'or' and 'not'; most of them are quite prepared to admit that these concepts are a special case falling outside the scope of the theory. On the other hand, some abstractionists feel no such hesitation. As logical concepts obviously cannot be abstracted from sensory experience (there are no instances of 'or' and 'not' provided by perception), the appeal must be made to 'reflection' upon our experience. Mill (1874), for example, uses such an explanation to account for the law of contradiction, which asserts that an affirmative proposition and the corresponding negative proposition cannot both be true. Mill considered this to be a generalization from experience, the foundation for it being that belief and disbelief are two different mental states excluding one another. Similar derivations of logical concepts have been attempted by James (1890) and Russell (1940).

The view that logical concepts derive from experience and that therefore, logic is based upon psychology, is known as psychologism (see Chapter 1). The issue will not be discussed fully here. It may be sufficient to raise two criticisms of the doctrine. In the first place, as Husserl (1900) argued, Mill's reduction of the axiom of contradiction to the experience that belief and disbelief are two different mental states is refuted by the simple observation that people often do hold contradictory beliefs without any recognition of their doing so. Now this, on Mill's theory that the two states of mind are mutually incompatible, would be impossible. Secondly, in all probability different individuals will have different experiences corresponding to the same logical concept. For instance, 'or' might suggest hesitation to one man but a threat to another (Geach). To be consistent, the abstractionist would have to admit that these individuals possessed different concepts. Yet this does not reflect the actual usage of logical concepts, which do not vary between individuals because of a dependence upon idiosyncratic experiences, but which, like mathematical concepts, are capable of being used by everybody in the same way. Of course, this is not to say that everyone uses these concepts perfectly efficiently, only that it is a reasonable expectation that everyone could, given the ability and tuition.

Both logic and mathematics may be characterized as being concerned with the study of rules of relation. The fact that the elements that they deal with are ordered by such rules lends the quality of necessity to logical and mathematical conceptualization. It is a matter of necessity, not of probability, that $2 \times 2 = 4$, because the result inevitably follows from the application of the rules of the system. We can, indeed, invent other systems with different rules, but this does not affect the issue, for abstractionism is silent about the existence of these rules, although they constitute the essential nature of logico-mathematical thinking.

'Simple' Concepts

Against this it may be argued that the theory of abstraction cannot account for such higher-order concepts but that it does explain simple, everyday concepts like 'colour' or 'man'. How else, it might be asked, could we develop these concepts except by abstracting resemblances from otherwise dissimilar stimuli?

In contesting that the theory of abstraction accounted for mathematical concepts, Cassirer noted that the theory assumes that which it has to explain, namely, the generality of mathematical rules. Likewise, Husserl (1901) maintained that the view that simple concepts, such as 'red', are formed through the recognition of similarities involves an infinite regress since, if to say that an object is red means only that its colour resembles that of other objects, all that I can say is that something is red because something else is red, and so forth, indefinitely. Consequently, it must be admitted that the generality of the concept is grasped, somehow, in the initial perception of the red object. We must be able to apprehend the general directly in a single act of perception:

> Thus we apprehend the species, 'red', directly, in itself, as it were, on the basis of a single perception of something red. We look at the red colour of an object given to us in perception, but we do this in a special kind of act; an act which aims at the 'ideal', the 'universal'. The abstraction in the sense of this act is completely different from mere pointing out or separating the perceived red from the rest of the perceptual context. In order to point out this difference we have repeatedly spoken of the *ideating* or generalizing abstraction.
>
> (Husserl, 1901, p. 223)

As Pivcevic (1970) says, this act of ideation to which Husserl refers is not to be regarded as a sort of 'sixth sense' but as an act of reason by which we turn things into examples.

Cassirer says that we turn things into examples by adopting a particular point of view. As he points out in Volume III of his major work, *The Philosophy of Symbolic Forms* (Cassirer, 1953b), the simplest concepts are never a mere amalgam of elements, but contain a particular organization of these. For example, when the Greek language designates the moon as 'the measurer' and the Latin language designates it as 'that which glitters', different intuitive concepts underline these different designations, but these concepts act in both cases only as a factor of comparison and correlation, only, that is, as a point of view. And, of course, points of view can be verified or superseded. It is in this sense that Cassirer sees that concept as essentially predictive, not reproductive. A concept is not so much a reproduction of reality, an established path, along which thought proceeds, as a capacity for discovering new paths; a concept does not provide a fixed and ready answer but only really establishes a point of view to guide thinking. It may turn out that a certain point of view is wrong; if, for example, certain languages designate the butterfly as a bird, focusing only on the point of view of flying, when other criteria become available through advances in zoology the original point of view will be superseded since it can now be replaced by one with a more complete meaning. This highlights the fact that there is no essential difference between the construction of everyday and the construction of scientific concepts. All concepts are hypotheses, capable of validation or invalidation.

Cassirer's (1953a) statement that 'all construction of concepts is connected with some definite form of construction of series' (p. 15) offers a formula which relates to the many different types of concept. The theory of abstraction ostensibly worked most effectively with concepts of concrete things, like tables and donkeys, but had great difficulty in accounting for logical and mathematical concepts. The weakness of the theory results from the fact that the only logical principle of order which the theory recognizes is the principle of similarity, and all the many other logical principles were either ignored or reduced to this. Cassirer's theory of the concept, however, makes it clear that a series of stimuli can be arranged according to the most diverse points of view, providing that the guiding point of view is maintained unaltered throughout the construction of the series:

> Thus side by side with series of similars in whose individual members a common element uniformly recurs, we may place series in which between each member and the succeeding member there prevails a certain degree of difference. Thus we can conceive members of series ordered according to equality or inequality, number and magnitude, spatial and temporal relations, or causal dependence. The *relation of necessity* thus produced is in each case decisive; the concept is merely the expression and husk of it. . . .
>
> (Cassirer, 1953a, p. 16)

IMPLICATIONS FOR THE PSYCHOLOGY OF CONCEPT LEARNING

These criticisms make it apparent that the principle of abstraction cannot account for the formation of even the simplest concepts and that there is no justification for retaining it in any psychological explanation of concept learning. Equally, it cannot suffice to resort to the principle of association. H. H. Kendler (1964) listed three properties of concepts implied by the mediational model: they are associations, cues and responses. But this list omits the most important property of concepts, namely, the fact that they are particular organizations of objects and events. The principle of association, as it has been pointed out on numerous occasions (see, for example, Humphrey, 1963), cannot itself account for the organized nature of thinking: we can and do distinguish between fortuitous associations and organized thinking. If the concept is, as Cassirer says, an expression of a particular way of organizing elements, then associationism is quite powerless to explain the concept.

The many experiments which demonstrate that subjects can be conditioned to associate certain stimuli with a particular response are not, therefore, answering the central question in the study of concept formation – the way in which elements become organized and thus distinct from chance associations. The recognition of this difficulty may be the cause of Heidbreder's (1946) strange pronouncement that a concept is 'a logical construct capable of interpersonal use' and that, 'so defined, concepts are obviously not the *subject matter* investigated in psychological research'. How experiments, in which the experimenter merely makes use of concepts that are not the subject-matter for experimentation, can hope to clarify our understanding of the attainment of such concepts, seems to be a paradox not fully appreciated by Heidbreder.

These considerations also show the ambiguities in the definition of the concept as 'a common response to dissimilar stimuli'. On the one hand, if stimuli are, in fact, dissimilar, any classifications of them that are achieved reflect the existence of different points of view or organizations, and it is therefore false to refer to these organizations merely as 'responses' which happen to become associated with a variety of stimuli. On the other hand, if it is maintained that there are, in some cases at least, resemblances between stimuli, which, when recognized, serve as the basis for classification and concept formation, then it is mistaken to refer to them as 'dissimilar stimuli'.

5

Concept shifts

The two theories of abstraction, we have noted, are distinguished by their conflicting accounts of the relationship between perception and thinking, the traditional theory assuming that concepts are formed when particular sensations are organized in thought, whereas the more recent theory affirms that thinking elaborates the forms of organization gained in perception. That this issue remains of fundamental importance may be judged from the controversy in contemporary theory and research over the importance of mediation in concept learning. Stated in its broadest terms, this controversy has to do with the relative weight to be attached to organization at the perceptual level (the viewpoint of differentiation theory) as against organization attributable to other variables (verbal or attentional mediation) that intervene between stimulus and response. Deductions from these alternative theories have been tested mainly in concept-shift situations, in which the subject learns one concept and is then required to learn another, but research on transposition and oddity learning is also relevant. A review of these theories and this research is essential, since, having accepted Cassirer's notion that the formation of concepts is always connected with some definite form of construction of series, it is necessary now to describe the mechanisms responsible for this construction, which means, precisely, accounting for the relationship between percepts and concepts.

THEORIES OF CONCEPT-SHIFT BEHAVIOUR

The three theories agree in asserting that concepts are formed through the organism learning to discriminate between stimuli and to attach different responses to different sets of stimuli. They disagree over the nature of the processes responsible for such stimulus-response connections, this disagreement being most evident in their interpretations of concept-shift behaviour.

The two major types of concept shift are intradimensional (ID) and extradimensional (ED) shifts. In both types, there is an initial phase, in which the subject learns a concept to a criterion, and a second phase, in which the subject has to learn a new concept, the cues for which are either along the rewarded dimension of the original concept (ID shift) or along another dimension, usually the one irrelevant in the

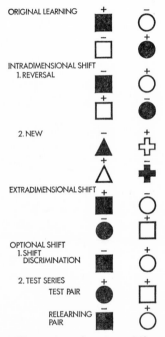

Figure 2. *Illustration of concept-shift paradigms.*

original learning (ED shift). The second phase of the experiment follows immediately after the first and the subject is not informed of the changes in the task requirements. Figure 2 illustrates the major forms of concept shift for a task involving shape and brightness dimensions. For human adults the task is to sort a series of cards correctly into two categories; after each response the experimenter indicates whether the subject was right or wrong. For young children and animals the task takes essentially the same form as for human adults except that the correct response is rewarded with a different kind of stimulus (food or something that children regard as a desirable possession, say, marbles).

In the example illustrated in Figure 2, the initial task requires subjects to choose cards with dark figures irrespective of shape. The reversal shift (one form of ID shift) requires the choice of the opposite value on the same dimension, that is, bright figures irrespective of shape. A second kind of ID shift, likewise, entails the subject responding to bright figures irrespective of shape but is characterized by the introduction of new shapes. In an ED shift (sometimes referred to as a non-reversal shift), on the other hand, the previously irrelevant dimension, shape, becomes relevant, the subject having to choose square rather than circular figures irrespective of brightness. The basic design, devised by Buss (1953), allows a comparison of the relative difficulty of reversal and ED shifts. Wolff's (1967) review contains an account of the variations on this design.

In an optional shift paradigm there are two phases after the original concept learning. In the shift discrimination phase only one pair of stimuli is presented: the previously negative stimulus becomes positive and the previously positive stimulus becomes negative; this means, in our example, that the subject can learn the shift by responding to shape (the circle) or to brightness or to both. The test phase involves rewarding responses to both of the stimuli that did not appear in the shift discrimination phase whilst maintaining the same pattern of reinforcement for the pair presented in the shift discrimination. If the bulk of the subject's responses in the test phase is to the stimulus that had been incorrect in the original learning, the subject is classified as a reverser; for example, if the subject responded to the bright square in the test pair, it is inferred that he learned the shift discrimination by shifting from dark to bright figures – a reversal response. If, on the other hand, the subject made more responses to the stimulus that had been irrelevant in the original learning, it would be inferred that he had learned the shift discrimination by responding to shape – an ED response. A third category of subjects contains those whose choices on the test series are inconsistent. The optional shift design was introduced by Kendler, Kendler and Learnard (1962).

Developmental Mediation Theory

Kendler and Kendler (1962) have formulated a theory which postulates developmental differences in concept learning attributable to the development of mediational processes. Two developmental levels are assumed. At the first, the organism is said to respond to stimuli directly; a single-link *S-R* model applies to this kind of behaviour, which, it is argued, is the only kind available to animals and young children.

At the second level, however, the organism is also able to respond to stimuli produced by its own responses; it is necessary, therefore, to postulate a mediational model, $S-r-s-R$, in which the implicit response, r, is assumed to modify the external stimulus to produce a transformed stimulus, s, that elicits behaviour. Although the trend of the Kendlers' theory appears to suggest that these mediational processes are mainly verbal, they do not discount other forms of mediation, for example, imagery. But, whatever the nature of this mediation may be, it leads to a higher level of cognitive functioning, since the existence of a symbolic system reduces the organism's dependence upon fluctuations in the environment. Because the effective stimulus is the mediational, rather than the direct, stimulus, behaviour, including conceptual behaviour, becomes both more flexible and more stable.

One consequence of the theory is the need to formulate a developmental account of concept-shift behaviour. It is predicted that the difficulty of ID and ED shifts is a function of the presence or absence of mediational processes. The non-mediational organism should find the ED shift easier, since, having learned to respond to one end of a dimension, e.g. brightness, the habit strength of this response will interfere more with the learning of the reverse concept, darkness, than it will with the learning of a new $S-R$ connection, e.g. responding to shape. The mediational organism, on the other hand, should execute ID shifts more rapidly than ED shifts, since the former enable him to utilize the same mediated response to a new overt response (e.g. 'bright – dark'), whereas the latter requires the acquisition of a new mediated response (shape) to a new overt response.

One source of ambiguity in this formulation relates to the assumption that the rates at which overt and mediational responses weaken or extinguish are different. H. H. and T. S. Kendler (1966), in reply to Mackintosh (1965), agree that the relevant assumption is to postulate that mediated responses extinguish more slowly than overt responses, since the subject can only utilize the same mediated response if the mediated response is still retained after the original overt responses are extinguished. But, the Kendlers argue, if differential extinction were the only factor, it would be expected that a reversal would occur once a subject shifted his overt response. This does not always happen, for there are cases in which the subject chooses an overt response consistent with a reversal shift, yet does not begin to reverse. The suggested absence of the mediated response in this case makes it strategic to consider the hierarchy of mediated responses available to the subject in addition to the relative rates of extinction of mediated and overt responses.

Attentional Mediation Theory

An alternative conception of discrimination learning is that the organism learns to make two responses, an attentional response to the relevant stimulus dimension followed by an instrumental response. Spence (1940) found it necessary to talk of a 'receptor-orienting' response in addition to instrumental responses, and Wyckoff (1952) demonstrated the 'observing response' in pigeons by requiring them to execute two responses to obtain reward: the animal had to depress a pedal to illuminate a key (the observing response) and then peck at the key when one of two colours appeared (the instrumental response). Attentional models of discrimination learning have adopted these ideas but emphasize that attention selects between stimulus dimensions and not between stimulus objects (Zeaman and House, 1963; Mackintosh, 1965). In the Zeaman and House model a dimension is defined to include stimulus compounds, such as 'black-tall' or 'white-short', in addition to the component dimensions like colour and size. It is argued that, since at the beginning of learning the stimulus dimensions present in the situation compete for attention, the subject must learn both to attend to the relevant dimension and to attach an instrumental response of approach or avoidance to the cues along that dimension. In this model, the mediational response is therefore the attending response which serves the function of increasing the probability that only relevant stimuli control the instrumental response.

The theory has a number of implications when applied to concept-shift behaviour. Of the two ID shifts, it is predicted that the one involving new stimuli along the same dimension will be learned more easily than the reversal shift because, although subjects in the latter condition have the advantage of looking at the relevant cues, they also have the disadvantage of a strong tendency to pick up the wrong one. The reversal shift may or may not be easier than ED shifts, for, although subjects in an ED shift may have the initial disadvantage of attending to irrelevant cues, they do not have the reverser's disadvantage of a strong habit to pick up the negative stimulus. The superiority of one or the other is thus dependent upon the nature of the situation and the subjects; exact predictions can be made by assigning weights to observing and instrumental responses. However, it is clear that an ID shift with new stimuli should be easier to learn than an ED shift. Finally, any experience that strengthens attention to the relevant dimension, such as overtraining, will facilitate reversal learning when the attentional response is relatively less well established than the instrumental response.

E

Differentiation Theory

Gibson and Gibson (1955a) believe the traditional view of perceptual learning to rest upon the mistaken assumption that stimulation must be mediated or somehow supplemented for perception to become more veridical. Consequently, perceptual learning can only be regarded as signifying a decreasing psychophysical correspondence between perception and stimulation and we are confronted with the paradox that behaviour becomes more intelligent or adapted the more it is divorced from perceived reality. However, the paradox can be resolved, they argue, if we reject the notion that stimulation provides us with sensations which only become organized after some kind of mediation. It is wrong to say that there is a stimulus and that a response becomes 'attached' to it. 'The organism discriminates and conceptualizes at the same time that he elaborates his repertoire of responses' (Gibson and Gibson, 1955b, p. 448). Perceptual learning must, therefore, be characterized as involving an increasing differentiation in the correspondence of stimulation and perception: the increase in the number of percepts a man has is matched by the number of different physical objects to which they correspond. Two general classes of stimulus variables are identified – variants and invariants. Variants provide information about the changing aspects of the environment, while invariants, defined as variables remaining constant through transformations in the stimulus array, may provide information about the permanent properties of objects. Thus, E. J. Gibson (1960) reasons that weight emerges as an invariant property of objects as the child lifts and carries objects of different size and shape and is able to detect a qualitative similarity across quantitative differences. In general, the child grasps the idea of a dimension through relating his experiences with a variety of stimulus objects exemplary of that dimension.

L. S. and T. J. Tighe (1966, 1968a) suggest that performance on concept-shift tasks will be a function of the degree to which the subject is able to detect the relevant dimension-reward relation. Relative ease of ID shift is predicted for the subject who has isolated the relevant dimension, since this remains relevant, whilst in an ED shift the subject must first redirect his attention (and perhaps further differentiate) the formerly irrelevant dimension. On the other hand, for the subject who has reached criterion in the original learning by responding to the relationship between a stimulus compound (e.g. 'dark-circle') and reward, it is predicted that an ED shift will be executed more rapidly since only one of these relations is changed in an ED shift while both are changed in the ID shift. Differentiation theory assumes that responding to stimulus compounds is developmentally prior to responding to component dimensions. A further prediction is that non-reinforced, perceptual pre-training designed to foster understanding of the dimensions involved in the concept shift will facilitate ID responding.

THE EXPERIMENTAL EVIDENCE

Comparison of these theories yields three general and interrelated questions:

1. Is concept-shift behaviour related to developmental level or does the operation of other variables override the developmental sequence? Two of the theories, developmental mediation and differentiation theories, hold that ED responding is developmentally prior to ID responding, while attentional theory asserts, more specifically, that reversal shifts may or may not be easier than ED shifts, although ID shifts with new stimuli along the same dimension should be easier than both reversal and ED shifts.

2. Is concept-shift behaviour largely predictable from a knowledge of the way in which the subject perceives the situation or is it necessary to postulate response-produced stimulation to account for this behaviour? Differentiation and attentional theories concur in their orientation to perceptual factors, while developmental mediation theory posits response-produced stimulation as a necessary feature of functioning at one developmental level.

3. Is the learning process more accurately described by postulating the intervention of mediational processes or by postulating the simultaneous differentiation of stimulation and responses? Developmental mediation and attention theories agree in assuming that mediational processes intervene between stimulus and response while differentiation theory insists that the organism increases its repertory of responses at the same time that it differentiates among its perceptions.

There is a certain parallel between these theories and those put forward to account for the child's understanding of conservation. Differentiation theory comes closest to operationalism with the view that development in the construction of invariants is brought about through the interaction of subject and environment. Attention theory resembles 'identity theory' in so far as both assume that successful performance is due to the child recognizing an aspect of the test situation which he was capable of discriminating at the beginning of the session: in both cases the subject fails due to responding to the wrong dimension. And, just as learning theory applied to conservation results in the conclusion that it is a form of behaviour learned through reinforcement and possibly imitation, so developmental mediation theory predicts relative ease of ID over ED responding due to the development of implicit associational processes. But if it is clear from this that similar issues are involved in the two cases, work on concept shifts has been much more concerned with the stimulus aspects of the test situation and thus permits us to approach the issues from the side that has tended to be neglected in the Piagetian research. At the same time, our discussions both of Piagetian psychology and the theories of abstraction point towards certain generalizations relevant to the three questions which it may be as well to state now. From these discussions it is anticipated (1) that there will be developmental differences in concept formation and shift tasks which will be related to the development of the ability to relate and organize stimuli; (2) that, since the central determinant of conceptual behaviour is the subject's ability to relate stimuli into series by his acting and operating upon the environment, response-produced stimulation, such as language, is not the process which brings this into being, although language training may be effective to the extent that it helps the subject to differentiate and relate environmental stimuli; (3) that the learning process, by which stimuli become distinguished and related, can only be regarded as one in which stimulation and responses become simultaneously differentiated: this means, contrary to developmental mediation and attention theories which assert processes intervening between stimulus and response whose functioning is not subject to developmental change, that what used to be called 'the higher mental processes' and are now referred to as mediational processes, notably language, imagery and operations, develop, not by being or becoming independent of environmental stimulation, but by referring to and thus coming to reflect more faithfully its underlying structures, whether spatial or temporal.

1. *Developmental Levels*

If age is related to behaviour on concept-shift problems, it should be possible to distinguish three developmental levels: infra-human organisms and young children should find ED easier than ID shifts; children at an intermediate stage, usually identified as occurring between the ages of 5 and 7, should exhibit no consistent preference, and older children and adults ought to execute ID shifts more rapidly than ED shifts. Reviews of the literature by Kendler and Kendler (1962), T. J. and L. S. Tighe (1966) and Wolff (1967) do, in fact, confirm that infra-human organisms acquire ED shifts more easily than ID shifts whereas adults learn ID shifts more easily. There is also support from the experiments on adults for the hypotheses, derived from Zeaman and House's model, that ID shifts with new stimuli are learned more easily than both reversal shifts and ED shifts. However, a great deal of uncertainty still surrounds the development of concept-shift behaviour in children: in particular, the hypothetical dominance of ED responding in young children and ID responding in older children has been questioned. It will be maintained that this uncertainty is not sufficient to warrant rejection of the developmental hypothesis. While the available evidence does not enable the matter to be settled with any degree of confidence, it is perhaps possible to determine which conclusions are justified through a closer analysis of the factors which appear to be responsible for divergent opinions about the relationship of concept-shift behaviour to age. Chief among these are (1) the adequacy of designs which compare ED shifts with reversal shifts, (2) the influence of a variable irrelevant dimension in the ED shift, and (3) the effects of overtraining.

Slamecka's (1968) thorough critique leads him to suggest that the problems connected with comparing ED shifts with reversal shifts are so intractable that the only strategic manoeuvre is to abandon this design. He has isolated five factors responsible for confusing the interpretation of such comparisons – the differential presence of intermittent reinforcement, differential opportunity for detection of shifts, obviousness of solution, partial stimulus novelty, and transfer of sorting responses. Take as an example the obviousness of solution factor. The subject in the reversal-shift condition responds consistently with the pre-shift habits until he suddenly encounters a series of non-reinforcements. It is possible, Slamecka suggests, that this alerts the subject to the changed situation and provides a cue to the solution, for, if the last few cards were all incorrectly sorted, it is obvious that they would be correctly sorted when placed in the opposite pile. The subject in the ED shift, on the other hand, only encounters an irregular sequence of reinforcements and non-reinforcements and is not, therefore, similarly alerted. This factor may be partly responsible for observed developmental trends, since the older child will possibly be more able to make the necessary deduction. Kendler, Kendler and Wells (1960), G. Marsh (1964) and Tighe and Tighe (1967) report that children under 5 learn ED shifts more readily than reversal shifts, while other investigators have been able to confirm the developmental priority of ED over reversal responding (e.g. Kendler, Kendler and Learnard, 1962; Cole, Gay and Glick, 1968; Guy, 1969; Kendler and Kendler, 1970).

On the other hand, a number of studies present data that conflict with the hypothesis of three, distinct stages in the development of concept-shift behaviour. Cobb (1965) found that children under 5 were able to perform reversal and ED shifts equally easily; Blank (1967) observed her 5-year-olds to learn reversal shifts with facility, and Suzuki (1961) found reversal shifts to be learned more easily than ED shifts by children between the ages of 5 and 7. Similarly, when ID shifts with new stimuli are employed, rather than reversal shifts, Trabasso, Deutsch and Gelman (1966) report that they are as easily learned by children under 5 as ED shifts, and Eimas (1966) reports that children in the transitional period perform them more easily than ED shifts.

These conflicting findings are not, at the moment, reconcilable. Wolff (1967) concludes that there is no acceptable evidence for the developmental hypothesis. My own opinion is that, in view of the well-established differences in the concept-shift behaviour of animals and human adults and of the other evidence to be reviewed in this section, rejection of the hypothesis would be premature.

Eimas (1965) has indicated a further procedural factor which may have contributed to the identification of a developmental sequence. Most of the experiments which have demonstrated that reversal shifts are learned faster than ED shifts have used an ED shift procedure in which the relevant dimension in the original learning (e.g. brightness) becomes irrelevant and variable within trials in the second phase (i.e. two values on this dimension are present on a given trial but neither is rewarded consistently over trials). But most of the experiments which have demonstrated ED responding dominant to ID responding in animals and young children have used an ED shift procedure in which the relevant dimension of the original learning becomes constant within trials in the second phase (i.e. only a single value of this dimension is present on a given trial). The former is termed a variable-irrelevant procedure, the latter a constant-irrelevant procedure. On this reasoning, the relative ease of ED and ID shifts may be contingent upon the procedures used irrespective of the subject's age or developmental status.

This argument was investigated by Dickerson (1966), who tested pre-school children with a variable irrelevant dimension during original learning and shift and found reversal shift to be easier than ED shift. In a further study, Dickerson (1967) interpreted the finding that ED shifts are learned faster when the irrelevant dimension of the shift problem varies between trials and is constant within trials, as supporting the view of Zeaman and House (1963) that the attentional response is evoked when both variable relevant and irrelevant dimensions are present. Studies by Saravo (1967) and Fritz and Blank (1968) also lend support to the view that observed developmental differences may be due, in part at least, to different procedures with the irrelevant dimension in the ED shift. However, Tighe and Tighe (1967) found that 4-year-olds accomplished ED shifts more rapidly than reversal shifts regardless of the state of the irrelevant dimension. Further, they criticize Dickerson for overtraining his subjects, since the evidence indicates that overtraining facilitates ID shifts in children and, in refutation of Eimas's argument, they point to experiments by Kelleher (1956) and Brookshire, Warren and Ball (1961) which do not confirm that animals learn ED shifts faster with a variable irrelevant dimension.

A later experiment by Eimas (1967) is of interest because it reveals the complexity of the interactions of age and procedure in these experiments. Using an optional shift design, Eimas found fewer reversal shifts after constant-irrelevant training but also discovered that relatively fewer reversal shifts were executed by younger children trained with a constant irrelevant dimension, a procedure × age interaction not predicted by attention theory. On this theory, it may be argued that the constant-irrelevant procedure results in putting into competition in the optional shift phase a previously irrelevant dimension and a novel dimension, both of which are strong determinants of attention. Attention theory predicts a lower level of response to the previously relevant dimension, i.e. fewer reversal shifts, than in the situation where the same relevant dimension has no strong rival for attention, and this is what Eimas found. But in order to explain the age × procedure interaction in the same terms it is necessary to introduce the additional assumption that novel stimuli exert greater control over attentional processes in younger children. If this is so, are we to conclude that the mediating attentional response itself is a developmental variable? Eimas thinks not. He believes it possible to maintain that the mediating attention response is independent of development but that 'over time, through maturation and/or experience, there are changes in the relative dominance of certain classes of stimuli or dimensions toward which attention is directed' (p. 339). The simple reply to this argument, however, is that, if there are such changes in stimulus dominance, it is not because they develop of themselves but because the perceiving subject is himself developing. Here is an example of how attention theory, although demonstrating the extent to which concept-shift behaviour is influenced by the stimulus situation, cannot, when confronted with developmental differences in the way stimulation affects the subject, escape the paradox of asserting that attention is a perceptual process which remains independent of development for the subject but follows a developmental course for the environment! The facts can be handled, however, by the assumption that stimulus effectiveness and perceptual response are parallel developments.

A third variable found to influence relative ease of ID and ED shifts is degree of training on the original concept. While it is well established that infra-human organisms and adult humans differ markedly in this respect when original learning is to a criterion, the available evidence, though open to a number of interpretations, does indicate that when criterion-trained subjects are given further, overtraining trials, the relative ease of the shifts may change markedly. In general, overtraining has been found to facilitate both ID and ED shifts in adults (Wolff, 1967), ID shifts in animals (Mackintosh, 1965), and ID shifts in young children (House and Zeaman, 1962; Furth and Youniss, 1964; T. J. and L. S. Tighe, 1955; T. S. and H. H. Kendler, 1966; Eimas, 1969). If the differences in the concept-shift behaviour of animals and men can be made to disappear with over training, should the developmental hypothesis be abandoned? Clearly not, since the opposite point of view would hardly do justice to the evidence. It remains a fact, as Kendler and Kendler (1966a) point out, that human adults and older children can reverse rapidly after a discrimination, whereas in all cases where lower animals reverse rapidly extensive amounts of previous discrimination training or overlearning are necessary. Tighe (1964) has found that both young and old rhesus monkeys execute an ED shift more rapidly than a reversal shift, in contrast to the normal course of development observed for criterion-trained humans of different ages. The Tighes and their associates have not been able to demonstrate the overlearning reversal effect in rats (Tighe, Brown and Youngs, 1965) or in monkeys (Tighe, 1964) using the same procedures found to be effective for young children (Tighe and Tighe, 1965). Moreover, the evidence that both ED and ID shifts may be facilitated by overtraining in adults, whereas only ID shifts are, in general, facilitated for young children and animals, itself indicates a developmental sequence.

What can be concluded from these three lines of inquiry is that the relationship between shift behaviour and age is not as straightforward as was perhaps first believed. The relative ease of ED shifts in animals and of ID shifts in adult humans led to the supposition that a transitional period of human development could be identified and related to chronological age. White (1965) has made a convincing case that many changes in behaviour occur between the ages of 5 and 7 and has talked of a transition from an 'associational' to a 'cognitive' stage. But concept-shift problems appear to be open to the influence of many other variables besides those subject to developmental variation within this age range, for example, obviousness of solution and the other variables identified or discussed by Slamecka (1968), the use of constant-irrelevant versus variable-irrelevant dimensions in ED shifts (Eimas, 1965), and the degree of training on the original task (Mackintosh, 1965; Wolff, 1967). The implication that may be drawn from these studies is, not that concept-shift behaviour is independent of development, but that it is necessary to specify more accurately than hitherto which developmental variables are operative under different circumstances and at different ages. The need for such a strategy is reinforced by studies which have used an optional shift design because, although these show a consistent increase with age in the percentage of optional reversers, the increases are relatively small. Thus Kendler, Kendler and Learnard (1962) observed an increase from 50 per cent to 65 per cent between the ages of 5 and 11 and Jeffrey (1965) an increase from 37·5 per cent to 81 per cent for the same age group. T. S. Kendler and H. H. Kendler (1966) found an average increase between 5 and 9 years of age from 45 per cent to 75 per cent and more recent studies (Kendler and Kendler, 1970; Tighe and Tighe, 1970) confirm these figures. Moreover, T. J. and L. S. Tighe (1966) showed that the probability of an optional reversal in 4-year-old children ranged from virtually zero along a dimension of relatively low salience (horizontal versus vertical stripes) to 1·0 along a dimension of relatively high salience (flat versus raised forms). Since the performance of 4-year-olds is so dependent upon the stimulus situation and since no one would maintain that large numbers of adolescents and college students are still responding in the manner of infra-human organisms to these problems, it is clearly necessary to specify more precisely the relevant variables for different ages and levels of development.

2. *Perceptual and Verbal Factors*

The second issue has to do with the relative importance of the subject's perception of the stimulus situation (irrespective of whether the perceptual process is couched in differentiation or mediational terminology) as against non-perceptual, response-produced stimulation. Since the most commonly investigated subclass of this latter category is language, we shall be concerned with the roles of language and perception in concept formation. The relevant research includes studies of the theoretical significance of verbal and perceptual training, of the

E*

relationship between shifts and dimensional preference, and of over-training.

On the whole, the evidence suggests that verbal training has either no effect upon concept-shift behaviour or is effective primarily through focussing the subject's attention on to the relevant dimension. Thus, although Kendler and Kendler (1961), T. S. Kendler (1964), Woerner (1963), Silverman (1966) and Milgram and Noce (1968) found overt verbalization of dimensional labels to facilitate performance, a number of other studies have found that overt verbal labelling was either ineffective (Kendler, Kendler and Wells, 1960; Lachman and Sanders, 1963; Cobb, 1965; Tighe and Tighe, 1970) or interfered with the acquisition of a new or reversed concept (O'Connor and Hermelin, 1959; Blank, 1966). In addition, studies comparing deaf and hearing children report no significant differences in performance (Rosenstein, 1960; Youniss, 1964; Furth, 1964; André, 1969), although André did report that only 40 per cent of the slow reversers verbalized correctly whereas 90 per cent of the fast reversers did so.

In contrast to these findings, techniques which involve non-reinforced perceptual practice, without overt verbalization, and which involve subjects making comparative, perceptual judgements of stimuli along dimensions, are quite consistently successful (Tighe, 1965; Tighe and Tighe, 1968a, 1969, 1969b, 1970; Caron, 1968; Osler and Scholnick, 1968). Other studies which directly support the hypothesis that the conceptual difficulties of the young child are due, not to a failure to label dimensions, but to a low probability of detecting the relevant dimensions because of a lack of discriminative experience are those of Johnson and White (1967) and White and Johnson (1968), who found a significant correlation between performance on a 'Concept of Dimensionality' test (a measure of the subject's ability to perceive particular stimulus values as ordered points along a dimension) and ease of reversal responding. Indirect support comes from a study by Blank and Klig (1970) who, in the light of Slamecka's (1968) critique, used a cross-modal shift paradigm involving form and texture dimensions. They reported that 4-year-olds are able to achieve cross-modal dimensional learning (tactual to visual) as readily as ipsi-modal dimensional learning. Since no relevant verbal labels could be elicited, Blank and Klig argue that at least some forms of dimensional learning in young children are non-verbally mediated: they suggest that their subjects were either using imagery to mediate specific dimensions or were effectively organizing the stimulus situation.

Results of studies on the effects of dimensional preference on concept shifts have frequently been interpreted as offering support for attention theory and evidence against the Kendlers' mediation model. Several studies have established that concept learning is faster when the subject's preferred dimension is relevant (Heal, Bransky and Mankinen, 1966; Smiley and Weir, 1966; Suchman and Trabasso, 1966; Wolff, 1966; Mittler and Harris, 1965; Trabasso, Stave and Eichberg, 1969). The prediction that subjects will also reverse more rapidly on their preferred dimension has been confirmed by Heal *et al.* and Smiley and Weir. An interesting qualification to this conclusion is suggested by the results of Trabasso *et al.* however. It was found that lower middle-class subjects, who are described as 'unsophisticated in psychological testing' and who preferred colour, learned to discriminate stimulus objects slowly and made ED responses regardless of the dimension upon which they were trained, whilst subjects who preferred form showed the anticipated behaviour. The authors are led to speculate that colour-preference may indicate a lower level of problem-solving maturity. In reply to these experiments, Kendler and Kendler (1970) have reasoned that the effects of dimensional preference on the shift behaviour of infra-human organisms and young children should be incorporated in the single-unit part of developmental mediation theory, but the dimensional dominance hypothesis cannot explain the shift behaviour of human adults who are most likely to make reversal shifts regardless of which dimension was initially relevant.

While reviews of the literature (Sperling, 1965; Wolff, 1967) conclude that there is no one satisfactory explanation of the effects of overtraining, several investigators have interpreted their data – showing the facilitation of ID shifts with overtraining in infra-human organisms and young children – as casting doubt upon a verbal mediational theory of concept-shift behaviour and as supporting either a perceptual differentiation interpretation, according to which overtraining facilitates the subject's isolation of the relevant dimension (Tighe and Tighe, 1965) or an attention theory explanation, according to which overtraining increases the probability that the relevant attentional response is transferred from training to reversal (Turrisi and Shepp, 1969). In either case it is unnecessary to postulate verbal mediation. In the same vein, Mumbauer and Odom (1967) conclude from their analysis of the interaction of verbalization, overtraining and dimensional preference, that verbalization and overtraining affect performance in a similar way through their interaction with dimensional preference.

An objection to the hypothesis that sensitivity to the relevant dimension is central in the relative ease of ID shifts has been voiced by H. H. and T. S. Kendler (1966a), who refer to findings that reversal shifts are easier for older children and adults even when unrelated stimuli are used. Bogartz (1965) found that if the subject learns one of two responses to half of the stimulus items in a list of nonsense syllables and the second response to the remaining half, it is easier for him to learn to reverse his responses to all the stimuli than to learn to reverse his responses to half of the stimuli and keep the same responses to the remaining half. Kendler, Kendler and Sanders (1967) verified Bogartz's findings and also demonstrated that reversal shifts are easier when the original sorting of words follows the ordinary conceptual categorization (e.g. into classes like 'clothes' and 'furniture') than when the original sorting does not follow these categories. Schaeffer and Ellis (1970) used 'unrelated' stimuli (pictures of a beige minibus, a mahogany-coloured guitar, a red chair and a multi-coloured plane) and reported that (1) without overtraining, 7- to 9-year-old children learned ED shifts more easily than reversal shifts, presumably because the subjects learned the *S-R* connections individually and the ED shift requires the learning of fewer such connections, but (2) with overtraining reversal shifts are learned more easily than ED shifts, either because this condition allows subjects to create 'stimulus clusters' among the stimuli or because of the operation of the 'obviousness-of-solution' factor. Schaeffer and Ellis conclude that a response to explicit dimensions is not crucial in the change from easier ED shifts to easier reversal shifts after overlearning.

In assessing the significance of these experiments let us first consider those using nonsense syllables. Slamecka (1968) concludes that these studies confirm that the shift effect can be produced with the basic design even when mediational aids to the dimensional properties of the stimuli are minimized, and therefore indicate that the basic design is rather inadequate as a critical test of the mediational position. But surely a more basic point emerges if we ask why the shift effect is still produced under these conditions. J. J. Gibson (1968) has proposed that conditioning and the learning of nonsense syllables may also be viewed as the detection of invariant relationships: Pavlov's dog learned to detect the bell-food invariant in the laboratory situation and Ebbinghaus's subject was required to detect the invariant association of certain nonsense syllables. Now, whilst the associations required of the subject in these experiments and the concept-shift experiments with nonsense syllables are arbitrarily laid down by the experimenter, whereas with dimensions such as colour and form the experimenter makes use of series which are not arbitrary, both types of task require that the subject detect relationships between stimuli. In both cases, presumably, the organism that has succeeded in learning the relationships involved will be able to reverse its responses more easily than learn a new invariant. One would think that the problem of detecting invariants in perceptual dimensions (and hence of reversing responses to them) is an easier task than detecting them in material in which the invariant to be detected is identifiable only through learning the reinforcement contingencies or the associations. Rather than being the basic unit of behaviour, this latter would appear to be a relatively difficult and specialized subclass of invariant relationship since its only rationale is contiguity. But the study of Kendler, Kendler and Sanders (1967) showing the influence of conceptual categorization and the Schaeffer and Ellis (1970) study are clearly not of this type. In both the subject could refer to perceived similarities, either indirectly through the use of words or through inspection of the pictures. We can agree that language may fulfil this function but, of course, this is a far cry from asserting that verbal mediation produces the perceptual organization which facilitates ID shifts.

In conclusion, there is little empirical support for the view that verbal factors are crucial for concept-shift behaviour but much to implicate perceptual factors. It is suggested that the major determinant of ID responding is the perception of stimulus relations either in the form of perceptual dimensions or in the form of experimenter-determined associations. Verbal processes may play a role either in directing attention to the stimulus relations or in serving as the material for experimenter-determined invariants.

3. *Mediation versus Differentiation*

Granted that there are developmental differences in concept-shift behaviour and that these are due mainly to differences between subjects in their ability to perceive stimulus relations, there remains the problem of whether these insights are conceptualized more validly in terms of mediational processes or in terms of the simultaneous differentiation of stimulation and responses. In the author's opinion, the latter is, ultimately, the stronger theoretical position.

To begin with, the available evidence suggests the importance, not just of perceptual factors, but, more positively, of perceptual ability. Experiments demonstrating the effectiveness of perceptual pretraining (Tighe, 1965; Tighe and Tighe, 1967, 1968a, b, 1969, 1969a, b) may be interpreted by reasoning that such training focusses the child's attention on the relevant dimension, but this interpretation misses the point that what appears to be effective, for young children at least, is that they make comparative perceptual judgements of the stimuli as they vary in their dimensional attributes. Significant in this connection are the experiments (Johnson and White, 1967; White and Johnson, 1968) showing a relationship between concept-shift behaviour and performance on a test designed to assess the subject's understanding of dimensionality. This work suggests the desirability of further studies relating concept-shift behaviour to the development of cognitive capacity.

Moreover, studies which derive from attention theory reveal developmental differences whose explanation requires the introduction of assumptions beyond those of the original theory. Two examples have already been encountered: in order to account for their findings, Eimas (1967) has been obliged to acknowledge that there are changes over time in the relative dominance of classes of stimuli to which attention is directed, and Trabasso, Stave and Eichberg (1969) to argue that colour preference may indicate a lower level of problem-solving ability. These particular findings illustrate the general necessity of accounting for the differential selectivity of attention at different levels of development. For to establish the selectivity of attention is not enough; it is necessary to attempt to understand what characteristics of the stimulation are salient and effective as the organism develops. And a comparative-developmental study of this kind need not involve the introduction of mediational processes, since the task can be accomplished by observing the correlation of effective stimulation and responses.

That attention theory faces the problem of explaining the development of selective attention is recognized by Jeffrey (1968), whose analysis is worth considering in some detail since it reflects the sort of difficulty which a mediational perspective encounters in attempting to explain the development of concept learning. Jeffrey accepts (1) that attention theories must be concerned with changes in cue salience due to maturation and experience. He believes (2) that it is the reaction of the child and not the stimulus that changes, so that (3) it is probably useful to postulate a mediating mechanism to account for changes in cue salience. This mechanism is the orienting reflex which is defined, after Sokolov (1963), as a pattern of psychological responses that occurs to novel stimulation. Jeffrey's thesis is that cue salience changes as a result of the serial habituation of orienting reflexes. An infant, for example, confronted with a novel object, directs his attention to a few stimuli that are most salient. With continued exposure or with development, the orienting reflex habituates to the salient cues, allowing less salient cues to elicit appropriate attending responses. With repeated experience the orienting reflex habituates more and more quickly to each separate cue of a stimulus complex and 'under certain conditions an orderly set of rapidly shifting attending responses should occur' (p. 325). One example given by Jeffrey is the dimension of colour: as habituation occurs more rapidly to different colours, the dimension will become isolated from the objects of which it is a part. In this way, it is maintained, attention theory can account for differences in cue salience as a result of experience.

The major criticism that can be made against this theory is the same one that Cassirer and Husserl directed against the theory of abstraction, namely, that the generality of the series of attending responses is assumed but not explained. The infant would not switch his attention from one colour to another unless the generality of the colour dimension was somehow grasped initially in each of them by what Husserl called an act of ideating abstraction. If the selectivity of attention were determined solely by the novelty of the stimuli, then the probability of the colour dimension, or any other, being formed would be low indeed. We are now in a position to see the connection between this criticism of abstractionism and the thesis that differentiation of stimulation parallels the elaboration of responses. Stimuli do not become organized through the 'chaining' of mediating responses because the subject's relationship with his environment is such that this organization is always already implicit in his response to stimulation. Therefore, development can only be conceptualized as the process in which this implicit organization is made explicit in two parallel directions: in the direction of an increasing differentiation of responses, whether of action, imagery or words, and in the direction of an increasing sensitivity to and differentiation of the complexity of the stimulus field. In other words, Jeffrey's statement (2) that it is the reaction of the child which changes while the stimulus situation remains the same must be replaced by one acknowledging that it is the subject-stimulus relationship which changes, and this replacement then makes unnecessary the proposition (3) of responses mediating between stimulus and response.

There is one hypothesis of differentiation theory, however, which receives no support from the experimental evidence, namely, that predicting the developmental priority of stimulus compounds over stimulus dimensions. Contrary evidence is presented by Colby and Robertson (1942), Kendler, Kendler and Learnard (1962) and House and Zeaman (1962). The hypothesis ought probably to be rejected, not least of all because it smacks too much of the associationism which differentiation theory claims to replace. Dimensions are, to be sure, abstracted from experience with a variety of stimulus objects. But the insight that the perception of a stimulus value of a dimension is never something absolutely particular but always implicitly points to the perception of other values along that dimension (rather than stimulus values along any other dimension), suggests that dimensional responding and dimensional preferences may be established relatively early in development, although an understanding of the organization inherent in dimensions is a later development.

The three theories have been related to studies of concept-shift behaviour. The main conclusions are: (1) there are developmental differences in concept-shift behaviour; (2) these are mainly attributable to developmental differences in the capacity to perceive stimulus relations; (3) this capacity does not depend upon linguistic ability, although language may help the subject to differentiate and relate stimuli; (4) the developmental process is to be described as taking the form of the parallel, progressive differentiation of stimulation and response. Of course, the validity of these conclusions must be tested against a wide range of problems. Two related problems are oddity learning, in which the subject has to learn to respond to the odd stimulus in three, irrespective of the specific stimuli involved, and transposition learning, which requires the subject to learn to recognize the equivalence of stimulus relationships across transformations in the stimulus values. A review of these areas of research is beyond the scope of this book, but it is of note that similar questions are of importance in this work to those encountered in the concept-shift literature. How, for instance, are the comparative and developmental differences observed for these tasks best described and explained? Are deficiencies in transposition learning attributable to mediational deficiences of a verbal nature? (Reese, 1962, 1968; Flavell, Beach and Chinsky, 1965). Or to deficiencies in the ability to order stimuli? (Tighe and Tighe, 1969a). To what extent can attention theory account for oddity learning? (Brown, 1970).

The customary means of dichotomizing theories of conceptual behaviour has been to oppose *S-R* theories to those which maintain that concepts are equivalent to hypotheses (e.g. Bourne, 1966). The present analysis suggests that this is no longer a crucial dichotomy since an *S-R* framework free from the limitations of abstractionism and associationism can conceivably encompass both a description of the development of stimulus-response co-ordinations and the affirmation that the subject may use the co-ordinations he discovers as hypotheses to guide his behaviour.

PART THREE

Thinking –
Human and Mechanical

6

Reasoning and problem-solving

INDUCTIVISM AND DEDUCTIVISM

Both the use of logical models to describe the development of thinking and the characterization of concepts as hypotheses form part of a general assumption that scientific and everyday thinking have certain features in common. Equally important and inseparable from this assumption is the further one, manifest in Piaget's adaptation model and the Gibsons' differentiation theory, that the proper way to account for the development of thinking is to postulate the simultaneous and parallel development of psychological mechanisms, whether perceptions or operations, and of sensitivity to environmental stimuli. The inseparability of these two assumptions allows us to recognize that the subject's competence is not an absolute possession; rather, it must be conceptualized and measured as a response to a variety of environmental conditions. Thus, scientist and layman alike do not possess a set of rules whose application ensures successful problem-solving, since there is a sense in which it may be said that the rules themselves emerge, alter or at least extend their scope in the process of problem-solving. This implies, of course, that the same sorts of limitations apply to scientific as to everyday thought, the former being superior in sophistication but not in kind. But, since this is a conclusion which conflicts with the two dominant conceptions of scientific inquiry, inductivism and deductivism, it becomes necessary to examine the psychological literature on inductive and deductive reasoning in order to assess the extent to which induction and deduction may be regarded as 'models of thinking' in science and in everyday life.

Inductivists assert that the scientist accumulates knowledge by careful observation of data; by inductive reasoning he passes from statements of particular facts to general statements which comprehend them. Mill (1874) believed that the laws of inductive reasoning allowed for the attainment of certain knowledge, but the most prevalent current belief is that induction leads only to statements of probability since we can never be sure that the evidence has been exhausted. Deductivism, on the other hand, maintains that particular truths are attained by relating hypotheses deduced from theories to the empirical evidence. Following Popper (1959), it is frequently argued that the criterion used in science is 'falsifiability', for, whereas the confirmation of an hypothesis does not necessitate that hypothesis being true (because false hypotheses can lead to true conclusions), its invalidation means that something must be wrong. Inductivism, therefore, states that progress is from the particular to the general, while deductivism insists that the particular is only attained through the erection of general theories. Now, it is undoubtedly quite reasonable to say that men form generalizations from particular observations or that we test hypotheses against experience, but the elaboration of either of these statements to serve as models of the process of scientific inquiry results in serious difficulties. As Medawar (1969) points out, just as a formal objection to classical inductivism is that no upper limit is set to the amount of factual information to be assembled, so the essential failure of deductivism is to set an upper limit to the number of hypotheses we might think of to account for our observations. Obviously, our observations are always guided by some criterion (tacit or explicit) of relevance just as our hypotheses must relate to the demands of the problem in hand. But whilst it is easy to see that inductivism and deductivism misinterpret the necessary relationship of theory and observation, it is another matter to embody the insights gained from a critique of these points of view into a convincing alternative perspective. Kuhn (1970) has suggested that one of the main reasons for the survival of these philosophies of science is precisely the absence of such an alternative. He asks:

> But is sensory experience fixed and neutral? Are theories simply man-made interpretations of given data? The epistemological viewpoint that has most often guided Western philosophy for three centuries dictates an immediate and unequivocal Yes! In the absence of a developed alternative I find it impossible to relinquish entirely that viewpoint. Yet it no longer functions effectively. . . . (p. 126)

Kuhn's work is an attempt to develop an alternative conceptual framework that will be more in accord with the history of science and the psychology of thinking. He argues that scientific theories are not rejected solely because the hypotheses they give rise to are invalidated, but also because the evidence begins to point to a new paradigm which promises a fuller explanation. New paradigms, such as 'Copernican astronomy' or 'relativity theory', are at once sufficiently systematic to represent a genuine alternative to the prevailing viewpoints and sufficiently open-minded to leave all kinds of problems awaiting resolution. When a science has emerged from its pre-paradigmatic stage, it unfolds in alternating periods of crises (paradigm change) and consolidation ('normal science'). Study of the nature of scientific revolutions, Kuhn suggests, will force us to revise the belief that observations remain fixed once and for all whilst the scientist's interpretations change. What occurs during a scientific revolution is not adequately described as a reinterpretation of unchanging observations for the change embraces both interpretations and observations: a new paradigm means a new way of perceiving and of operating upon the world.

Do psychological experiments on inductive and deductive reasoning confirm the necessity of introducing this alternative conception? If our analysis is correct, then this literature should reveal no straightforward distinction between induction and deduction, not because people are insufficiently competent at either, but because these paradigms do not, as they stand, present a sufficiently accurate account of the way in which people think. Thus, in deduction, inferences are valid by virtue of their form, as, for example, in syllogistic or propositional logic; but, witness our consideration of the relationship between logic and psychology, such models are only effective in conjunction with one which is able to specify the influence of personal and environmental factors on performance. Similarly, as the discussion of concept formation made clear, to arrive at general statements from particular observations always presupposes an interpretative model, hypothesis or strategy, that is, some system of competence. The significance of experiments on deductive and inductive reasoning lies precisely in their demonstrating these facts and, hence, in their suggesting the necessity for an alternative paradigm in the study of thinking.

EXPERIMENTS ON DEDUCTIVE REASONING

Psychologists concerned with deductive reasoning have assessed the capacity of their subjects on problems connected with the rules of syllogistic reasoning and of propositional logic. The main propositional operators ('and', 'not', 'either . . . or', 'if . . . then') and some of the ways in which these can be symbolized have been outlined in a previous chapter (p. 72). The most investigated operation is that of implication, 'if p, then q' ($p \supset q$). The implying proposition is called the antecedent and the implied proposition the consequent. Since both antecedent and consequent can be either true or false, there are four possible outcomes of this operator. Consider, for example, the assertion: 'If I did not buy a dog, I bought a cat'. (1) If both antecedent and consequent are true, we would say that the assertion is true. (2) If the antecedent were true and the consequent false, we would say that the assertion is false. (3) If the antecedent were false and the consequent true, the assertion is true (I have bought a dog and a cat). (4) If both antecedent and consequent are false, then, again, the assertion will be true. Thus, the only case in propositional logic in which 'If p, then q' is false is that in which p is true but q is not. This means, essentially, that a valid inference depends upon meeting the falsifying contingency, $p\bar{q}$. These combinations are customarily represented in the form of a truth table:

$p \supset q$	1	0
1	1	0
0	1	1

Two cases which meet this contingency are known as (1) *modus ponens*, which states that from the antecedent of a true implication we may infer its consequent ('If p, then if p implies q, then q'), and (2) *modus tollens*, which states that from the denial of the consequent of an implication we infer the denial of its antecedent ('Not q, but if p then q, therefore, not p'). A further principle, termed the *principle of syllogism* because of its similarity to the Aristotelian syllogisms, states: that what implies the antecedent of a true implication implies its consequent ('If q implies r, and if p implies q, p also implies r'), and also, that what follows the consequent of a true implication follows from the antecedent ('If p implies q, and q implies r, then p implies r').

The Aristotelian syllogism consists of two premises and a conclusion. Logicians divide the propositions that enter into a syllogism into four types:

    (1) Universal affirmative (or A) propositions, e.g. 'All ps are qs'.
    (2) Universal negative (E) propositions, e.g. 'No ps are qs'.
    (3) Particular affirmative (I) propositions, e.g. 'Some ps are qs'.
    (4) Particular negative (O) propositions, e.g. 'Some ps are not qs'.

The truth of the syllogism derives from its adherence to the rules governing the valid interrelationships of the propositions (see any introductory textbook on logic, for example, Prior, 1955) and not, of course, from whether any particular proposition is actually true or not.

A few investigators have been impressed by the capacity of their subjects to reason deductively. Stewart (1961) administered a questionnaire containing examples of *modus ponens*, *modus tollens* and the 'principle of syllogism' and found subjects (university students without training in formal logic) to be capable of recognizing valid forms of inference. In subsequent research (Stewart, 1965) he has explored the thesis that the communication of ideas from person to person takes place through deductive systems of thought; in a conversation between two persons, Stewart argues, each participant assumes that the other will affirm all the logical consequences of what he has said and deny everything which is contradicted by his previous statements. Henle (1962) has questioned the belief that the existence of errors in syllogistic reasoning signifies the irrelevance of logic to the actual thinking process. She asked forty-six graduate students to evaluate the logical adequacy of deductions presented in the context of everyday problems and, from an analysis of their errors, concluded that error need not involve faulty reasoning but may, rather, be a function of the subject's interpretation of the task, as, for instance, when the subject restates a premise or introduces a further one. Thus, although the experimenter infers faulty reasoning from observed errors in syllogistic reasoning, the errors may in fact arise because subjects have undertaken a task other than the one the experimenter intended. Smedslund's (1969) paper includes a defence of the usefulness of deductive systems in the description of personal and interpersonal activity.

However, most studies of deductive reasoning have concentrated on those factors which limit the subject's ability to think logically. This tradition began with demonstrations of variations in capacity with different types of problem-material and has resulted in studies which show the influence of the subject's emotions and prejudices. But, perhaps more significantly, it has revealed that the logical interconnectedness of rules does not imply that they are psychologically equivalent: this is true with respect to the understanding of implications and of the so-called 'three-term series problem'.

The effect of changed material upon reasoning was investigated by Thorndike (1922), who administered algebra problems in conventional and altered forms, e.g. using $b_1 + b_2$ instead of $x + y$. Even such a slight change was found to impede reasoning. This conclusion was confirmed by Wilkins (1928) in relation to syllogistic reasoning: the easiest material was found to be the familiar and the concrete, whilst symbolic material was almost as difficult as unfamiliar material.

Janis and Frick (1943) observed a significant interaction between subjects' attitudes to the conclusions of syllogisms and their judgements of the validity or invalidity of these syllogisms. Specifically, it was found that there are more errors in judgements of logical validity when the subjects agreed with the conclusions of invalid syllogisms than when they agreed with valid syllogisms and, correlatively, they made more errors on valid syllogisms whose conclusions they disagreed with. Morgan and Morton (1944) noted an increase in errors when syllogisms dealt with personal and emotional convictions. This conclusion was confirmed by Lefford (1946), who found that neutrally toned syllogisms were more often correctly solved than emotionally toned syllogisms and that there was little relationship between the ability to reason accurately in non-emotional and emotional situations, and by Thistle-thwaite (1950), who observed the influence of prejudice in the use of the rules of implication. Henle and Michael (1956), however, have voiced the criticism that the important question is to do, not with the determination of the reasoning process by attitudes, but with the manner in which these two interact. The fundamental error of these early investigations lies in the assumption that attitudinal influences are arbitrary in the sense that they themselves are not contingent upon the logical characteristics of the problems. But, as Henle and Michael say, the adoption of this assumption results in a failure to overcome the dichotomy between motivational and cognitive processes, since motivation is regarded as a purely extraneous influence. A more fruitful approach, they suggest, is to inquire about the changes produced by motives in accordance with the logical structure of the problems.

A similar dispute surrounds the 'atmosphere effect', first postulated by Woodworth and Sells (1935). This is defined as the drawing of conclusions on the basis of the global impression produced by the premises: an affirmative premise is said to create an affirmative atmo-sphere, a particular premise a particular atmosphere, and so on. In a later paper, Sells (1936) introduced the supplementary principle of 'caution': this is defined as the tendency to accept weak and guarded conclusions, that is, particular, more readily than strong (universal) conclusions. The implication of this account of syllogistic reasoning is that we can explain the way in which people 'reason' without any reference to the rules of logic. This supposition was challenged by Chapman and Chapman (1959), who argued that the results attributed to the 'atmosphere effect' are primarily a function of the test format used by Woodworth and Sells. If a universal conclusion is accepted, then, logically, a particular one corresponding to it must also be accepted. Therefore, to be self-consistent on Woodworth and Sells' test format, which required the subject to indicate the truth or falsity of a conclusion, all subjects who regarded a universal conclusion as acceptable for a given pair of premises would necessarily adopt the corresponding particular conclusion. Thus the acceptance of particular conclusions should never be less than that of universal conclusions on this test format. The obtained order of errors (I conclusions always exceeding A, and O conclusions exceeding E), explained as due to the atmosphere effect, might then be due to the successful maintenance of self-consistency on the part of the subjects. Chapman and Chapman tested their hypothesis by assuming that, if error patterns are primarily due to the atmosphere effect, they ought to be found also in a multiple-choice format in which the subject is presented with two premises and can choose from among various possible conclusions. Their results did not conform to the pattern obtained by the earlier investigators. On the other hand, they were able to identify two main sources of error: the interpretation of A and O propositions to mean that the converse is also true (e.g. 'All As are Bs' to mean 'All Bs are As') and the use of probabilistic inference as well as strict deductive reasoning. These are inductive procedures and, as such, have no place in deductive reasoning tasks; but from the point of view of the subject, who, anyhow, has no means of knowing that they are disallowed, their use is eminently reasonable.

The difficulty of discerning a clear distinction between inductive and deductive reasoning in the way in which people actually think is also demonstrated by the work of Wason and his colleagues. They have observed that negative statements are responded to more slowly than affirmative statements, even after practice and the amount of information conveyed by both kinds of statement have been equated (Wason, 1959, 1961; Wason and Jones, 1963). In the latter study both statements made in English and statements in which neutral signs stood for assertion and denial were used. Through analysis of the subjects' introspections the authors were able to identify two factors that may be responsible for the subjects' difficulties with negative statements: (1) a tendency to translate negative statements into affirmatives because of the role which denial plays in language, and (2) an inhibition of response specifically associated with the prohibitive connotations of the word 'not', an interpretation also put forward by Eiferman (1961), who found that response latencies to the Hebrew negative term normally used in all contexts were significantly greater than those for the negative term normally used in the same language in all contexts except the prohibitive.

Discrepancies between the logical use of implication and its application in 'everyday' thought have also been noted. Wason (1966) presented subjects with a series of cards that was to enable them to falsify the assertion, 'If there is a vowel on one side of the card, then there is an even number on the other side'. On the front of the first card appeared a vowel (let p stand for this assertion), on the front of the second a consonant ($\bar{p}$), on the front of the third an even number (q) and on the front of the fourth an odd number ($\bar{q}$). The subject was instructed to select all those cards, but only those cards, which would have to be turned over in order to discover whether the assertion was false. It may be recalled that within the propositional calculus there is only one combination which is false, namely when the antecedent (p) is true and the consequent (q) is false, i.e. $p\bar{q}$, while the other three combinations are true. Thus, since only values of p and values of $\bar{q}$ allow a valid inference, the selection by the subject of q (affirmation of the consequent) is fallacious, as is the failure not to select $\bar{q}$ (*modus tollens*). In fact, Wason found that nearly all subjects selected p, between 60 and 75 per cent selected q, only a minority selected $\bar{q}$, and hardly any selected $\bar{p}$. Wason explains these results by making two assumptions. The first accepts that individuals are not constrained by the rules of the propositional calculus; instead, they may be guided by a tacit belief that a conditional sentence can have three outcomes: $p.q$ is true, $p.\bar{q}$ is false, and $\bar{p}$ with either q or $\bar{q}$ is irrelevant. This assumption may explain why the consequent is affirmed – q is selected in order to see whether it is associated with p making the conditional true – and it also may explain why the antecedent is so infrequently denied – $\bar{p}$ is irrelevant to the truth or falsity of the sentence. The second assumption is introduced in order to explain the infrequent use of $\bar{q}$ to deduce $\bar{p}$. It is that individuals are biased through their experience to expect a correspondence between sentences and states of affairs, so that in adulthood we seldom make use of the falsity of a proposition in deductive reasoning. But this is precisely what the selection of $\bar{q}$ entails. The comparative lack of success of experimental attempts to induce subjects to recognize the propositional-logical characteristics of the task has led to the conclusion that deep-seated habits of thought are involved (Wason, 1968, 1969; Wason and Johnson-Laird, 1970). Support for Wason's first assumption comes from a study by Johnson-Laird and Tagart (1969), who found that subjects judged stimuli to be irrelevant when they falsified the antecedents of conditional sentences.

Johnson-Laird and Wason (1970) propose that the subject gains insight into the task in a number of stages. (1) He must realize that the cards are reversible; once he grasps that the cards must be turned over, he has the information which permits him to escape from the results of his initial selection. (2) He must be able to resolve the apparent conflict between his correct evaluation of p (q) and $\bar{q}$ (p); this leads to the partial insight that cards which could falsify should be selected. (3) He must resolve the conflict between his correct evaluations of q (p) and $\bar{p}$ (q) in order to gain the complete insight that only cards which could falsify should be selected. Although such views are reminiscent of Piagetian notions of reversibility and cognitive conflict, the authors are critical of Piaget's assumptions about the efficiency of adult subjects in using propositional logic. Our consideration of this issue in Chapter 3 allows us to acknowledge that the demonstration of errors in adult reasoning does indeed indicate that a purely deductive, logical model cannot be used *in vacuo* as a description of the way in which people think, whereas a logic based upon the adaptation model could incorporate the kinds of variation in performance discussed in the above experiments.

This conclusion may also be drawn from work on the three-term series problem (sometimes called the linear syllogism), although there is some dispute over the psychological mechanisms involved in the solution of the problem. The deduction requires the serial ordering of three terms (A, B, C) from two premises stating their relationship on a particular dimension. The dimensional relationship of the terms, for example, 'is taller than', 'prettier than', etc., is indicated by the symbol $>$. According to Hunter (1957), the easiest form of this problem occurs when the grammatical object of the first premise is the grammatical subject of the second, that is, either $A > B$, $B > C$, or $C < B$, $B < A$, and the difficulty of the other forms of the linear syllogism is a function of the number of mental operations the subject has to carry out to translate them into this form; thus, $B > C$, $B < A$, requires two operations – reversal of the second premise to $A > B$ and a re-ordering of the two premises to produce $A > B$, $B > C$. However, De Soto, London and Handel (1965), Handel, De Soto and London (1968) and Huttenlocher (1968) report that linear syllogisms of the form $A > B$, $C < B$, $A > B$ are the easiest and propose that performance on these tasks is dependent upon the ease with which the subject can represent the relationships involved spatially. This involves ordering the terms on either a vertical or horizontal axis. Some terms are inextricably linked with spatial preferences (e.g. 'better' is consistently placed at the top of a vertical axis) while others do not have a consistent spatial assignment (e.g. the same person may visualize the 'lighter haired' on top if the premise is, 'Tom has lighter hair than Bill', but may visualize the 'darker haired' on top if the premise is, 'Bill has darker hair than Tom'). The theory predicts that syllogisms containing relational terms assigned to the top of the vertical axis, or the left of the horizontal axis, will be easier to solve because of these directional preferences. There is some empirical support for this prediction.

On the other hand, Clark (1969), whilst not denying that spatial imagery may occur to some subjects during these problems, maintains that the mechanisms responsible for solution are those mental operations that are used regularly in understanding language. These are (1) the principle of the primacy of functional relations (Miller, 1962; Chomsky, 1965), according to which functional relations like 'subject of', 'predicate of', 'main verb of', 'direct object of', are stored in memory in a more readily available form than other kinds of information; (2) the principle of lexical marking, according to which the senses of certain 'positive' adjectives, like 'good' and 'long', are stored in memory in a less complex form than the senses of their opposites; (3) the principle of congruence, according to which, when the subject is asked a question, he seeks from his previous knowledge information which is congruent, at the level of functional relations, with the information asked for in the question. One application of this theory, and a crucial one in the comparison with spatial imagery theory, concerns the substitution of terms such as 'not as bad as' for 'better'. According to the notion of directional preference, problems like 'A is better than B and B is better than C' should be easier than ones like 'C is worse than B and B is worse than A' because the former allow the subject to follow his directional preference (they are 'top-down' problems) while the latter go against the directional grain (they are 'bottom-up' problems). Clark argues, however, that the crucial theoretical comparison occurs between top-down problems such as 'A is not as bad as B and B is not as bad as C' and bottom-up problems like 'C is not as good as B and B is not as good as A'. Spatial imagery theory predicts the former to be the easier but Clark's theory predicts the opposite on the assumption that the underlying adjective in the first problem is 'bad' whilst the underlying adjective of the second is 'good'. Clark's results support the latter prediction, as do experiments by Jones (1970).

Despite the uncertainty surrounding the mechanisms involved in solving these problems, experiments upon them and upon the other problems reviewed in this section do confirm that deduction is only one of these mechanisms and that, consequently, a purely deductive scheme for the description of thinking is limited. It is limited, but this does not mean that it is wrong or unnecessary. In fact, the variations in performance described by the experimenters can only be seen as such against the framework provided by a deductive system, for their subjects' performance combines the deductive and the inductive.

EXPERIMENTS ON INDUCTIVE REASONING

Thinking in Open and Closed Systems

An insight into the manner in which this process should be characterized may be gained from an examination of Bartlett's (1958) views on thinking in open and closed systems. For Bartlett, thinking is the process by which an attempt is made to extend evidence which the subject perceives as, in some sense, incomplete: the subject's perception of a gap in the evidence is assumed to motivate the search for evidence that will fill the gap. There are three ways in which this process of gap-filling may take place – interpolation, extrapolation, and by looking at the evidence from a special and often unusual point of view. These mechanisms are said to apply to both closed and open systems. A closed system possesses a limited number of items, the properties of which are known to begin with and do not change in the course of solving the problem. Examples of problems of this type include those requiring the subject to fill in a series between two given items (for instance, a series of numbers between 1 and 17) and those which are concerned with the addition of letters substituting for numbers; these latter are sometimes referred to as 'cryptarithmetic problems', the best-known one being that in which DONALD added to GERALD produces ROBERT, where D = 5 and every number from 1 to 10 has its corresponding letter. In both cases the subject has to make use of his existing knowledge of the rules of arithmetic. He does not have to learn new procedures and in this sense it may be said that the structural properties of the closed system are given. In contrast, the properties of the open system are only discovered as the subject's thought progresses. The thinker in an open system is an explorer rather than a spectator; such thinking characterizes the significant intellectual achievements of both art and science.

According to Bartlett, the essential difference between the processes of thinking in closed and open systems is that in the former the thinker is in search of something which he must treat as being in some way 'there' all the time, whereas in the latter the properties of the material are not known until they are discovered. But, whilst this way of distinguishing the two modes of thought does accurately express a subjective impression to which they give rise, it does not, I believe, define exactly enough the difference from the viewpoint of the psychological processes involved. For the thinker in an open system is surely also guided by a sense of what is 'there': if not, he would neither perceive a problem nor recognize the solution when he found it. Thus the psychological distinction between thinking in closed and open systems must relate to differences in the sense of what is 'there' to guide thinking, rather than to that sense being present in one and absent in the other. More specifically, in a closed system the thinker may work within the framework provided by his existing knowledge, whereas in an open system he is aware of the limitations of his existing knowledge and it is precisely the awareness of these limitations which points the way towards a solution of the problem. Looking at thinking as a process in which there is a necessary relationship between closed and open system thinking, we require to understand how the closing of one system necessitates the opening of another.

It is over this point that the difference between Bartlett's account and the present one is most marked. Bartlett recognizes a stage of routine thinking, which adds little or nothing to what is known already, and a stage in which previously unexplored relations begin to be studied. But the emergence of this latter stage appears to bear no relationship to that preceding it: Bartlett localizes the new development 'in some other branch of science and perhaps in some hitherto disconnected part of what is treated as the same branch' (p. 136). This description contrasts sharply with Kuhn's account of the alternation of periods of normal science and of crisis, but perhaps the necessary relationship between routine and crisis in the process of thinking has been most succinctly stated by Whitehead (1938). He has argued that thinking becomes routine and the need for new perspectives urgent, not simply because the application of one set of techniques results in the exhaustion of a particular set of evidence, but, more significantly, because those techniques begin increasingly to reveal inconsistencies in the evidence which, in turn, reflect upon the presuppositions on which the techniques are based:

Also scientific practice is founded upon the same characteristic of omission. In order to observe accurately, concentrate on that observation, dismissing from consciousness all irrelevant modes of experience. But there is no irrelevance. Thus the whole of science is based upon neglected modes of relevance, which nevertheless dominate the social group entertaining those scientific modes of thought. For this reason, the progress of systematized knowledge has a double aspect. There is progress in the discovery of the intricacies of composition which that system admits. There is also progress in the discovery of the limitations of the system in its omission to indicate its dependence upon environmental coordinations of modes of existence which have essential relevance to the entities within the system. Since all things are connected, any system which omits some things must necessarily suffer from such limitations. (p. 101)

Thus, advances in thought are often due to oversimplification. A good example of this has been the widespread acceptance of the Aristotelian view that there are discrete classes of events and things over the opposing view, discernible in Plato, that there are no clear distinctions among species. Whitehead comments that of course Plato was right and Aristotle wrong: there are no clear divisions when you push your observations beyond the presuppositions on which they rest. But, since we always think within limitations, acceptance of the Aristotelian class concept has been justifiable.

How, then, are we to interpret the roles of induction and deduction? Deductivism is correct in stressing the need for theory (or, more simply, a point of view) to guide observation; thinking can only advance to the discovery of new relationships in this way. On this account, therefore, induction corresponds to that phase of thinking during which the pre-suppositions of the theory are accepted without question; this is the viewpoint of common sense which confines itself merely to 'observing the evidence' and which is as fruitful as its underlying presuppositions allow it to be. Deduction corresponds to that phase in which certain presuppositions are made explicit and systematic; hypotheses are tested and deductions made according to the principles of the system. A useful theory is one which leads both to an extension of understanding in respect to the evidence constructed as relevant to the theory and to a recognition of the omissions of the theory. Stating the distinction in this way implies that the psychologist may claim to study induction under circumstances in which he can reasonably assume that his subjects have already achieved competence in the use of a particular system of thought, so that their task in the experiment is to apply this existing knowledge to new material or to unfamiliar problems with familiar material. The problems used by Bartlett in his study of thinking meet this definition, as do games, such as chess (De Groot, 1965) and peggity

(Rayner, 1958). We shall concentrate upon studies of concept attainment.

Studies of Concept Attainment

The distinction made by Bruner, Goodnow and Austin (1956) between concept formation and concept attainment should be understood along the lines suggested by our discussion of Bartlett's distinction between closed and open systems. Concept formation is defined as the inventive act by which classes or categories are constructed, whereas concept attainment refers to the search for attributes that distinguish exemplars from non-exemplars of the class one seeks to discriminate. For example, the discovery that some substances can be categorized as 'fissile' and others as 'non-fissile' is an act of concept formation, whilst the determination of the qualities that are associated with fissile and non-fissile substances is an act of concept attainment. In the latter case, it is assumed that the person already knows what the concept 'fissile/non-fissile' means; his only task is to discover the defining attributes of the concept in order to predict whether any given substance belongs to the fissile or the non-fissile group. Now it seems reasonable to argue that some concept learning consists of relating an already well-defined concept to new instances and should be distinguished from concept formation. It is reasonable as long as it is remembered that the difference between formation and attainment is one of degree and not of kind. A person does not form a concept and then apply it; he forms it *through* application. The difference, then, is that in concept formation this application results in an amplification of the concept itself, whilst in concept attainment this does not happen to the same extent. Thus we can see that the physicist, testing substances with his concept, 'fissile/non-fissile', may simply be classifying substances according to a pre-arranged scheme, but he may also be extending the meaning of that scheme, at least for himself, in the same way, to use another of Bruner's examples, that a child comes to learn more about the differences between cats and dogs when he learns to distinguish them by criteria other than parental decree. As Pikas (1966) has noted, it may be difficult to draw a precise distinction between cases that can be classed as 'concept attainment' and cases that can be classed as 'concept formation'.

The authors identify three major types of concept: conjunctive, disjunctive, and relational. A conjunctive concept is one of which all the relevant attributes are jointly present. For example, in the card-selection task used by Bruner *et al.* (1956) in which there are various combinations of figures that vary in shape, colour and number and which are surrounded by one, two or three borders, a conjunctive concept might be 'all cards containing three red circles'. A disjunctive concept is defined by the presence of any one of a given number of relevant attributes; it might be three red circles or three circles or red circles or three figures, etc. A relational concept is defined as a particular relationship between attributes, for instance, 'all cards with fewer figures than borders'. The subject's task is to select those cards that will enable him to attain the concept. Using this task the authors were able to demonstrate (1) the existence of certain problem-solving strategies; (2) that subjects are relatively inefficient in using the information gained from negative instances, and (3) that disjunctive concepts take longer to attain than conjunctive concepts.

Behaviour on the task was found to conform moderately well to four theoretically-isolated strategies. In the simultaneous scanning strategy the person's choice of cards is determined by the aim of eliminating as many concepts as possible and, consequently, of avoiding choices which eliminate no hypotheses. For example, if the choice had been narrowed down to three possibilities – 'cards containing red', 'cards containing circles' or 'cards with red circles' – the choice of a card displaying a red circle would convey no information even if the concept to be attained were 'cards with red circles'. It is assumed that this strategy involves great 'cognitive strain', since an understanding of the many possible combinations of attributes places a heavy load upon memory and concentration. The strategy of successive scanning, however, involves considerably less cognitive strain, for it consists of testing a single hypothesis at a time, for example, choosing cards containing red to determine whether they are positive instances. Because any one choice is also likely to induce a lot of irrelevant information, this strategy is not as economical as that of simultaneous scanning. A third strategy, conservative focussing, does ensure that the subject will derive some information from each of his choices and at the same time avoid excessive cognitive strain. This involves using a positive instance as a focus and then making a series of choices, each of which alters one attribute value of the focus card. An alternative to conservative focussing is focus gambling, in which the subject uses a positive instance as a focus and then changes more than one attribute value at a time. This entails greater risk since, although it may on occasion lead to relatively fast concept attainment, it may also result in the subject needing many more trials; this is because encountering a negative instance necessitates reverting to choices that will convey some information towards explaining the negative instance. Bruner *et al.* found that the less time

F

allowed to the subject for a decision, the more likely he is to move from a safe strategy, such as conservative focussing, to a risky one, such as focus gambling.

The finding that subjects do not use the information obtained from negative instances as efficiently as that derived from positive instances was explained to be the result of a distrust of transformations carried out 'in the head'. The finding is consistent with the results of other studies (Smoke, 1932, 1933; Wason, 1959, 1961; Freibergs and Tulving, 1961; Wickelgren and Cohen, 1962; Wason and Jones, 1963) but the explanation does not appear to be sufficient. The warrant for this opinion comes from Donaldson's (1959) studies of matching problems. One of these problems involves supplying the subject with the information that each of five persons goes to a different school: person A goes to school 4, B to 2, C to 1, D to 3 and E to 5. The subject's task is to supply the information necessary for the solution of the problem in such a way that the lowest possible 'score' was incurred. He could either supply positive information like A goes to 4 ($A = 4$) or negative information, for example, A does not go to 2 ($A \neq 2$). The subjects were told of the scoring system, used by the author, which gave a value of five points to each positive piece of information and one point for each negative assertion. Thus it was advantageous for the subject to use negatives in order to obtain a low score. Among the errors found by Donaldson were: (1) positive/negative redundancy, which is the failure to realize that a positive statement linking two characters makes any negative statement involving either character superfluous – thus, if $C = 1$, it follows that $C \neq 2$, that $D \neq 1$, etc.; (2) negative/negative redundancy, which consists in failing to realize that a combination of negatives makes redundant further negatives implicated by the combination. Thus, one subject, who showed understanding of positive/negative redundancy, seemed to think that the assertion, $A \neq 2$, $A \neq 1$, $A \neq 3$ and $A \neq 5$, involved a score of twenty points since there would be one point for every negative and four points for every letter. He showed no awareness that the first four negatives enable him to reduce the number of negatives for the subsequent letters. In general, subjects could understand the way in which negatives combine to be equivalent to a positive assertion without necessarily realizing that the provision of negative information which duplicates a derived positive also introduces redundancy. The hypothesis of Bruner *et al.* does not apply since both types of error involve transformations 'in the head'. Donaldson proposed that the failure might be due to a feeling that negative information is less reliable than positive information for complicated transformations or to a feeling that positive statements involve a finality that negative assertions lack.

That subjects learn conjunctive concepts more readily than disjunctive concepts has been confirmed by Wells (1963), who also found that exclusive disjunctive concepts (A or B but not both) take longer to solve than inclusive disjunctive concepts (A or B or both). Neisser and Weene (1962) and Bourne (1970) have extended this line of inquiry and proposed that the difficulty of a concept is in part a function of its place in a logical hierarchy. Neisser and Weene distinguished three levels of complexity for concepts involving two attributes. The univariate level (e.g. A must be present; A must not be present) is the simplest. Next is a group of six bivariate attributes made up directly from the univariate ones by negating, conjoining or disjoining them (e.g. A must be present and B not present), while the most complex level occurs when certain conjunctive pairs are disjoined (either A or B must be present but not both together; both A and B must be present, unless neither is). Experimental results indicated that the order of difficulty of concepts varies directly with their complexity. Bourne (1970) suggests that his experimental data show that inter-rule (and interproblem) transfer is traceable to the acquisition by subjects of a simple but powerful problem-solving strategy. In the course of learning different rules for the combination of two relevant attributes, 'subjects acquire a mode of responding which is best described as an intuitive version of the logical truth table' (p. 552). Once this strategy is established, each new rule-learning problem is solved by reference to this truth table, which comes, therefore, to act itself as a superordinate concept. Bourne contends that a number of such superordinate systems may develop, each of which is characterized by its own logic (a three-valued logic, an n-valued logic, etc.).

The difficulty of a concept-attainment task depends, however, not only upon its logical complexity but also upon the sheer number of relevant and irrelevant attributes. Whilst there is agreement about the relationship between complexity so defined and performance, there is some controversy over the precise nature of this relationship. A number of mathematical models have been proposed. According to Bourne and Restle (1959), difficulty of concept attainment is dependent in a straight-forward manner upon the number of irrelevant cues and inversely related to the number of redundant relevant cues. A redundant relevant cue is one that duplicates another; thus, for example, in a problem which requires red patterns being placed in one category and green patterns in another, the colour dimension is relevant. If all red patterns happen to be triangles and all green patterns squares, the problem can be solved by the subject using either the colour or the shape dimension, in which case we say that both colour and shape are relevant and redundant. This model assumes a steady increase in performance on concept-attainment tasks, but a later model by Restle (1961, 1962) adopted the assumption that subjects test instances against hypotheses. A similar model has been proposed by Bower and Trabasso (1964), which, like attention theory in respect of concept formation, distinguishes between the processes of stimulus selection and conditioning. Stimulus selection is said to proceed in an all-or-none fashion, so that, before the subject chooses the relevant dimension, the probability of his making errors remains constant; once he has hit upon the relevant dimension, the probability of error is zero. Reviewing these mathematical models, Van de Geer and Jaspars (1966) comment that their virtue lies in their specifying the remote consequences of our assumptions, but that their increasing sophistication means that more and more refined observations are needed to obtain a crucial differentiation of the various alternatives.

STRUCTURE AND PROCESS

The distinction between deductive and inductive reasoning contrasts problems which can be solved by reference to a purely deductive system with problems which require the person to make inferences from his observations. The experiments on problem-solving and reasoning reviewed in this chapter are important for two main reasons. They reveal the limited usefulness of straightforward deductive and inductive models for describing the activity of problem-solving – since experiments on deductive reasoning show that subjects are influenced sufficiently by their experience for their reasoning to differ from that described by a purely deductive system, whilst experiments on inductive reasoning lead to the view that an understanding of the strategies used by adult subjects in attaining concepts involves reference to higher-order concepts of a logical and deductive nature. Evidently, then, there is no clear distinction between inductive and deductive reasoning. But these experiments are also significant in their implications for the development of a perspective which will avoid the limitations of inductivism and deductivism. This alternative theory has two essential premises: that the process of thinking can be regarded as the collection and transformation of information, and that its structure involves a hierarchical organization of strategies. These features have impressed students of both deductive and inductive reasoning. Johnson-Laird and Wason

(1970), for example, have proposed that subjects' reasoning on deductive tasks can be described as a set of hierarchically-organized strategies for processing information, while Bartlett's (1958) cryptarithmetic problems and the concept-attainment tasks of Bruner *et al.* (1956) have been treated similarly, the former by Simon and Newell (1971), the latter by Hunt (1962) and by Wickelgren and Cohen (1962). One of the most compelling reasons for the adoption of information-processing terminology is that it permits us to pursue the analogy between human strategies and computer programmes. This analogy provides the subject-matter of the next chapter. The pertinent point here is that an evaluation of the fertility of this viewpoint should include a judgement of the extent to which it meets the limitations of the deductive and inductive models. These limitations, it may be recalled, arise from a misconception of the relation of theory to observation. We must find a way of expressing the reciprocal relationship of strategies and instances if we are to avoid the errors of either conceptualizing strategies as being rigidly imposed upon instances or of instances impressing themselves upon an organism that has no particular point of view.

Of course, subjects do occasionally behave in one of these ways or the other and this fact must be encompassed by any theory. But this is not achieved by making a sharp distinction between these two modes of thought and asserting that these represent the nature of thinking in general. This fault is inherent in rigid dichotomies such as that between deductive and inductive thinking, or between closed and open systems, or between concept formation and attainment. Whitehead (1938) puts this matter concisely when he argues that

> Too much attention has been directed to the mere datum and the mere issue. The essence of existence lies in the transition from datum to issue. This is the process of self-determination. We must not conceive of a dead datum with passive form. The datum is impressing itself upon this process, conditioning its forms. We must not dwell mainly on the issue. The immediacy of existence is then past and over. The vividness of life lies in the transition, with its forms aiming at the issue. (p. 131)

This argument has a vital implication for the analogy between computer programmes and human strategies. However interesting and fruitful the comparison may be between the ways in which humans solve chess problems or attain concepts and the ways in which computers may be programmed to do so, the most fundamental test of this analogy will be provided, not by those problems for which the machine's environment is already structured and defined, but by those problems which require this process of structuring to be made during their solution. It will be, in other words, the simulation by machines of the reciprocity of strategies and circumstances that may eventually convince us that a machine has exhibited 'the vividness of life'.

7

Computer simulation of thought processes

'CAN MACHINES THINK?'

The question is nonsensical and intriguing. It is nonsensical because it involves a misuse of language and a confusion of two levels of discourse. For a machine, however it is constructed, is to be compared with a brain and we ask, not whether a brain 'thinks', but whether and in what manner a *person* 'thinks'. The question remains intriguing, however, since we do accept that human thinking is related somehow to natural brain activity and, consequently, that it is sensible to inquire whether, and under what conditions, some kind of thinking is similarly related to artificial brain activity. This inquiry involves both empirical research and some speculation. The question may be pursued empirically largely because one of the most promising aspects of the language of information and control theory is that it provides a discourse to which physical and psychological processes may be referred. In this sense it provides a common language, partly because it is sufficiently general in its terminology to enable us to describe those characteristics common to widely different systems – biological, physical, psychological and social – and partly because it is sufficiently precise to enable us to define our hypotheses about cognitive processes in such a way that they may be tested out through being embodied in an artificial brain. Hopefully, simulation will result in advancing our understanding of thinking and of its physical and physiological basis. But the inquiry also entails some speculation since, as MacKay (1951, 1962) has observed, no matter how knowledgeable simulation makes us, we have still to face the question of why we attribute thought to persons, rather than brains, natural or artificial. What is the proper relationship between discourse about persons and discourse about brains? What is involved in the transition from talking in bodily terms to talking in personal terms? And have speculations about these questions any implications for a psychological theory of thinking? Accordingly, in this chapter we shall be concerned with (1) defining the terminology of the information-processing approach; (2) reviewing some of the major developments in the field of computer simulation of thought processes, and (3) considering the relationship between the language of this approach and the language of personal activity.

The development of the analogy between computer programmes and human thought has aroused a great deal of controversy. On the one hand, those working within the field tend to maintain that eventually machines will be capable of demonstrating all those qualities which we now believe to be distinctively human. Minsky (1966), for example, holds that when machines have been constructed which can improve upon their own programmes we shall begin to see all the phenomena associated with the terms 'consciousness', 'intuition' and 'intelligence', and Simon (1969) argues that the simulation of human intelligence is feasible because the behaviour of an organism is fundamentally quite simple, its apparent complexity stemming from the fact that it must adapt to the details of the environment in which it exists. He believes it will be possible to detect through simulation those characteristics which are independent of specific content. On the other hand, it has been frequently asserted that there are necessary limitations to artificial intelligence. Popper (1950) sees the creation of interests, purposes and problems as being the prerogative of human brains. Wisdom (1952) maintains that imagination, the peculiar feature of which is that something 'unreal' has 'real' effects, defies reproduction by any known artefact. Muses (1962) believes that creative, extrapolative thinking is likely to remain a distinctively human achievement because it is a capacity that can never be fully formalized. Taub (1961) makes a similar point when he says that experience is, in the last analysis, primarily aesthetic, an affair of feeling and not of formal logic.

There are, perhaps, two major reasons why statements referring to the intrinsic limitations of machines are mistaken. In the first place, as MacKay (1955, 1962) has suggested, predictions of impotence of the form, 'You'll never get a machine to do *x*', can never resolve the issue, for any detailed test-specification for particular behaviour is implicitly equivalent to a description of at least one mechanism to meet it. It follows that predictions of impotence are doomed to fail as soon as the speaker has specified what behaviour he would regard as satisfactory. Secondly, our concept of a 'machine' is changing all the while as a result of human ingenuity, so that we cannot specify at the present time just what sort of machine man may be compared to in the future.

Clearly, if this is so, then no limitations may be imposed *a priori* on the extent to which we may judge human and artificial activity to be similar or identical.

However, there is no doubt that some types of performance have proved easier to simulate than others. It has proved relatively straight-forward to programme computers to display planned, purposeful and intelligent behaviour for specific problem areas, such as chess playing and concept attainment, but attention has only recently been directed to devising artefacts which can be programmed to solve a variety of problems. The accomplishment of this objective seems to be bound up with the problem of artificial perception, for only when a machine can 'share our world', to quote Gregory (1971), will it be able to generate procedures for the execution of a variety of tasks, both simple and com-plex, which relate to that world. It will be argued in this chapter that the concept of the feedback loop provides the necessary theoretical foundation for the attainment of this objective, but that the first attempts at the computer simulation of thinking have failed to meet sufficiently the specifications derivable from this concept and, con-sequently, have been only partially successful.

THE CYBERNETIC HYPOTHESIS

The cybernetic hypothesis states that the fundamental structure of the nervous system is the feedback loop. Although the term 'cybernetics' was coined by Ampère (1834) in the last century to denote the science of government, it was not until the middle of this century that the field of cybernetics became clearly delineated. Its establishment owes much to Cannon's (1932) demonstration of the existence of homeostatic mechanisms in the regulation of bodily functions, for example, the control of temperature, and to the work of Wiener (1948) and Ashby (1952), showing how the servo-mechanisms of the engineer relate to neurophysiological functioning and, hence, to psychology. Because of these and other developments, the concept of the feedback loop came to be regarded by many as replacing the concept of the reflex arc as the fundamental structure of behaviour.

In a reflex arc a stimulus is said to elicit a response through activating receptors and afferent nerves which, in turn, through the medium of connective areas, elicit efferent activity. It has already been argued (in our examination of Piaget's theory of adaptation and the Gibsons' differentiation theory, pp. 120-1) that such a view is mistaken and that we need to view the development of behaviour as a progressive and

F*

simultaneous differentiation of stimulus and response. That the identical reasoning underlies the notion of a feedback loop is perhaps most evident when one considers the classic exposition of this concept contained in Dewey's (1896) critique of the reflex arc concept. Dewey reasoned that stimulus and response are not separate entities which become causally related; we must not conceive stimulus, central connections, and response as separate and complete entities in themselves, but as distinguishable functions within a single, concrete whole. Consider, for example, the child who withdraws his hand from a lighted candle. On the reflex arc interpretation, it is alleged that the light is a stimulus to a grasping response and the resulting burn a stimulus to the response of withdrawing the hand. This description is inadequate, says Dewey, because we do not begin the behaviour sequence with a sensory stimulus but with a sensori-motor co-ordination, the movement of the body determining the quality of the experience. Thus the stimulus, far from being an independent existent, 'emerges' out of a sensori-motor co-ordination. And just as the response is necessary to constitute the stimulus, so the stimulus must persist as a value related to the response in order to control it. What we observe, then, is a circuit, not an arc, and this is because stimulus and response are not distinctions of existence but distinctions of function, both emerging as aspects of an act of co-ordination. From this it can only be concluded that the differentiation of stimulus and response is at once mutual and parallel. The child, for instance, who is extending his scheme of seeing and reaching, may sometimes in the past have found something to eat and may sometimes have burned himself; it is not only the response that is uncertain in this situation, for the stimulus is equally uncertain. Because stimulus and response are correlative and contemporaneous, one is uncertain only in so far as the other is. As Dewey puts it: 'The search for the stimulus is the search for exact conditions of action; that is, for the state of things which decides how a beginning co-ordination should be completed' (p. 363).

The parallel between Dewey's 'forming co-ordination' and the feedback loop has been noted by Slack (1955) and by Miller, Galanter and Pribram (1960). A physiological example of a feedback loop is the way the sympathetic nervous system regulates body temperatures: the temperature-sensitive nerve endings in the body feed back information to the nervous system which regulates temperature by controlling the size of the blood vessels near the surface of the skin; these corrections are fed back, and so forth. James Watt had relied upon a similar mechanism to maintain constant the speed of his steam engine despite variations in load. The effectiveness of Watt's 'Governor' was dependent upon the engine causing two weights to rotate at the end of two levers. The faster the engine speed, the further the weights swung out, thus moving levers which supported them. The faster these levers moved, the less steam was admitted, thus reducing the speed of the engine. Watt's engine is an example of negative feedback, since the regulation is attained by returning the output to the input and subtracting it from the input. In positive feedback, on the other hand, the output is returned and added to the input.

Miller, Galanter and Pribram draw the most general conclusions from these ideas. They conclude that even the neural mechanism

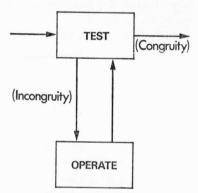

Figure 3. *The tote unit* (reproduced by arrangement with Holt, Rinehart & Winston, Inc., New York, from Miller, Galanter and Pribram, 1960).

involved in reflex action cannot be diagrammed as a simple reflex arc or as a chain of stimulus-response connections, for a much more complex kind of monitoring or testing is involved. They argue that the response of the effector depends upon the outcome of a test and is most accurately conceived as an effort to modify the outcome of the test. In other words, the action is initiated by an incongruity between the state of the organism and the state that is being tested for and the action persists until the incongruity is removed. The general pattern of reflex action, therefore, is to test the input against some criteria established in the organism, to respond if the result of the test is to show an incongruity, and to continue to respond until the incongruity vanishes. This process is represented by the TOTE unit. The Test-Operate-Test-Exit unit is a feedback loop or, in the authors' words, 'an incongruity-sensitive mechanism'. The generality of the unit derives from the fact that we do not have to restrict ourselves to assuming that it is nervous energy or even information which flows along the arrows in the diagram; rather, it is an intangible something called 'control', which may best be defined as the order in which certain tasks are carried out. For example, to hammer a nail involves locating the hammer, placing the nail, etc., in short a whole series of hierarchically organized TOTE units. The generality of the concept means that it can be applied to reflex behaviour, sensori-motor skills and problem-solving strategies, such as those described by Bruner, Goodnow and Austin (1956). Miller, Galanter and Pribram define a plan as 'any hierarchical process within the organism that can control the order in which a sequence of operations is to be performed' (p. 16). Any plan complicated enough to be interesting will include steps which are executed as means to attaining a goal.

How is this reasoning relevant to electronic computers? The answer is that a plan is for an organism what a programme is for a computer. Therefore, we may hope that the development of computer programmes to solve problems will prove useful in enabling us to formulate our ideas about human problem-solving more precisely. But note that this is only useful and interesting if the computer is programmed to 'create' its own plans. Suppose, for example, that we wish to use a computer to make calculations involving logarithms. A decision must be made whether to store a table of logarithms in the computer's memory or whether to provide the computer with a formula for calculating logarithms as they are needed. If the table is used, the logarithm will be rapidly found if it is in the table, but the computer will be unable to handle any numbers whose logarithms it has not been given. If the formula is used, the process will be slower but the computer will be able to discover the logarithms of numbers it has not seen before. This is the great advantage of formulae, rules or metaplans. They are easily stored and when it is time to use them they can be applied to a great many unforeseen situations. Miller and his associates maintain that it is impossible to conceptualize the range and diversity of human intellectual performance without postulating the existence of plans that generate plans.

THE LOGIC OF COMPUTER SIMULATION

The development of the analogy between human plans and computer programmes stemmed from a number of sources. Craik (1943) expressed the belief that the brain imitates or models external processes. Referring to mechanical analogies, such as an anti-aircraft 'predictor' or Kelvin's tidal predictor, Craik identified three phases in the modelling activity:

the *translation* of the external processes into their representatives in the model (e.g. positions of gears, etc.), *inference*, defined as the ways in which the representatives move to other positions (movement of the gears), and *retranslation* of the mechanical processes into physical processes of the original type (formulae for tidal movements). Craik hypothesized that humans model reality in the same manner: at the neurophysiological level, the process is represented by excitations of nervous nets; at the psychological level, thought itself models or parallels reality through the mediation of symbolism. Consequently, when we study the way in which machines handle symbols, we are modelling human thought processes, and the more successful our ability to produce machines that 'think' and 'solve problems' the deeper our understanding of these thought processes. This insight, together with the work of the mathematician, Turing (1936), who demonstrated that a machine could be constructed that could simulate any behaviour which was precisely described, and that of McCulloch and Pitts (1943), who showed that any such behaviour could be realized by a suitable neural network, formed the foundations for the theory of automata, since human plans, computer programmes and nervous nets could be regarded as isomorphic.

The symbols processed by a digital computer are discrete, all-or-none signals (e.g. 1 or 0), whereas an analogue computer represents the values of variables by physical quantities that vary continuously. The digital computer has proved more flexible and hence more popular. It consists essentially of a memory, an interpreter or control unit, which is the device for following the programme of instructions fed into the computer, and input and output units, which allow communication between the computer and its environment. To solve a problem on a computer, the programme and the data are stored in the computer's memory. A programme is a set of instructions arranged as a branching list, a branch instruction containing two further instructions, the one or the other of them to be executed depending upon whether or not the condition stated in the branch is satisfied. The form of a branch is: 'If y, then branch to x; otherwise go to z'. A typical programme contains many loops. For example, a programme for a man walking the length of a street would be:

1. Step with left foot, then 2.
2. Step with right foot, then 3.
3. If end of street, do 4; if not do 1.
4. Terminate.

We can see that this loop (statement 3), as any other, must contain a conditional branch, for, if it did not, the loop would continue indefinitely (Newell and Simon, 1963).

Newell and Simon (1961) have put the case for computer simulation thus:

> We postulate that the subject's behaviour is governed by a program organized from a set of elementary information processes. We encode a set of subprograms (subroutines) for a digital computer, each of which executes a process corresponding to one of these information processes. Then we undertake to write a program, compounded from these subroutines, that will cause the computer to behave in the same way that the subject behaves – to emit substantially the same stream of symbols – when both are given the same problem. If we succeed in devising a program that simulates the subject's behaviour rather closely over a significant range of problem solving situations, then we can regard the program as a theory of the behaviour. How highly we will prize the theory depends, as with all theories, on its generality and its parsimony – on how wide a range of phenomena it explains and on how economical of expression it is. (p. 2013)

The programme is a theory stated in such a way that it can be tested through simulation. Having to write his theory in the form of a programme, the investigator must define his ideas precisely; running the programme enables him to compare the output of the computer with that of humans and to modify the programme, if needs be, to produce greater similarity between the two.

There is reason to believe that the course of simulation has not run as smoothly as this. Murdock (1967) and Frijda (1967) have drawn attention to the subjective nature of many of the comparisons between human protocols and computer outputs. Hunt (1968), reviewing the field, cautions that 'teachers of general psychology should be aware that, as of this date, no programme has been shown to simulate human problem solving, although there are several programs which solve problems' (p. 160). Frijda is critical of the assertion that a programme is a theory, arguing that many of the lower-order operations of a programme are determined by the particularities of the programming language, the mode of operation of the computer, and the special limitations inherent in serially operating digital machines. If much in a programme is not theory, it is clearly the task of the programme's author to state just what the theory is. In the first flush of enthusiasm for computer simulation insufficient attention has been directed to problems of this sort.

CONCEPT ATTAINMENT

A number of authors have applied the language of artificial intelligence to the analysis of concept attainment. Wickelgren and Cohen (1962) suggest that this application will be useful since performance on concept attainment tasks is dependent upon the ways in which subjects store and retrieve information. In the same year, Allen (1962) wrote a programme for the strategy of simultaneous scanning and Wickelgren

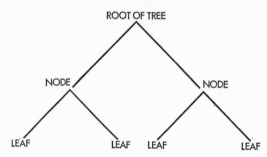

Figure 4. *Elements of the tree structure.*

(1962) for that of conservative scanning, although neither author presented comparative analysis of human protocols and machine outputs. However, Simon and Kotovsky (1963) proposed a theory in the form of a computer programme for the acquisition of concepts for sequential patterns, one part of the programme simulating the process of sequence production, the other the process of rule acquisition. This programme was found to predict quite successfully the order of difficulty obtained for human subjects. Two factors appeared to contribute to the difficulty of the task – the number of symbols in the sequence and the load imposed upon short-term memory. Gregg and Simon (1967) criticized the Bower and Trabasso (1964) model of concept attainment on the grounds that it is silent about the strategies that subjects use. They recommended instead a 'process model' which does make definite assumptions about strategies, and they demonstrated that these additional assumptions permit a more adequate description of the data from a number of experiments.

Perhaps the most active proselytizers of the artificial intelligence approach to concept attainment are Hunt and his associates (Hunt,

1962; Hunt, Marin and Stone, 1966; Hunt, 1971), who have proposed that any concept can be regarded as a sequential decision tree. A decision tree consists of a series of *nodes* (Fig. 4). The root of a tree is the node at which the tree starts; from each node two lines extend downwards to two lower nodes until an endpoint or *leaf* is encountered: a leaf is a node with no nodes beneath it. A decision tree for a concept-attainment problem represents a series of tests made upon descriptions of objects. Each node is associated with a test to establish whether an object is or is not included in a set of objects defined by a particular descriptive statement. For example, the statement 'Professors are clever or industrious' may be represented by a simple tree (Fig. 5).

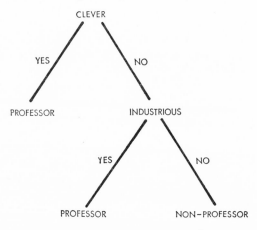

Figure 5. *Tree structure for the concept: 'Professors are clever or industrious'.*

The other binary concepts identified and investigated by such workers as Neisser and Weene (1962) and Bourne (1970) may be represented in this way. Hunt, Marin and Stone (1966) propose a general method of writing programmes for what they call 'concept-learning systems'. Essentially, a concept-learning system examines stored information in order to attain a concept, the computation involved taking the form of a decision tree. These authors examined different types of concept-learning system (the differences relating to search procedures and memory capacity) and confirmed that the general paradigm provides a way for writing workable concept learners, since the programmes were capable of recognizing complex logical patterns on the basis of experience with relatively few objects. They applied a version of Turing's test (Turing, 1950) for simulation: this requires that the observer cannot discriminate computer output from human performance. Selecting at random one subject from each of their experimental groups, Hunt *et al.* found that his responses corresponded as much with the output of a programme which assumed perfect memory for all information as with the responses of his fellow subjects. They admit, however, that this was partly due to the existence of a wide range of individual differences: people were so different in their approaches that one could not predict the course of one's performance from that of another's. But they did find that the order of difficulty of the concepts for their subjects was almost identical to the order of difficulty found by Neisser and Weene (1962), except that in the latter study the biconditional problem was consistently more difficult than the exclusive disjunction; Neisser and Weene's results, in this respect, were more in line with the simulation than the experimental results of Hunt and his associates.

Hilgard and Bower (1966) have pointed out that it was unrealistic to assume perfect memory for all information presented. The 'Distributed Memory' model (Hunt, 1971) may provide a more realistic framework. This model includes a long-term memory, in which information is stored permanently, an intermediate-term memory, which, roughly, stores a general picture of current events, and a short-term memory, which holds an exact picture of very recently received input. It is proposed that in concept-attainment tasks a hypothesis exists as a decision rule in intermediate-term memory. When the description of an object arrives in short-term memory, the hypothesis is used to classify it. If the classification is correct, a new object is sought; if incorrect, a new hypothesis is constructed based on the current contents of short-term memory. In constructing the new hypothesis some use may be made of data in intermediate-term or long-term memory. The programme which constructs the hypothesis corresponds to a strategy and, if this strategy is successful, it will be stored in long-term memory. Hunt suggests that the Distributed Memory model accounts for the difficulties which human subjects experience in concept learning; for example, the inhibition of learning consequent upon a short interval between the signal indicating the correct classification of an object and the presentation of the next object (Bourne and Bunderson, 1963) is predictable because this is the time during which the learner must do the processing required to check his classification and perhaps develop a new rule. Further, the difficulties experienced with more complex decision trees (Neisser and Weene, 1962; Hunt, Marin and Stone, 1966) may be related to the extra demands placed upon memory. Williams (1971) has presented evidence on the predictive power of a programme based upon the Distributed Memory model for conjunctive concept learning.

There is one limitation to work on the computer simulation of concept attainment that arises from the concept-attainment paradigm itself. This is the problem of representation, the way in which the subject defines the problem to be solved or perceives the stimuli to be classified. In a concept-attainment problem the subject searches for a classification of already well-defined stimuli. Now, the assumption that all subjects perceive the stimuli similarly may pass as plausible with familiar material or, at least, material that consists of familiar dimensions, such as colour and size, but it becomes increasingly doubtful the more complex and novel the stimuli are. In concept-formation problems, on the other hand, Dewey's maxim that 'the search for the stimulus is the search for exact conditions of action' applies, for the stimuli are ill-defined as long as the response (the classification) is unclear. In the previous chapter we agreed with Bruner that, since some concepts at least are learned by searching through familiar material, experiments on concept attainment are valid enough. But, since concept attainment would be impossible without concept formation (one has already formed the concepts to be attained) we must regard concept formation as the more fundamental process. Hence, as Hunt (1971) recognizes, the problem of how representations are generated urgently awaits solution. We shall see that this same conclusion emerges from investigation of deductive reasoning and problem-solving.

DEDUCTIVE REASONING AND PROBLEM-SOLVING

One of the earliest uses of computers was for proving theorems in logic or mathematics. The Logic Theorist of Newell, Shaw and Simon (1963) consists of a programme for proving the theorems contained in Whitehead and Russell's (1927) *Principia Mathematica*. In considering this work, the crucial distinction between an algorithm and a heuristic must be borne in mind. An algorithm is a systematic plan that guarantees the solution of a given problem; for example, a simple algorithm for opening a combination safe is to try all the combinations. A heuristic, on the other hand, does not guarantee solution but it may be considerably quicker. Thus, it is possible to construct an algorithm for playing chess (Shannon, 1950) but, given that humans are slow, serial processers of information, this approach is not practical. Heuristic methods, however, are selective and may yield a solution in a reasonable time.

Consequently, Newell *et al.* made the assumption that human problem-solving could be modelled by constructing heuristic programmes.

They distinguished three major heuristics for theorem-proving. The first is the substitution method, which consists of starting with a previously proved theorem or axiom and, by legitimate substitutions, attempting to derive the statement needing proof. The second method, detachment, makes use of the fact that, if one problem, A, implies another, B, and if A can be proved, then so can B. The third method, that of chaining, makes use of the transitivity of the relation of implication. Thus, if the theorem to be proved is 'A ⊃ C', one searches for a theorem or axiom of the form 'A ⊃ B', so that 'B ⊃ C' may be established as a new subproblem. This procedure is 'chaining forwards'. 'Chaining backwards' for the same problem would involve finding a theorem of the form 'B ⊃ C', so that 'A ⊃ B' could be established as a new subproblem. The organization of the Logic Theorist's sequence of operations, its executive routine, utilized these three heuristic methods in the same order for each new problem: substitution was followed by detachment which was followed by chaining. Of the first fifty-two theorems of *Principia Mathematica*, proof was found for thirty-eight. These proofs were obtained by various combinations of methods but substitution was an essential component in all of them. Hunt (1968) reports that all but one of the failures were due to the physical limitations of the computer and that the remaining theorem can be proven using an augmented version of the programme (Stefferud, 1963). Simon and Newell (1971) suggest that the importance of this early research is the demonstration that difficult problems may be solved by a slow information-processing system. This demonstration defined the terms of the next stage of the inquiry – that of discovering the heuristic processes actually used by humans to solve problems. Work has, of course, continued on theorem-proving (see, for example, Robinson, 1967; Meltzer and Michie, 1971).

Newell and Simon observed that a human subject brings to a problem both specific knowledge relevant to the problem-area and a number of broadly applicable problem-solving techniques. A computer which performs one specialist task very well but is helpless at any other problem is not, therefore, representative of human problem-solving. A theory that purports to be an explanation of human problem-solving must contain: (1) some general problem-solving techniques; (2) some way of acquiring knowledge of specific task environments and (3) some means of improving both its general and specific techniques. The General Problem-Solver (Newell, Shaw and Simon, 1959; Newell and

Simon, 1961, 1963) represents an attempt to progress towards meeting these specifications, for it is a programme that can operate upon any problem that is stated in a certain general form. Following the descriptions of human problem-solving given by Duncker (1945) and Bartlett (1958), the basic assumption was made that much human problem-solving proceeds by erecting goals, detecting differences between the present situation and these goals, finding plans to reduce these differences, and applying these plans. This basic organization is exemplified in a programme that plays chess. The goals – for example, the safety of the king, the promotion of pawns – are arranged in order of importance. Associated with each goal is a move-generator which proposes alternative moves relevant to the goal. A value is obtained for each move from a series of evaluations related to the goal. Finally, a choice is made by adopting the first move which meets a predetermined criterion of acceptability. Newell and Simon suggest that the same general, qualitative features are apparent in the chess-playing of this programme and that of humans.

But problem-solving does not begin when the subject organizes his plans to attain a goal; it begins when he perceives the problem. Simon and Barenfeld (1969), noting this omission in the theory, remark that in the first few moments of a chess game a skilled player is occupied with perceiving the essential properties of the situation, a fact observed also by De Groot (1965) and his colleagues, who report that, after scanning the board for five seconds, a grand master can reproduce the position of the pieces without error and that the weaker the player, the more errors are made in the reproduction. It may be reasonably assumed that these individual differences reflect variations in the capacity to extract organized networks of relationships from the stimuli: the skilled player is able to recognize such configurations whilst the less skilled must describe the board in a larger number of simple units. Simon and Barenfeld argue that existing computer programmes for heuristic search and learning must contain the basic processes to simulate this behaviour and they outline a programme which models the eye movements made by subjects during the first five seconds of the game.

Although this extension of the theory to include the initial 'perceptual' phase of problem-solving is, no doubt, useful, there remains a fundamental problem of perceptual representation that lies beyond the present scope of Newell and Simon's work. In order to understand this problem, it is necessary to consider the concept of a 'problem-space'. According to the authors (Simon and Newell, 1971; Newell and Simon, 1971), there are a few characteristics of the human information-processing system that are invariant over task and problem-solver. Thus, the system operates serially, there is a small, short-term memory capacity, and an infinite long-term memory with fast retrieval but slow storage. These characteristics determine that a task environment is represented as a problem-space, that is, as a space of possible situations to be searched serially in order to find one that corresponds to the solution. A problem-space can, then, be envisaged as a series of inter-connected nodes after the fashion of a decision tree except that in Simon and Newell's analysis the problem-solver who reaches a particular node must decide to choose a particular operator or to abandon the node in favour of another. The possible structures of the problem-space are determined by the structure of the task environment. Consider, for example, the DONALD + GERALD cryptarithmetic problem (see p. 147). Since there are 9! = 362,880 ways of assigning nine digits to nine letters, thousands of combinations would have to be tried if one were to attempt to find the solution in this way. But the task structure admits heuristics which serve to structure the task to the extent that all subjects substitute numbers for letters in approximately the same sequence. Subjects, in fact, make use of their knowledge that, if two digits in a single column are already known, the third can be found by applying the ordinary rules of arithmetic; thus, knowing that $D = 5$, we can obtain the right-most column: $5 + 5 = T$, hence $T = 0$, carrying 1 to the next column, and so forth.

But how does a problem-solver come to enter a problem-space in which the nodes are defined as different assignments of letters to numbers? How does he become aware of the relevance of arithmetical operations for solving the problem? Simon and Newell admit that the theory explains behaviour only after the problem-space has been postulated; it does not explain how the problem-solver constructs his problem-space in a given task environment. Now, the problems which beset human subjects are extremely varied in nature. To begin to account for the ability to enter diverse problem-spaces, it would appear essential to postulate modes of operation which have wide-ranging applicability besides those routines for specific and well-defined tasks. What could be the nature of such operations?

Michie (1970) contends that it is precisely this lack of specification of the stimulus-world, common in real-life problems, which prevents reaching a solution through having the computer represent sequences of events along future action-paths. Alternative courses of action can be specified only to the extent that the problem-space is specified. This fact, it is argued, forces an approach through formal deductive reasoning, in which the problem is regarded as a theorem to be proved. This process involves formulation of axioms, statement of the problem, and formal proof. Michie refers to a study by Popplestone which consisted of writing a programme for a robot whose world consisted of two places only, called 'here' and 'there'. The robot was, in fact, a hand capable of three actions: 'goto', a plan which moves the hand to the stated place, 'pickup', which transfers into the hand a thing chosen at random from the place where the hand is, and 'letgo', which has the obvious meaning. Suppose that all the things 'here' are green and that a plan is required to bring about the situation in which 'there' consists of at least one green thing. Popplestone found that an extensive set of axioms and inferences was needed to generate this plan by formal reasoning. It was necessary, for example, to state as axioms the propositions that, after going to a place, the hand will be at that place, and that, if a thing is held, then it is held after the hand goes to a place. Axioms such as these were followed by statements outlining the problem and then by statements leading to a proof. The 'answer' is the situation resulting from the following chain of actions: do a letgo, then go 'here', then a pickup, and then go 'there'. Michie suggests that the length of this deductive sequence appears less formidable if one remembers that the different intermediate stages would be acquired by humans on a number of different previous occasions and that, in any case, it seems likely that we combine planning by theorem-proving with the heuristics of planning by simulation.

Much remains to be done, however, before mechanized reasoning approaches the capacity for generalization possessed by human plans; for example, the fact that Popplestone's simple robot can be programmed to leave at least one green object 'there' does not facilitate the formation of a similar plan involving, say, 'red' substituted for 'green' and 'here' and 'there' interchanged throughout. We must await further advances in the field of machine intelligence. In addition, there may be a productive interaction between these computer studies and work on the development of intelligence by Piaget and others. For these latter are concerned with the problem of how the organism learns from and generalizes its experience (Piaget, for instance, asserting that it is through the co-ordination of actions and the subsequent internalization of these co-ordinations that the general structures of logical and mathematical thought arise) and this is something which machines do not do very well, whereas the necessity for stating these processes in the language of artificial intelligence may, in turn, inspire a more precise description of the developmental process.

The present limitations of intelligent machines are best summarized by comparing their capabilities with Dewey's specifications for the major theoretical concept of the cybernetic hypothesis – the feedback loop. We have noted that to use this concept is to recognize stimulus and response as different aspects of the same process, for stimuli become defined and capable of controlling behaviour to the extent that the organism acts upon its environment. On this paradigm, to form a concept or to solve a problem is to understand more precisely the stimulus conditions related to an act of categorization or co-ordination. However, the problem-elements in the environment of a computer programmed to attain a concept or play chess are already defined: Hunt's programmes assume that the concepts are formed (but not attained), Newell and Simon's that the problem-space is defined and entered without difficulty. Of course, these are still genuine problems and the work of these investigators has contributed to our under-standing of them. It is equally to their credit that their work should also lead to a greater understanding of the limitations of some of the assumptions upon which it was based initially.

SEQUENTIAL AND PARALLEL PROCESSING

The sequential organization of the General Problem-Solver has been criticized as being too single-minded to be an accurate representation of human information processing (Neisser, 1963; Reitman, 1965). It appears essential to incorporate parallel or multiple processing into computer models of thinking.

Convincing evidence comes from animal studies for the need to postulate two modes of visual processing (e.g. Schneider, 1968; Trevarthen, 1968). Focal vision is defined as the capacity of the organism to examine and discriminate the detailed features of objects, whilst ambient vision is characterized as the capacity to make simultaneous differentiations of wide scope but of low discrimination. Ambient vision is involved, for example, in climbing or running over rough ground: one is not aware of the details of the environment but, neverthe-less, this information is utilized in order to maintain a steady course. Experimental brain surgery has revealed that ambient vision in primates is controlled largely by a midbrain visual mechanism and that focal vision is under control of the fovea and the cortical visual areas. This distinction is reminiscent of Polanyi's (1967) analysis of focal and subsidiary awareness. When, for example, hammering a nail, our aware-ness of the hammer and our awareness of the nail are fundamentally different: we have a focal awareness of the nail (the object of our activity) but a subsidiary awareness of the hammer (the instrument of our activity). This distinction is readily demonstrated if, while engaged in this task, focal attention is shifted from the object to the instrument. And this is true of any skilled activity – there is a necessary and complementary relationship between two kinds of awareness which, if disturbed, leads to an impairment in performance.

Neisser (1963, 1967) has suggested that there are two types of cognitive process. Following Freud's distinction between the primary and secondary processes, he characterizes the one as a relatively well-ordered and efficiently-adapted thought process and the other as a profusion of simultaneous activities. In computer programming, these are called sequential and parallel modes respectively. The contrast between them is well demonstrated in letter-recognition problems. A sequentially programmed computer can solve these as long as the input is restricted to printed characters in particular founts. When, however, the computer is given hand-printed characters to identify, such a programme will score almost at random, because all sorts of distortions are present in normal hand writing. Although people can identify 96 per cent of randomly-selected hand-printed characters, even without the aid of context, a sequential programme is unable to cope with them, since a process which goes consecutively from one decision to the next must go astray if a single decision is wrong. Only when no uncertainty exists is such a programme dependable. A multiple-process programme, on the other hand, examines the input for many different properties simultaneously; thus, the presence of variability and uncertainty need not lead the programme into error for letters are effectively defined by the totality of their features combined by a single weighted sum. Neisser's thesis is that human thinking is a multiple activity, that, awake or asleep, a number of more or less independent trains of thought usually co-exist, although, ordinarily, there is a main sequence in progress (the secondary processes), dealing with some material in a step-by-step fashion.

Argus is a programme designed to explore means of modelling the interaction of sequential and parallel processes (Reitman, 1965). The main aspects of the system are the sequential executive, a network of active semantic elements (hot: cold; short: tall, etc.), and the channels of communication between them. The executive solves problems in a step-by-step fashion by utilizing available strategies. The network consists of a number of semantic elements, each of which derives its meaning solely from its interconnections with other elements in the total cognitive structure, Argus having neither perceptual inputs nor behavioural outputs. The current state of each semantic element is also specified. Interaction between the executive and the semantic elements is through the medium of signals sent by the elements to a main signal cell, for once the activity of an element exceeds a certain threshold it transmits a signal to this cell. The executive checks the main signal cell and makes its decision according to the signals it finds there and the dictates of its current strategy. This is a most schematic portrait of Argus but it may be sufficient to convey that it is a design which allows for many possible forms of interaction between spontaneous cognitive activity and the sequential strategies appropriate to a particular problem. Reitman acknowledges that Argus is very far from an explanation of the phenomena that motivated work on the system but, nevertheless, the problems with which it is concerned are real ones.

PERSONAL KNOWLEDGE

The empirical evidence suggests that computers can model various aspects of human thinking but that certain problems remain, for example, the representation of problem-spaces, the construction of general plans, and the interaction of sequential and parallel processes. May we assume that these and other limitations will be overcome as work progresses or are there essential differences between men and machines which ensure that some of them will remain?

One point of view states that persons do possess qualities which entail that they will always be in advance of the machines they construct. This argument, which rests upon an appeal to Gödel's theorem, states that, since we always know more than we can formalize, our knowledge will always be greater than that of machines which embody the results of our formalized knowledge. This argument may also be associated with the assertion that creativity and imagination are human prerogatives and quite beyond the reach of machines (Muses, 1962; Beloff, 1962; Butcher, 1968). Two main criticisms have been directed to these views (MacKay, 1962, 1965). In the first place, it is not clear why future machines that are capable of representing the world and of acting upon it should not also be capable of showing creativity and the ability to progress from one formalized system to another. But secondly, it is argued, there is here a confusion of the language of personal and impersonal knowledge. A more defensible thesis is that a purely impersonal and objective account of human behaviour will never remove the necessity for an account in terms of personal intentions and activity because the language of personal activity is not reducible to, although it may be in some sense compatible with, the impersonal language of science. To understand fully the implications of this point, we must understand the relationship between these two languages. We shall follow the interpretation given by Macmurray (1957, 1961).

We may choose to interpret human behaviour impersonally and deterministically: to do this is to assume that the laws which govern this behaviour, like the laws which natural objects obey, are discoverable through objective techniques of investigation. Alternatively, we may choose to construe the other person as an agent who has intentions, makes choices and acts purposefully on the world. That these are distinct types of knowledge is clear from the impossibility of reducing personal action to the level of objective knowledge. To attempt this is to reduce action, which is intentional, to behaviour, which merely happens, and this leads inevitably to a paradox, since if we are thought of exclusively in impersonal terms, then it can only be said that events happen, not that we are responsible for our actions or that these accomplish or fail to realize our intentions. Consequently, 'if we are thought of as parts of the scientist's world, then we cannot make mistakes or be in error or have illusions, not even the illusion that we are free to act. We cannot, then, frame a hypothesis and make an experiment to discover whether it is true or not. In the "scientific" world there is no place for scientists' (Macmurray, 1961, p. 220). Note that it is the assumption that all knowledge is scientific knowledge which leads to this paradox. To construe man impersonally and objectively is, of course, a legitimate and useful activity (as when, for example, one analyses a person's problems in order to help him), but to construe him solely in this way is false.

Because the scientific pursuit of entirely objective knowledge which motivates the approach to man through artificial intelligence can escape paradox only when we assume that there also exists a form of knowledge which may be termed 'personal', we must say, not that men will always be in advance of the machines they construct, for this is like saying they will always be one step ahead of their brains, but that a purely impersonal account of man will always require to be complemented by a personal account. We cannot say that there are necessary differences in the capacities of men and machines, but that there are two systems of concepts that serve to define impersonal and personal knowledge, the first of which we use when construing the other (man or machine) as a determinate object, the second when we construe the other as engaging in dialogue with us or as having intentions towards us and the world. The former may develop into the formal and impersonal language of science, whilst the latter is the language of personal experience, by which we characterize ourselves as subjects who, though also influenced by events beyond our control, are yet capable of acting responsibly and of searching for and discovering meaning.

The two accounts may eventually be shown to be isomorphic but, unfortunately, whenever a psychological theory has been understood as exemplifying one or the other of these modes of thought, the erroneous assumption has usually been made that the relationship between the two is one of conflict or indifference, so that the problem of understanding how they may be regarded as complementary has seldom been broached. The situation that has resulted from this failure has been discussed with fitting irony by the Austrian novelist, Robert Musil (1953):

> So there are in reality two outlooks, which not only conflict with each other but – what is worse – usually exist side by side without exchanging a word except to assure each other that they are both desirable, each in its place. The one contents itself with being precise, and sticks to facts; the other does not content itself with that, but always looks at the Whole and draws its knowledge from what are called great and eternal verities. Thereby the one gains in success, and the other in scope and dignity. It is clear that a pessimist might also say that the results of the one are worthless and those of the other not true. For where will it get one, on the Day of Judgment, when mankind's works are weighed in the balance, to come forward with three treatises on formic acid – or thirty, for that matter? On the other hand, what can one know about the Day of Judgment if one does not even know what may have come of formic acid by then? (p. 313)

The research that has been reviewed to this point has been conducted within the framework of impersonal knowledge, some authors seeking affiliations between the psychology of thinking and biology whilst others have drawn upon advances in formal logic and cybernetics. Henceforth, the nature of personal knowledge is our central preoccupation. This transition involves a shift of attention from Piaget's epistemic subject to the individual subject and his experience. Consequently, it involves the study of the different ways in which individuals 'make sense of' the world, that is of modes of thought and of individual differences in cognitive style. It involves also an analysis of how persons come to think originally about things and events – the problem of creative thinking and the creative use of language. And, finally, it is concerned with establishing a systematic account of the nature of cognitive experience, that is, with the phenomenology of thinking.

PART FOUR

Personal Knowledge

8

Creative Thinking

TACIT AND EXPLICIT KNOWLEDGE

To say that a person has shown creative thought is to judge that which he has produced as original with respect to previous relevant products and significant with regard to any future ones. This is true whether the product is a style of artistic expression, a theory in science, or an original way of solving a problem whose solution is already known. In all these cases the successful thinker breaks away from traditional modes of thought, in some instances to the extent of making necessary a revision of our most fundamental ideas. But whilst it is clear that the creative process results in our attending to a meaning which we previously ignored, it is far from obvious, when one seeks an explanation of this process, how it can be meaningfully asserted that a man passes from a state of ignorance to one of knowledge. It was Plato who first pointed out the contradiction that seems to be inherent in talking about discovery. He says (in the *Meno*) that to search for the solution of a problem is absurd, for either you know what you are looking for, and then there is no problem, or you do not know what you are looking for, and then you cannot expect to find anything. He asks: 'How will you set about looking for that thing, the nature of which is totally unknown to you? Which among the things you do not know is the one you propose to look for? And if by chance you should stumble upon it, how will you know that it is indeed that thing, since you are in ignorance of it?' (quoted by Merleau-Ponty, 1962, p. 371). The paradox implies that creative thinking is meaningless or impossible. The conclusions seem inescapable but we know they are false, for people have persisted in solving difficult problems or in creating new forms of expression in the arts.

The paradox arises from the assumption that all knowledge is capable of explicit statement and may be resolved, as Polanyi (1958,

1959, 1967) has shown, by formulating the distinction between tacit and explicit knowledge. Let us return to the statement of the paradox to see how this distinction applies. Most of us would wish to say that in solving a problem there is a sense in which we do know what we are looking for and a sense in which we do not know. Our thought is, in some way, guided to the solution of the problem and yet the solution comes as something of a surprise and an illumination. Now, tacit knowledge may be defined as 'the intimation of something hidden, which we may yet discover' (Polanyi, 1967, pp. 22-3). As an example of tacit knowledge, Polanyi quotes some experiments by Lazarus and McCleary (1949, 1951) in which subjects, presented with a large number of nonsense syllables, received an electric shock after certain of the syllables. It was found that, after a while, the subjects showed signs of anticipating the shock at the sight of these particular syllables, but, on questioning, they could not identify them: they had come to know when to expect a shock but could not tell what made them expect it. Polanyi argues that this was due to the fact that the subjects knew the electric shock by attending directly to it but knew the nonsense syllables associated with the shock only by relying upon an awareness of them for attending to the shock, that is, upon a tacit awareness of them in relation to a focal awareness of the shock itself. The distinction between tacit and explicit knowledge is no less evident with respect to practical activities. If we are using a tool, say a hammer, our knowledge of the hammer and our knowledge of the object of our hammering are fundamentally different. There is a focal awareness of the object but a subsidiary awareness of the hammer, a distinction which becomes all .too apparent if one transfers one's focal attention from the nail to the hammer.

Thus, just as the Gestalt psychologists pointed to the existence of figure and ground as the necessary organization of the perceptual field, so Polanyi distinguishes between the tacit and explicit components of the activity of knowing. The tacit is the ground against which the explicit emerges and is defined. Plato's paradox arises from the assumption that all knowledge is explicit but, granted that our explicit knowledge rests always upon a tacit framework, it follows that we can have a tacit foreknowledge of yet undiscovered things.

> The pursuit of discovery is conducted from the start in these terms; all the time we are guided by sensing the presence of a hidden reality towards which our clues are pointing; and the discovery which terminates and satisfies this pursuit is still sustained by the

same vision. It claims to have made contact with reality: a reality which, being real, may yet reveal itself to future eyes in an indefinite range of unexpected manifestations.

(Polanyi, 1967, p. 24)

These ideas suggest certain specifications for the psychology of creative thinking. They suggest that the creative thinker is a person who is able both to formulate a problem as explicitly as possible and to remain sensitive to the clues provided by tacit awareness. This implies the capacity to be guided by clues discerned at this level of awareness and the capacity to raise these to the level of explicit awareness. Thus conceived, the creative process involves a number of phases in which conscious control is exercised, relaxed and exercised again, and the creative thinker possesses the skills appropriate to each of these phases. As it happens, the psychological study of creative thinking has followed two distinct courses – study of the creative process and study of individual differences in thinking abilities – and there has not been as much interchange between these two as might be reasonably expected. Nevertheless, despite this and despite the existence of numerous apparently contradictory theories and studies of individual differences, certain generalizations are suggested by the available evidence and the prospects are encouraging.

THEORIES OF CREATIVE THINKING

In the psychological literature the creative process is very commonly characterized as falling into four phases. These phases were first discussed extensively by Wallas (1926), mainly with respect to reports from eminent scientists such as Poincaré and Helmholtz concerning their own experiences, but in the following year Lowes (1927), in his study of Coleridge, outlined a similar scheme for the description of artistic creation. The first phase Wallas called preparation. During this time the person immerses himself in his subject-matter, becoming acquainted with the problems and complexities of a particular field, so that the problem, whose solution he seeks, can be formulated in as precise and knowledgeable a way as possible. The danger at this stage is that one may, to continue the metaphor, remain submerged for ever under the weight of the literature. The second phase is one of incubation. The idea is that, after the conscious mind has done its work in the first phase, the unconscious now takes over and makes those unexpected connections that constitute a genuine discovery. This leads

G

to the third phase, that of illumination, in which the solution to the problem is grasped or intuited. Inspiration cannot be consciously controlled, although a number of thinkers have adopted particular and sometimes peculiar strategies in order to assist inspiration on its way. Kneller (1965) reports that Schiller used to fill his desk with rotten apples, Dr Johnson would surround himself with a purring cat, orange peel and tea, while Kant, in writing *The Critique of Pure Reason*, adopted the ploy of concentrating upon a tower visible from his window. The final phase is that of verification, for, although the inspiration may have provided an intuition of the correct solution, this must now be tested deductively or against the available evidence; similarly, the artist must translate his vision into actuality by conscious elaboration.

This account may appear to place the different aspects of the creative process too rigidly into separate compartments, but Wallas himself contended that these four stages constantly overlap, so that at any one moment a man may be incubating one problem, preparing for a second and verifying a third. Moreover, he devoted a large part of his discussion to what he termed 'intimation' in order to indicate that the boundary between unconscious and conscious processes is not a rigid one. He argued, following William James (1890), that intimation occurs in the 'fringe' of consciousness which surrounds focal consciousness, and suggested that it is by paying attention to our intimations that we succeed in realizing our thoughts. Wallas's description of the creative process is, of course, a complex theory. The idea that there are four phases receives support from the introspections of eminent scientists and artists (see, for example, Harding, 1940, Ghiselin, 1952, and Vernon, 1970, for accounts of these). Although there is no experimental investigation of all four phases, there are two lines of experimental analysis that are directly relevant to the preparation and incubation phases.

In the first place, experiments which have derived largely from Gestalt theory and explored some of the conditions responsible for rigidity in thinking, are perhaps instructive of the difficulties which must be overcome in the incubation and inspirational phases. Thus, experiments on 'functional fixedness' (Duncker, 1945; Birch and Rabinowitz, 1951; Adamson, 1952; Saugstad and Raaheim, 1960; Ray, 1967) demonstrate the importance of previous experience for original problem-solving. The term 'functional fixedness' refers to the tendency to perceive and utilize an object in its habitual function only, with the result that novel but appropriate functions are ignored. Duncker's 'box problem', for example, requires the subject to mount three candles vertically on a screen, at a height of about five feet, using any of a large number of objects lying on a table. Among the objects are five tacks, five matches, and three paste-board boxes of varying sizes. The solution consists in mounting one candle on each box by melting wax on the box and sticking the candle to it, then tacking the boxes to the screen. Functional fixedness prevails when objects are used in their usual functions first and in their unusual functions later, but when this procedure is reversed and the unusual function occurs first, fixedness is prevented (Van de Geer, 1957; Duvall, 1965). Flavell, Cooper and Loiselle (1958) have found that fixedness varies inversely with the number of varied pre-problem experiences with an object. A similar demonstration of the effects of set or *Einstellung* on problem-solving has been made by Luchins (1942) with the well-known 'water-jars problems', which require subjects to find out how to obtain required volumes of water, given certain empty jars for measures. Luchins' procedure was to create a set in his subjects for solving such problems in a certain way and then to present problems capable of being solved by simpler techniques. Maier (1930, 1931), too, has demonstrated the influence of such directional factors in inhibiting an original solution.

Secondly, some experiments have investigated the effects of incubation. The effect of short-term incubation on a task in which subjects had to think of as many consequences as possible of an unusual event (e.g. all power-stations closing down) has been investigated by Fulgosi and Guilford (1968). They found that a 20-minute interval on this task produced significant gains, although these were apparently greater for the production of obvious consequences than for the production of remote ones, while a 10-minute interval was not effective. Dreistadt (1969) found a combination of pictorial analogies and incubation to be effective for one of his problems.

However, the concept of incubation has little explanatory power itself, for it suggests only that 'something' is happening between posing the problem and solving it, but does not specify what this might be. Introspective reports frequently refer to the fact that the relaxation of conscious direction results in a proliferation of ideas, but this leaves unexplained how these ideas may combine to provide the solution to problems defined consciously. Three major theories have been proposed to account for this process – associationism, psychoanalysis and cognitive theory.

Associationist Theory

Theories of creative thinking based upon the principle of association have been proposed by a number of authors. Campbell (1960) has argued for the efficacy of blind variation and selective retention, whilst

Maltzman (1960) has proposed that a person's 'originality' may be improved by training him to produce different associations to the same stimuli. But perhaps the most influential work has been that of Mednick (1962), who defined the creative thinking process as 'the forming of associative elements into new combinations which either meet specified requirements or are in some way useful' (p. 221). He suggests that a creative solution may be achieved in three ways: by serendipity, when a contiguous event elicits (usually accidentally) the requisite associations; by similarity of the associative elements, or by the requisite elements being evoked contiguously through the mediation of common elements. Mednick accounts for individual differences in creative thinking by

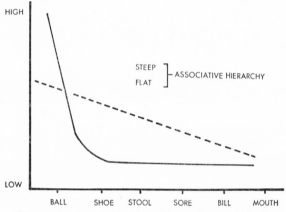

Figure 6. *Associative hierarchy to the word 'foot'.*

assuming that there are consistent individual differences in the production of conventional and remote associations to stimuli. Some subjects rapidly produce conventional associations but produce remote associations with difficulty or not at all, while others may be less dominated by convention and produce the remoter associations with greater alacrity. As Fig. 6 shows, the associative hierarchy of the former subjects is a steep one, but the latter show a flat associative hierarchy. The person with a flat slope will have more uncommon associations and hence he is likely to be more creative than the man whose associative slopes are mostly steep. According to Mednick, whether a creative solution to a problem is achieved or not depends upon the success of trial-and-error procedures in meeting the specified requirements. He has also argued (1962, 1969) that the creativeness of a product is some function of the number of requirements that the product meets.

The Remote Associations Test (RAT) of Mednick (1962, 1968) was devised on the basis of this theory. The test items consist of sets of three words drawn from mutually remote associative clusters, the task of the subject being to find a fourth word that serves as an associative link between them; thus the three stimulus words, 'surprise', 'line' and 'birthday', all associate with the response, 'party'. The relationship of the RAT to the theory from which it was derived has been confirmed by some studies but some predictions are not supported. Confirmation of the link between test and theory comes from studies showing significant correlations between RAT scores and associative productivity (Mednick, 1962; Mednick, Mednick and Jung, 1964; Desiderato and Sigal, 1970) and from studies demonstrating improvement in RAT performance following associative training (Freedman, 1965; B. J. Miller *et al.*, 1970). On the other hand, it would be predicted from Mednick's theory that high RAT scorers should show superior performance on tests involving mediational processes, but, although Higgins and Dolby (1967) found that this relationship obtained for a learning task which involved mediated associations, Jacobson *et al.* (1968) were unable to support this hypothesis when they utilized paired-associate tasks designated to foster the use of mediational processes in concept learning. And further, there is no support for the idea that high RAT scorers have flatter associative hierarchies than low scorers. Olczak and Kaplan (1969) found no support for this prediction and suggested that either the test measures extent rather than slope of hierarchy or that the slope of an individual's hierarchy is not a general trait but is dependent upon the particular stimulus context. This last suggestion has been confirmed by Piers and Kirchner (1971), whilst, earlier, Riegel, Riegel and Levine (1966) had demonstrated that under some conditions, for example, when asked to name the functions of objects, subjects scoring highly on a creative personality scale which has been found (Walker, 1962) to correlate with RAT performance are actually more restricted in their output than low scorers.

Perhaps the major difference between high and low RAT scorers has to do with attention deployment. Mendelsohn and Griswold (1964) had undergraduates memorize 25 words whilst subject simultaneously to the interference of hearing another list of 25 words being played on a tape recorder. Thereafter, they solved 30 anagrams, for which 10 of the solutions had been in the memorized list, 10 in the interference list, and 10 were new or neutral. The authors found that high RAT scorers utilized the cues both from the memorized and interference lists to a greater extent than did low scorers and attributed this superiority to the wider deployment of attention among these subjects. This study is open to the criticism that there was no direct control for intelligence, which previous studies had found to correlate with RAT performance to the order of ·41 (Mednick, 1963) and ·31 (Rainwater, 1964). But subsequent investigations by Mendelsohn and Griswold (1966) and Laughlin (1967) confirmed the earlier finding and demonstrated that it was not attributable to differences in intelligence. In a later study by Laughlin, Doherty and Dunn (1968), the RAT was found to be a more sensitive predictor than intelligence for incidental concept learning, while intelligence was a more sensitive predictor than the RAT for intentional concept formation. It seems plausible to express the essential difference between incidental and intentional learning by saying that the one involves learning at the level of subsidiary awareness and the other learning at the level of focal awareness. It appears, therefore, that the person who scores highly on the RAT is also capable of making effective use of stimuli existing at the level of subsidiary awareness.

Expressing these results in this way enables us to avoid the contradiction which inevitably results from the acceptance of the doctrine of associationism. Consider, for example, Wallach's (1970) argument. His summary of the literature concludes with the assertion that the generation of associations itself is the crux of the creative process, during which sensitivity to relevance is not important: 'What matters most is the generating of associates; once produced, the evaluation of their relevance and appropriate action in the light of this judgment seems to pose little difficulty' (pp. 1254-5). Now, it is probably true that evaluative attitudes are relaxed and that subjects are able subsequently to apply criteria of relevance with varying degrees of difficulty, but what is not clear on the associationist account alone is how a phase of association without any evaluation or sensitivity to relevance can *ever* lead to a recognized, relevant solution. For this doctrine asks us to assent to two incompatible ideas: that thinking consists of associations and that we are capable of discrimination between those associations which are relevant and those which are not. But if the first notion were true, the second could not be, for we would not be able to judge relevance. If associationism were true, there would be no means of telling whether it was true or not. To say, therefore, that the work of creative thinking is done in a 'non-evaluative' phase must not mislead us into believing that thought ceases to be directed in some way during this phase. But this direction is not at the level of explicit knowledge. Somehow, a person's appreciation of the realities of a problem can provide a direction for thought processes at a phase in which the problem is withdrawn from focal awareness.

Psychoanalytic Theory

The problem of reconciling conscious and unconscious control of thinking has occupied a prominent place in psychoanalytic conceptions of the creative process. In his study of Leonardo da Vinci, Freud (1910) had attempted to relate the inhibitions of the artist's sexual life to his childhood experiences and to his artistic activities. The validity of some of Freud's specific conclusions may be doubted (see the note accompanying Freud's paper in the Standard Edition of the Complete Works), but the generalization that a person's emotional relationships with others during childhood can influence his modes of thought in adult life is now widely accepted. However, the major limitation of this kind of analysis is that it does not explain why an individual with Leonardo's conflicts is sometimes able to express them in creative, artistic or scientific activity rather than merely as neurotic symptoms. Clearly, as criteria of relevance and originality are applied to the former but not to the latter, some framework is needed which expresses the differing relationships between unconscious and conscious processes in neurosis and in genuine creative work. In Freudian theory this involves an analysis of ego functions and of the distinction between primary and secondary processes.

In his essay on 'The Unconscious' Freud (1915) defined two types of mental process – the genetically earlier, primary process, in which combinations between ideas are determined by their fulfilling some desire, and the secondary process, in which there is adaptation to the demands of the situation. The primary process is said to be governed by the pleasure principle and the secondary process by the reality principle. The chief mechanisms of the primary process are condensation and displacement and we may see these in operation in dreams. Thus it often happens, for instance, that a number of different persons form a composite figure in a dream, this figure serving the purpose of laying special emphasis upon some characteristic that links the different persons. Such condensation can, of course, also occur with objects or places. Freud says that 'it is as though a new and fugitive concept were formed, of which the common attribute is the kernel' (1929, p. 144). Displacement occurs either when something is expressed, not directly, but by allusion to something else, or by a shift in emphasis from an important to an unimportant element. The primary process is characterized by large amounts and freedom of cathexis (charge of energy), the secondary process by small amounts and limited freedom. The ego operates under the influence of necessity and the development of the ego corresponds to the development of the capacity to delay gratification of the instinctual desires of the id, that is, to obey the reality principle. Gill (1963, 1967) has argued that, although primary and secondary processes are theoretically distinguishable, condensation and displacement should not be described as mechanisms of the primary process alone, since, of necessity, a production involving condensation and displacement will be a compromise formation, expressing the functioning of both primary and secondary processes. This follows from the fact that one can see the mechanisms of the primary process at work – in a dream, a joke or in neurotic symptoms – only in so far as they are influenced by some inhibition emanating from structures controlled by the secondary process.

In attempting to correct the deficiencies of the psychoanalytic theory of art evident in Freud's study of Leonardo, Kris (1953) drew upon Freud's own suggestion that in humour the ego makes use of pre-conscious activity (Freud, 1905) to propose that in all creative thinking the ego achieves some measure of control over the primary process. He invented the term, 'regression in the service of the ego', to refer to the capacity of gaining easy access to unconscious material without being overwhelmed by it. It is this capacity which characterizes the creative person and the creative process, for dream content and the joke are simply compromises between unconscious material and ego functions and in mental illness the person is overwhelmed by the forces of the unconscious. As Bush (1969) has pointed out, the concept of regression in the service of the ego as used by Kris appears to involve a number of different phenomena: it refers to the removal of defensive barriers between the ego and the id which stimulates the development of ideas which, initially, are not entirely unconscious or conscious but exist at a preconscious level; or it refers to a regression of the ego functions of perception and thinking to more primitive levels; or to the emergence of preconscious or unconscious material into consciousness in the phase of illumination.

There have been several critical discussions of the concept (Rapaport, 1951; Bellak, 1958; Shafer, 1958; Weissman, 1967; Bush, 1969). Rapaport (1951) posed the crucial question when he supposed that, if primitive thought content is to serve creative ends, then it must possess a measure of reality orientation. But it is difficult to see how any of the meanings of Kris's concept of adaptive regression can be interpreted to meet this criterion. How can the regression of ego functions or the emergence of unconscious ideas into consciousness lead to the solution of significant scientific and artistic problems or of important, everyday affairs? There would seem to be two significant answers to this problem – one which stresses the role of ego functions and the secondary process, the other which suggests that a revised conception of the primary process is needed.

Weissman (1967) maintains that Kris was able to avoid this problem only by equating creativity with the stage of inspiration and by ignoring the stage of verification, at which criteria of relevance are of central importance. He proposes that it is more valid to conceptualize the entire creative act, including inspiration and verification, as a positive ego activity which utilizes special ego functions, particularly a dissociative function, defined as the ego's capacity to dissociate itself from its established object relations and from its conventional responses to the demands of the id and the superego. Similarly, Bush (1969) believes that there has been an overemphasis on the role of regression in creative thinking. The tendency to dichotomize primary and secondary processes too sharply that has been criticized by Gill (1963, 1967) is perhaps largely responsible for this, but important also has been the implicit equation of the secondary process with *conventional* thinking and perception. Given these two assumptions, the source of original ideas can only be the primary process. However, just as people differ in their openness to the primitive within themselves, so they differ also in their openness to what is outside themselves. Accordingly, Bush believes that the role of the secondary processes in creative thinking requires more intensive investigation; also, the relationship between primary and secondary processes must be defined more precisely before we can grasp in full the complexity of the creative process.

An alternative conception, however, retains an emphasis on the primary process. Ehrenzweig's (1967) view of the primary process allows him to discuss the creative process as an essential part of the ego's normal functioning. The starting-point of his analysis is the distinction between the two kinds of attention: focused attention is analytic and organizes the world into figure and ground; unfocused attention is syncretistic and, through the mechanism of unconscious scanning, is able to attend to the details of a scene without imposing an organization into figure and ground. The term, syncretism, as used by Piaget (1928) and Werner (1948), refers to a type of perception or reasoning which assimilates a multitude of diverse things into a global structure (as does the dream through condensation and displacement). But while these theorists tend to view syncretism as an immature mode that is replaced by an analytic attitude, Ehrenzweig maintains that the positive function of syncretism is to unite a total

G*

structure in a single, undifferentiated view. That this is an achievement and not an immaturity is evident, for example, in the way in which a caricature can infringe the rules of analytic perception and yet convincingly represent a face; or in the capacity of the artist, who draws an ambiguous figure with alternating figure and ground, to comprehend unconsciously the alternate views in single glance; or, again, in modern art or serial music which defy the analysis of focused attention and which require to be comprehended on a global, undifferentiated level. Ehrenzweig argues that the mechanisms which permit these achievements are the mechanisms of the primary process, but this is not now regarded as an archaic and wholly irrational function of the unconscious, since this could only lead to the concept of ego regression in order to account for creative thinking. What is original in Ehrenzweig's conception is the idea that in creative work the ego controls the activity of the primary process itself, since it 'decomposes itself' (i.e. abandons focused attention and the good *gestalt*) in order to provide material for elaboration by the primary process. Thus, in place of adaptive regression, there is a reciprocal interaction between primary and secondary processes.

However, a number of investigators have interpreted their experimental findings in terms of adaptive regression rather than in terms of these alternative conceptions. Unfortunately, most studies have been carried out with the Rorschach and are open to different interpretations. Pine and Holt (1960) claimed that the Rorschach could be used to measure individual differences in both the degree to which primary processes are expressed and the degree of control over such expressed primary processes, whilst a score taking into account both these measures could be taken as an operational measure of regression in the service of the ego. Consequently, they administered the Rorschach along with tests of imaginative ability, hypothesizing that, while the tendency to express primary processes would be unrelated to imaginative ability, the ability to control primary process material would be positively related. These hypotheses were confirmed for the males but not for the females of the sample. Some empirical support also comes from a study by Silverman (1965), although Rogolsky (1968) concluded from an analysis of his subjects' protocols that creative individuals 'seemed to be adapting more than regressing'. However, the results of a study by Gray (1969) seriously challenge the interpretation that the Rorschach reveals adaptive regression. Gray found that an initially significant relationship between measures of creativity and of primary process activity was based upon a common third variable, namely, productivity: the greater the number of words a subject used and the more responses he made upon the creativity tests, the higher did his creativity score and primary process score tend to be and the more did they tend to intercorrelate. Gray is careful to point out that this should not lead us to define creativity solely in terms of productivity, but, clearly, this variable is a more parsimonious explanation of the Rorschach investigations than is the concept of adaptive regression.

Similarly, studies which have used other measures of adaptive regression have failed to consider the possibility that other interpretations are equally plausible. For example, Wild's (1965) finding that artists are able to shift more easily between regulated and unregulated thought than comparison groups might just as easily be interpreted in terms of greater general flexibility of response among these subjects, unless it can be shown that their flexibility is limited specifically to shifts between earlier and later developmental phases. Or consider the study of Gamble and Kellner (1968), who used the Stroop Colour-Word Test (Stroop, 1935a, b) to test the hypothesis that in a task situation requiring the active subordination of a developmentally advanced operation (word reading) to a developmentally primitive operation (colour naming), high creative subjects, as defined by the RAT, would perform significantly better than low creative subjects. The Stroop test consists of three cards. Card A contains 100 colour words ('red', 'blue' and 'green') which are printed in black ink and arranged in random order. The subject has to read the words aloud as quickly as possible. Card B is made up of 100 rectangular patches of the colours, red, blue and green, and the subject is required to name the colours correctly as quickly as possible. Card C consists of 100 colour words ('red', 'blue' and 'green') printed in ink the colour of which is different from the colour designated by the word. The subject has to name as quickly as possible the colour of the ink in which the word is printed. Gamble and Kellner argue that, as responding to colour is developmentally earlier than reading names, any superiority of the high RAT scorers on Card C may be attributed, when intelligence and other confounding variables are controlled, to the subject's ability to utilize the lower level of cognitive functioning through adaptive regression. The results were as predicted. But the authors' interpretation would have been more convincing if they had also shown that their high RAT subjects were *not* superior at focusing upon material related to developmentally-later processes as well. If high RAT scorers did show this general ability, the concept of adaptive regression would be redundant and could be replaced by one couched in terms of attention deployment or response inhibition.

The distinctive feature of the contribution of psychoanalysis to our understanding of creative thinking lies in its emphasis on the role of the primary process in the incubation and inspiration phases. The criticisms directed at the concept of regression in the service of the ego suggest that further clarification of the relationship between primary and secondary processes is necessary. Investigations are called for which study how problems that remain unsolved at the level of explicit awareness are transformed through primary process functioning, and how such transformation is effective in fostering an intuition of a solution and its subsequent elaboration. The study of subjects' dream-work after failure in problem-solving or the experimental reduction of problem-elements to the level of primary process functioning, for example, through subliminal or tachistoscopic presentation, might prove effective techniques for gaining the necessary empirical support for psychoanalytic contentions.

Cognitive Theory

Contemporary cognitive theories are concerned with the different ways in which people perceive and think about things and events, that is, with the question of cognitive style. From this standpoint, creative thinking results from the adoption of those cognitive styles which most effectively lead to the detection of novel information. We have seen that associationist and psychoanalytic theories both distinguish between 'regulated' and 'unregulated' thought and that both implicate attention deployment as a crucial variable. Investigations of cognitive style enable us to pursue these themes still further, since they employ measures which relate directly to attention deployment and to cognitive level. Two of the most influential theorists are Witkin and Gardner. Witkin *et al.* (1954, 1962) distinguish two modes of perception, a field-dependent mode in which perception is strongly dominated by the overall organization of the field with the result that the parts of the field are experienced as 'fused', and a field-independent mode in which there is a clear differentiation between figure and ground. Gardner *et al.* (1959) have suggested a dimension of individual differences based upon Piaget's notions of perceptual centration and decentration (e.g. Piaget, Vinh-Bang and Matalon, 1958). According to this theory, accuracy of perception depends upon the capacity to decentre attention and scan a greater area of the field. Gardner argues that there are consistent individual differences in the extent to which attention is decentred: some individuals scan broadly others narrowly.

Field dependence is measured by several tests. The most commonly used are the Embedded Figures Test, which requires the subject to locate a simple figure in a complex design that is organized to conceal the figures, and the Rod and Frame Test. The apparatus for the latter consists of a luminous rod and frame, which are the only objects visible to the subject in a completely darkened room. The subject's task is to adjust the rod to an upright position while the frame is tilted; successful performance is interpreted as revealing analytic ability – the ability to perceive a part of the field as discrete from the remainder – whilst failure is said to indicate global perception. Scanning has also been assessed by a variety of measures, including recording movements of the eyes, number of separate centrations, etc., and these have been found to be intercorrelated (Gardner and Long, 1962a; Luborsky *et al.*, 1965). There is some evidence to suggest that Witkin's field-articulation dimension is distinct from Gardner's scanning control: Gardner (1961), in a factor analysis of a number of tests, found two factors corresponding to field articulation and scanning, while Gardner and Long (1962b) found that number of centrations in a size-matching procedure showed non-significant correlations with mean solution time on the Embedded Figures Test. Accordingly, it appears useful to distinguish between narrow attention in the sense of limited scanning and narrow attention in the sense of reduced responsiveness to compelling irrelevant stimuli (Wachtel, 1967).

This distinction is important when the results of studies relating cognitive style to creativity are considered. For (1) we would not expect that the focusing of attention involved in analytic perception is itself related to creative thinking, although (2) the expectation that flexibility, defined as the ability to switch attention from analytic to global modes, would be related appears plausible. But (3) from the previous discussion of attention deployment we could anticipate that the kind of broad attention discussed by Gardner would be related to creative thinking ability. Evidence on these hypotheses is still accumulating but certain trends are apparent:

(1) There appears to be no straightforward relationship between field articulation and creativity, for studies using a variety of indices of creative thinking indicate that high scoring subjects on the creativity measures may be either field-dependent or independent (Bieri, Bradburn and Galinsky, 1958; McWhinnie, 1967, 1969; Spotts and Mackler, 1967; Klein, 1968; Bloomberg, 1967, 1971).

(2) Haronian and Sugerman (1967) maintain that, while field dependence is characterized by a rigidity that prevents any change in one's attitude towards a task, field independence permits, although it does

not guarantee, a mobility of attitude in response to different instructions; flexibility is thus regarded as a dimension along which a subject may score if he performs above a certain threshold on the field-articulation dimension. Bloomberg (1971) attempted to assess the implications of this reasoning for creative thinking. He assessed field articulation by the Rod and Frame Test, and flexibility by the discrepancy between the number of Necker cube reversals when subjects were instructed to focus passively and the number of reversals they produced when asked to produce them as rapidly as possible. However, Bloomberg found this measure of flexibility to relate to intelligence but not to creativity. He echoes those working within the psychoanalytic framework when he concludes that a measure of flexibility is needed which assesses the capacity to integrate the more primitive, global level of functioning with the higher, more differentiated level.

(3) Direct support for the hypothesis linking width of attention deployment to creative thinking comes from a study by Ward (1969), in which three creativity tests were administered; each test required subjects (children) to name as many ideas as they could for a simple problem. Two of the tests were given in a 'barren' experimental setting and the results from these served as the means of dividing the sample into 'creative' and 'uncreative' subgroups. The third test was given to some subjects under the same condition but to others in a 'cue-rich' testing environment. Ward found that his creative subjects gave more responses in a rich than a poor environment, while uncreative subjects were not affected by the environmental variations. He argued that scanning the environment for task-relevant information is an important strategy of the creative thinker. This interpretation is also supported by Strauss (1969) in a study of intentional and incidental learning: scanning control was found to be linearly associated with ease of solution of peripherally-cued anagrams but not related to solution of focally-cued ones. Although, no doubt, further studies will be forthcoming, it is perhaps already significant that, whilst direct measures of attention deployment have been found to relate to incidental cue utilization, tasks which measure the focused attention that accompanies analytic thinking do not show this relationship consistently. Thus Strauss (1969) found field articulation to be associated with incidental cue utilization for males but not for females, while Marx (1970) has found a measure of conceptual complexity to relate to utilization of incidental cues only when intelligence is not partialled out.

In Summary

Although the three theories contain conflicting assumptions – the one stressing unregulated associations, another, the activity of the unconscious, and the third, cognitive structure and styles – their application to the study of creative thinking has encouraged a convergence of opinion in, perhaps, three major respects. In the first place, there is strong support for the ideas that width of attention deployment relates to the ability to utilize incidental cues in problem-solving and that this capacity is a feature of the cognitive style of the creative thinker. Secondly, it seems desirable to distinguish two types of attention which relate to two different cognitive modes: on the one hand, there is a mode of thinking, described variously as 'unregulated', 'global' and 'syncretistic', which is accompanied by diffuse awareness; on the other hand, regulated, analytic thought occurs within focal awareness. A recurrent theme in the literature is that the creative thinker is more able to gain access to the former mode. But, thirdly, he must be able, not only to gain access to it, but to integrate it with explicit, analytic thinking. Measures of adaptive regression and flexibility may reflect this capacity to some extent, although it is doubtful whether they exhaustively define the integrative abilities necessary for creative thinking.

PSYCHOMETRIC APPROACHES TO CREATIVITY

The development of measures of creativity has, however, derived more from the psychometric tradition of ability testing than from theories whose hypotheses have been experimentally tested. Of course, these techniques for investigating the intercorrelations of different measures may be construed as means of testing the underlying assumptions of the measures, so that eventually there may exist tests of individual differences which relate to various aspects of the creative process in a systematic manner. But there are no such tests in existence at the moment and, accordingly, confusion may be avoided if one remembers that any existing creativity test is not really a test of creativity in the full sense of this term. This is simply to repeat what has been said about the concept of intelligence, namely, that the proper, evaluative meaning of the term always refers to an ideal performance (Hebb's (1949) Intelligence B) which is incompletely embodied in tests (Vernon's (1969) Intelligence C). It is important to bear the distinction between these meanings in mind when considering the psychometric issues related to creativity testing.

The first of these issues has to do with the relationship between intelligence and creativity: is creativity independent of intelligence, or do intelligence and creativity measures correlate so highly that creativity is merely another name for intelligence, or are the two related and yet distinguishable? The second issue poses the question of whether creativity is a unitary dimension or whether creativity tests form a number of dimensions, whilst the third asks whether creativity tests measure an ability, like intelligence, or a personality characteristic, like extraversion. Before considering the evidence on each of these questions we must outline the major tests of creativity.

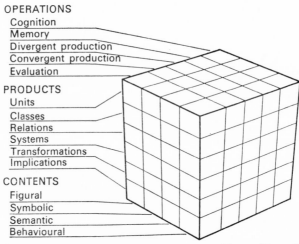

Figure 7. *Guilford's model of the structure of intelligence* (from Guilford, 1966).

Undoubtedly the greatest impetus for the development of creativity measures came from the factor analytic studies of Guilford and his associates (Guilford *et al.*, 1951; Guilford, Wilson and Christensen, 1952) which ultimately led to the postulate of a three-dimensional model of the structure of the intellect (Guilford, 1966, 1967). The model is three-dimensional because it permits the assessment of subjects' performance on tests which are classified by (1) the supposed *operations* or psychological processes involved, (2) the *contents* of the items, and (3) the *products* of the subjects' operations upon the contents. As there are four types of content, six products and five operations, the structure of intellect may be represented as a cube with 120 units (Fig. 7) corresponding to specific abilities. The main criticism that has been directed at Guilford's model is that it fails to take into account the existence of a general factor running through diverse tests and of group factors which are intermediate in range between the general factor and the host of specific factors. Hierarchical models of the structure of the intellect (Burt, 1940; Vernon, 1950) do incorporate such features. The absence of a general factor has caused Eysenck (1967) to liken Guilford's model to 'Hamlet without the Dane', whilst Varela (1969) has proposed that squashing Guilford's cube into a doughnut might do more justice to the generality of intellectual performance across tests.

Of more immediate interest, however, are Guilford's descriptions of the operations involved in convergent and divergent production. The distinction between these two rests upon the fact that some tests, notably the traditional tests of intelligence, demand that the subject's thought converges upon the one correct answer, while other tests measure the ability to think of many different answers to the same question. Thus, the Unusual Uses Test requires the subject to think of as many uses as possible for a number of common objects (a brick, a button, etc.), and in the Consequences Test subjects are asked to give as many consequences as they can imagine for an unusual event, such as people no longer needing or wanting sleep. Guilford's tests of divergent thinking can be scored for *fluency*, the sheer number of responses produced, for *flexibility*, the ability to vary ideas over a wide range, and for *originality*, defined as the production of responses that are statistically unique or unusual for the sample subjects. Guilford's ideas also provided the basis for the Minnesota Tests of Creative Thinking (Torrance, 1962, 1968), which have been specially designed for use with children. Among the new tests devised by Torrance are the Ask and Guess Test, which calls for questions about the causes and consequences of events depicted in pictures, and a Product Improvement Test which calls for novel ideas for improving objects, such as children's toys.

Although most of the significant research in this area (e.g. Getzels and Jackson, 1962; Wallach and Kogan, 1965; Hudson, 1966, 1968) has been with measures of divergent thinking, non-divergent tests of creativity have also been utilized. Thus, Gough (1961), using the Barron-Welsh Art Scale (Barron and Welsh, 1952), found creative scientists to prefer the complex asymmetrical figures preferred also by artists, and Eisenman (1969) has found that preference for complex figures is related to both the Barron-Welsh Scale and to fluency and originality scores on the Unusual Uses Test. Although it has been questioned whether the Barron-Welsh Scale measures preference for complexity or for asymmetry (Moyles, Tuddenham and Block, 1965), the existence of this and other tests of creative thinking besides the divergent tests obviously raises questions concerning the unitary nature of the test dimension.

Intelligence and Creativity

It is known that different measures of convergent thinking intercorrelate and yield a general factor (g) of ability. In order to have demonstrated that our measures of creativity form a dimension distinct from intelligence, they must have met two criteria: they must correlate highly among themselves and these correlations should be appreciably higher than the correlations between creativity and intelligence measures (Wallach and Kogan, 1965). A different technique for investigating this issue is to carry out a factor analysis of the test intercorrelations in order to interpret the underlying dimensions of test performance: if it can be shown that the creativity measures define a dimension or factor, upon which intelligence measures load negligibly, and which accounts for a significant degree of the variance in performance, then we can conclude that a dimension of ability has been isolated that is independent of intelligence.

The results of a large number of studies do not meet these criteria. Thus, Getzels and Jackson (1962), using a variety of divergent thinking tests, claimed to have isolated a creativity dimension, but critics (Thorndike, 1963; R. W. Marsh, 1964; Wallach and Kogan, 1965) were quick to point out that the intercorrelations among their creativity measures were no higher than the intercorrelations among creativity and intelligence tests. Edwards and Tyler (1965) and Hasan and Butcher (1966) were unable to confirm the results of Getzels and Jackson, the latter finding that their creativity measures, including four tests used in the American study, correlated with intelligence to the extent that the two concepts appeared to be equivalent. Likewise, Wallach (1970), reviewing studies using the Guilford and Torrance batteries, concludes that in neither case has it been demonstrated that what these investigators call 'creativity' is not more economically described as 'intelligence', although it should be noted that this view is contradicted by Madaus (1967) and Dacey, Madaus and Allen (1969), who found low correlations between IQ measures and the Minnesota Tests.

However, there are two reasons why the notion of a distinct creativity dimension should not be abandoned. In the first place, a number of studies support the hypothesis that the two criteria are met by creativity tests the more they are administered in a playful, non-evaluative context. Wallach and Kogan (1965) were able to induce their subjects,

10- to 11-year-olds, to regard the divergent thinking tasks as games, rather than tests: in this atmosphere, the average correlation between the intelligence measures was ·51, between the creativity measures, ·41, and between the intelligence and creativity measures, ·09. This finding has been confirmed by Ward (1968) with 7- and 8-year-olds and by Wallach and Wing (1969) with undergraduates. Boersma and O'Brien (1968) compared the pattern of test intercorrelations found for subjects in non-evaluative and evaluative contexts and noted a substantial reduction in the correlation between IQ and creativity variables in the former. Two variables might be effective in producing this typical finding: the reduction of anxiety in non-evaluative contexts or the extension of time allowed for the tasks. At present it is impossible to say which of these is the more important. On the one hand, Kogan and Morgan (1969) report the predicted differences in correlational patterns between the two conditions only for males and only when test anxiety was employed as a moderator variable. On the other hand, Van Mondfrans *et al.* (1971) compared the standard testing conditions with a Game-like, an Incubation and a Take-home condition and were able to isolate the relaxation of time limits as the critical factor in producing high inter-test correlations for the creativity measures and low correlations between these and IQ variables. This issue deserves further study.

The concept of an independent dimension of divergent thinking ability is also supported by factor analytic studies of either the original Wallach and Kogan data (Ward, 1967; Fee, 1968) or of test batteries given under non-evaluative conditions (Cropley, 1968; Cropley and Maslany, 1969; Kogan, 1971; Hargreaves and Bolton, 1972).

The second variable influencing the relationship between creativity and intelligence is the range of intelligence of the sample under investigation. In particular, there is convincing evidence that the correlation between these dimensions decreases with increasing intelligence. MacKinnon (1962), in his studies of the personality characteristics of creative architects, concluded that, beyond a certain threshold of IQ, being more intelligent or less intelligent is not crucially determinative of the level of an architect's creativeness, as judged by his peers. Yamamoto (1964, 1965a) found a consistent decrease in the size of the correlation between creativity and intelligence with increase in IQ level, thereby supporting the threshold hypothesis, as do other studies which use measures of divergent thinking (e.g. Richards, 1970; Hargreaves and Bolton, 1972). On the other hand, a study using the RAT (Ginsburg and Whittemore, 1968) found no such relationship.

Is Creativity Unitary or Multidimensional?

This question has already received a part-answer. The fact that tests of divergent thinking have been found, especially under non-evaluative conditions and with subjects of high IQ, to correlate highly among themselves and to form a factor of ability independent of intelligence, indicates that there is a unitary dimension of test performance. But, of course, just as the existence of a general dimension of convergent thinking does not preclude distinctions between, say, verbal and performance intelligence, so the existence of a dimension of divergent thinking may embrace similar factors, whose generality is intermediate in the same fashion. Thus, Fee (1968) has found factors of verbal and of visual creativity, while Dacey, Madaus and Allen (1969) isolate verbal and non-verbal divergent thinking factors. There is, however, little support for the existence of separate factors corresponding to fluency, flexibility and originality, for most workers find high correlations between these variables (Torrance, 1962; Mackler and Spotts, 1965; Dacey, Madaus and Allen, 1969; Wallach and Wing, 1969).

The relationship between divergent and non-divergent tests of creativity is still obscure. Using an adaptation of the Barron-Welsh Art Scale, Hargreaves and Bolton (1972) found no relationship between this measure and divergent thinking among children, although earlier Barron (1953), Eisenman (1969) and Eisenman and Schussel (1970), using adult subjects, had. Similarly, Cropley (1967) has contended that the RAT relates more to intelligence than to divergent thinking – a view which receives support from the study of Phillips and Torrance (1971), who found no relationship between RAT performance and divergent thinking ability – while, on the other hand, Wallach's (1970) and the present review of associative theories of creative thinking are in accord with the hypothesis that the RAT taps both convergent and divergent skills. In view of the fact that test atmosphere and range of intelligence have proved to be important influences on divergent thinking, studies of the RAT and divergent thinking which systematically manipulate these variables might well help to clarify these contradictory findings.

The following tentative conclusions may serve to summarize these two sections. (1) The correlation between intelligence and creativity, as defined by performance on tests of divergent thinking, decreases with increase in intelligence and decreasing test atmosphere. (2) Different tests of divergent thinking and different measures (i.e. fluency, flexibility and originality) within the same test correlate highly among themselves to form a unitary dimension, although verbal and non-verbal components may be distinguished. (3) The relationship between divergent and non-divergent tests awaits further clarification from studies which control for test atmosphere and range of intelligence.

Personality and Creativity

That there are significant differences in personality between creative and non-creative persons has been shown both by studies which have used divergent thinking scores as criterion measures and by those which have employed ratings by qualified judges. Getzels and Jackson's (1962) study, whatever its statistical limitations, did succeed in demonstrating the existence of a personality structure associated with divergent thinking. They selected from their sample of adolescent boys two subgroups: subjects in a 'High Intelligence' group had IQ scores falling within the top 20 per cent of the sample and divergent thinking scores below the top 20 per cent, while 'High Creativity' subjects were the top 20 per cent in divergent thinking who had IQ scores below the top 20 per cent. The latter were found to exhibit a much more playful and less conforming approach to a variety of tasks. For example, subjects were shown a Thematic Apperception Test card which most interpreted as a man seated in an aircraft. The stories of the two groups of subjects about this picture were quite distinctive. Thus, a high IQ subject responded, fairly conventionally:

> Mr Smith is on his way home from a successful business trip. He is very happy and he is thinking about his wonderful family and how glad he will be to see them again. He can picture it, about an hour from now, his plane landing at the airport and Mrs Smith and their three children all there welcoming him home again.

On the other hand, a 'High Creativity' subject allowed his imagination greater scope:

> This man is flying back from Reno where he has just won a divorce from his wife. He couldn't stand to live with her anymore, he told the judge, because she wore so much cold cream on her face at night that her head would skid across the pillow and hit him in the head. He is now contemplating a new skid-proof face cream.
>
> (Getzels and Jackson, 1962, p. 39)

Other authors (e.g. Hudson, 1966, 1968; Cropley, 1967) confirm that divergent thinkers have a more adventurous and relaxed personality than convergers.

Among studies which have correlated experts' ratings of creativity in various professional activities to personality are those of Roe (1951a, b, 1953), MacKinnon (1962) and Cattell and Butcher (1968). Roe, using projective tests such as the Rorschach and the Thematic Apperception Test, found that the most distinctive characteristic of her eminent scientists was independence and self-sufficiency. This conclusion has been verified by studies relying upon personality questionnaires: MacKinnon stressed the creative scientist's independence of thought and action, his relative freedom from conventional restraints and his strong motivation to achieve in situations calling for independent judgement; Cattell and Butcher confirmed that those who attain scientific eminence are significantly above average in ego strength, intelligence and dominance, but lower on extraversion, and refer to the evidence of other studies which indicate similar personality profiles for talented scientists and artists, with the exception that the latter, not surprisingly, score more highly on measures of emotional sensitivity.

To the author's knowledge, there are as yet no studies of twins and siblings which might enable us to assess the role of hereditary factors in determining this disposition towards originality, but there is some evidence on the importance of environmental factors. Cropley (1967) reviews studies which show that divergent thinking is correlated with egalitarian child-rearing practices, while a number of studies (e.g. Lichtenwalner and Maxwell, 1969; Eisenman and Cherry, 1970; Eisenman and Schussel, 1970) find first-born and only children to be more creative than later-born children. Presumably, early experiences may influence personality development through reinforcement or the child imitating his parents and they may also influence the person's self-perception. Hudson (1966, 1968), exploring the personalities of convergers and divergers, suggests that the many factors which affect the development of personality and cognition exert an influence on our sense of identity, that is, upon our perception of ourselves in relation to others. Specifically, he suggests that the differences between divergers and convergers represent the poles of a single system of values, at the one end of which are convergent thinking, respect for authority, self-control and the masculine virtues of the scientist, at the other, freedom of expression and behaviour, divergent thinking, and the feminine sensitivity of the artist. Mackay and Cameron (1968) have found that, when first-year undergraduates elect to specialize, arts students tend to be divergers and science students to be convergers, but further studies are needed to substantiate Hudson's major thesis that the need for personal identity is an important motive in the organization of intellect and of values.

One of the most interesting implications of work on creativity is its bearing upon the concept of cognitive ability. As Warr (1970) has commented, the distinction between a measure of ability, defined as an index of how well a person *can* think, and a measure of cognitive style, defined as an indication of how he habitually *does* think, has now become a fluctuating and dubious one. To think creatively must mean to exercise an ability and yet, in view of the research reviewed in this chapter, it seems probable that the exercise of this ability is enhanced or inhibited by one's approach to life and style of behaviour. Ultimately, then, it may be we shall have to revise the concept of an ability which sees it as a determinate quality possessed by the subject in the same way that he possesses a pancreas or a hooked nose. This idea will be taken up again in the final chapter when we examine Merleau-Ponty's (1962) view that the central concepts of psychology refer to phenomena which are ambiguously intermediate between the determinate and the chosen.

PROSPECTS

In discussing the computer simulation of thought processes, a distinction was made between impersonal and personal accounts of thinking. The study of creative thinking presents the first clues towards a systematic characterization of personal knowledge, for it suggests ways in which conscious experience must be described and analysed. In particular, the distinction between the two kinds of awareness emerges as a fundamental one. With respect to empirical research, there are some encouraging convergences between the experimental and the psychometric traditions; for example, the concept of incubation appears to relate to the finding of the facilitating effects of non-evaluative contexts for divergent thinking; or again, the notion that flexibility is independent of field articulation once a threshold of field independence is reached resembles the threshold hypothesis linking convergent and divergent thinking. But much remains to be done to connect the two traditions. We can await with interest the results of studies which explore the implications of diffuse attention deployment for performance on a wide range of creativity tests; we can hope that these measures will be validated, not only against such criteria as teachers' ratings or number of publications (Yamamoto, 1965b), but also against behaviour in problem situations of the sort investigated in experiments on functional fixedness; and we can anticipate that creative thinking will be studied more and more as a part of the total personality.

9

Language and thought

The problem of the relationship between language and thought is an ancient one and it is still contested. At one extreme some authors, for example Müller (1887), have maintained that language and thought are identical and that thinking cannot occur without language. At the other extreme, the two are regarded as entirely independent: language makes no significant contribution to thinking; thus Berkeley, quoted by Cohen (1954), believed that words are an impediment to thinking. A third view admits a reciprocal relationship between the two. This notion was supported by Sir William Hamilton (quoted by Black, 1962) when he compared the relationship between language and thought to that between an arch of masonry and a tunnel: '. . . every movement forward in language must be determined by an antecedent movement forward in thought, still, unless thought be accompanied at each point of its evolution by a corresponding evolution of language, its further development is arrested'. This idea that language and thinking are mutually dependent was taken up by Révész (1954) in a symposium on the subject. He argued that thinking and speech cannot be identical because their ontogenesis is different and because words are often inadequate expressions of thoughts and emotions, but nor can they be distinct and independent processes because there are many congruities between them and because disturbances of speech and thought often go together. Therefore, Révész says, they must be two distinct processes which are dependent upon one another.

Miller and Lenneberg (1958), commenting upon these deliberations, raise the possibility that discussing the relationship between language and thought might be as unproductive as discussing the relationship between, say, walking and swimming. We can readily recognize these as distinct activities which have a common basis – the movement of legs –

but these facts appear to have little theoretical relevance. However, there are perhaps two good reasons for not taking this possibility too seriously. In the first place, there is a genuine problem, open to empirical investigation, involved in describing the conditions under which language and thinking relate. For example, we have seen in relation to the work inspired by Piaget's theory that, although thinking may be regarded as a system of operations, this does not imply a denial of the usefulness of language, especially at the level of formal operations when the child becomes capable of manipulating symbols. Or again, in creative thinking the incubational and inspirational phases appear from many accounts not to involve verbal mediation, but no one could deny the role of language in the elaboration and verification of these 'non-verbal' intuitions. Consequently, it is reasonable to ask about the conditions under which language assists thinking. Secondly, the assertion of the reciprocal dependency of language and thought points to a phenomenon which has intrigued a number of authors. Wittgenstein (1953) expresses this meaning when he says that 'it is in language that an expectation and its fulfilment make contact' (p. 131e). We are capable, he states, of understanding a word 'in a flash', although its precise meaning is not yet fully definable, but will only emerge through the whole subsequent use of the word. Paradoxically, then, the meaning of a word lies in its future use, yet the meaning must already be present as we grasp it in a flash as the fulfilment of an intended meaning. This is, as Ehrenzweig (1967) has noted, exactly the same paradox which confronts any explanation of creative thinking in general; its resolution depends, as we saw in the previous chapter, on the distinction between two kinds of awareness and the thesis that it is in undifferentiated, unfocused awareness that such ambiguity of meaning arises. Merleau-Ponty (1962) saw clearly the implication of these views for the problem of the relationship between language and thought when he recognized that we must grant to language its capacity to accomplish thinking rather than regarding it as being simply the expression of a meaning already grasped by pure thought. The mysterious property of language is that it accomplishes the transition from the tacit to the explicit.

In this chapter we shall examine some of the empirical evidence for the relationship between language and thinking. This involves: (*a*) an examination of linguistic competence, as defined by Chomsky (1965) and his critics, and of its relation to general cognitive competence; (*b*) a review of cross-cultural and experimental evidence on the influence of language on the development of thinking; and (*c*) a discussion of some of the interpretations placed upon Goldstein's (1948) findings concerning language disturbances, with especial reference to Merleau-Ponty's contention that 'language accomplishes thinking'.

LINGUISTIC AND COGNITIVE COMPETENCE

The distinction between competence and performance was stated in the following manner by Chomsky (1965):

> Linguistic theory is concerned primarily with an ideal speaker-listener, in a completely homogeneous speech-community, who knows its language perfectly and is unaffected by such grammatically irrelevant conditions as memory limitations, distractions, shifts in attention and interest, and errors (random or characteristic) in applying his knowledge of the language in actual performance. . . . To study actual linguistic performance, we must consider the inter-action of a variety of factors, of which the underlying competence of the speaker-hearer is only one. In this respect, study of language is no different from empirical investigation of other complex phenomena. We thus make a fundamental distinction between *competence* (the speaker-hearer's knowledge of his language) and *performance* (the actual use of language in concrete situations). . . . The problem for the linguist, as well as for the child learning the language, is to determine from the data of performance the underlying system of rules that has been mastered by the speaker-hearer and that he puts to use in actual performance. (pp. 3-4)

The subject's competence, his knowledge of a language, involves the capacity to relate deep and surface structures appropriately and the ability to assign these structures to an infinite range of sentences. The deep structure of a sentence is associated with meaning and the surface structure with sound. For example, the surface structure of the sentence, 'A wise man is honest', might consist of the subject, 'a wise man', and the predicate, 'is honest'. But the deep structure of the sentence is different, for it expresses those underlying propositions which, though not explicitly asserted, nevertheless express the meaning of the sentence. In this particular instance, the deep structure extracts from the complex idea that constitutes the subject of the surface structure an underlying proposition with the subject, 'man', and the predicate, 'be wise'. The deep structure of the sentence can be shown in the form of a tree-diagram, (1) in Fig. 8, as can the surface structure (2) where S = sentence, NP = noun phrase, and VP = verb phrase. Thus a person who knows a specific language has control of a grammar that generates an infinite number of deep structures and relates them to surface structures. According to Chomsky (1968), some of the characteristics of the deep structure are universal, presumably because they derive from innate abilities.

To talk of a subject's 'knowledge of the language' as underlying his actual performance, especially when this notion is combined with the idea of innate linguistic abilities, might be interpreted to imply that the competence of the actual speaker-hearer is identical to the competence of the ideal speaker-hearer, except that in the case of the former the

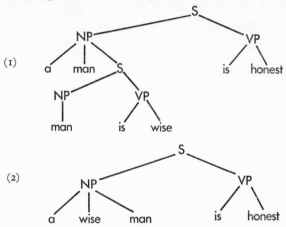

Figure 8. *Deep and surface structure for the sentence 'A wise man is honest'* (© 1968 by Harcourt Brace Jovanovich, Inc., and reproduced with their permission from Chomsky, 1968).

expression of this absolute competence in performance becomes distorted through limitations of memory, attention, etc. But this interpretation seems quite unwarranted. Cowan (1970) argues that when a linguist asserts that he aims to describe the competence of the ideal speaker-hearer, he is not saying something about a 'mental reality' underlying performance but making an assertion about the status of linguistic theories which, like other scientific theories, may be regarded as having some independence from the data to which they refer: the theory is elaborated and tested against the data. Cowan suggests, in particular, that a theory of linguistics developed on the basis of intuitions about what is grammatical and what is not will almost inevitably *not* correspond exactly to the language as defined in the subject's performance, since such intuitions are only one source of information about the speaker-hearer's competence. In fact, he argues, there may be conflicts or incompatibilities between the rules provided by judgements of grammaticality and the rules observable in actual behaviour, with the result that, for example, a construction judged to be grammatical might never actually be uttered. Along the same lines, Bever (1970) points out that, even if our linguistic intuitions are consistent, there is no reason to believe that they are direct behavioural reflections of linguistic knowledge, for the behaviour of having linguistic intuitions may introduce its own properties. Bever, and also Watt (1970), consider evidence which suggests that ongoing speech behaviour does not utilize the kinds of transformations yielded by our intuitions about grammatical acceptability. Moreover, he considers that these intuitions may be subject to contextual restraints. For example, take the three sentences:

(*a*) Who must telephone her?
(*b*) Who need telephone her?
(*c*) Who want telephone her?

Sentence (*b*) preceded by (*a*) may be judged ungrammatical but, contrasted with (*c*), it will probably be judged as grammatical. Bever concludes:

> Since there are many sources for intuitional judgments other than grammaticality, and since grammaticality judgments themselves can be influenced by context, subtle intuitions are not to be trusted until we understand the nature of their interaction with factors that are irrelevant to grammaticality. (p. 348)

These reservations about the competence-performance distinction also hold for semantics. Katz (1966) has proposed that, just as we can form empirical generalizations about the syntactic structure of linguistic constructions, so the existence of 'semantic markers' enables us to construct empirical generalizations about the meaning of linguistic constructions, that is, about semantics. For example, the words 'man', 'bachelor', 'bull' and 'priest' have the semantic marker, 'male' in common: this is, says Katz, an empirical generalization about the semantic usage of a natural language. Someone who knows a language can provide a multitude of such judgements concerning the various expressions of the language. Katz constructed a quite complex system for accounting for these judgements – a semantic theory which, through comparison with the semantic judgements of the speakers of the language, permits us to verify which constructions are meaningful and which anomalous. However, as Lackowski (1968) points out, this enterprise is based on the assumptions that the markers and the selection rules for each word are either there or not and that the only remaining problem is that of devising analytic techniques. But this scheme is called into question if there is some ultimate and irresolvable uncertainty on the part of the speaker as to whether or not a particular marker or selection restriction is to be associated with a word. Lackowski maintains that uncertainty is inevitable because the knowledge one has of a language cannot be clearly distinguished from other knowledge. Thus, for instance, an informed speaker might agree with Katz that the phrase, 'silent paint', is anomalous, but, were he to be shown a new kind of paint which made a crackling sound when touched, he might well alter his decision and, by generalization, also be more cautious in semantic judgements of related expressions, e.g. 'silent plaster'.

The implications of these critical discussions are that linguistic competence is necessarily connected with other forms of cognitive competence and that these associated abilities are to be studied as they interact during the subject's performance. These conclusions concerning the relationship between linguistics and psychology parallel those concerning logic and psychology, for in both cases the formal model is to be understood, not as a description of the subject's real ability, once distortions due to performance variables have been accounted for, but as a theory about certain of the abilities (logical or linguistic) which the subject may apply to the problems that confront him. As performance on any one problem is likely to involve a number of abilities other than the purely logical or linguistic – memory, perceptual-motor speed, etc. – the purpose of experiments must be to analyse their interaction under a broad range of conditions. It is necessary to study the influence of cognition upon language as well as the influence of language on cognition. The first of these problems has scarcely been recognized (McNeill, 1970), but there are signs of increased attention to the possibility of studying the reciprocal interaction of thinking and language evident, for example, in the studies of Donaldson and Wales (1970), Sinclair-de-Zwart (1967) and Cromer (1968). Cromer's (1968) study of the development of temporal reference during the acquisition of language strongly suggests the desirability of studying the interaction of cognitive ability and linguistic ability. Cromer found that, before the child had achieved certain abilities, he used temporal referents in a limited way. Thus, the words 'before' and 'after' are used to relate two objects in space before they are used to relate two events in time. Moreover, although the child is exposed to linguistic forms related to time, these are not assimilated. Once certain cognitive abilities have been acquired, however, the child is able to use correctly those forms which previously he used only in a limited way and, at the same time, those words to which he has been exposed now become part of his speech. One of the cognitive abilities which Cromer suggests is important and which may be a precursor of what Piaget calls decentration is the ability to 'de-actionize' time (Bruner, Olver and Greenfield, 1966), a process in which time comes to be separated from action, so that time can be treated according to its distinctive features, and action can be analysed in terms of cause and effect.

There has, on the other hand, been a great deal of interest in the influence of language upon cognition, and it is to this question that we now turn.

THE INFLUENCE OF LANGUAGE ON THINKING

The Whorfian Hypothesis

The idea that the language system we use influences the way in which we experience the world has been voiced on a number of occasions. Sapir (1927) argued that we see and hear and experience things as we do largely because the language habits of our community predispose certain choices of interpretation. The idea was elaborated by Whorf, one of Sapir's students, and it is now known commonly as the Whorfian hypothesis.

Whorf (1956) presented some evidence for the hypothesis. In one study he compared the language of the Hopi Indians with English and other European languages. The latter he abbreviated to SAE or Standard Average European on the assumption that there is very little difference between the European languages with respect to the traits compared. Whorf set out to answer two questions. Are our concepts of time, space and matter given in substantially the same form to all men or are they in part conditioned by the structure of particular languages? And are there any traceable affinities between cultural and behavioural norms on the one hand and large-scale linguistic patterns on the other? To answer these questions he examined linguistic usage in Hopi and SAE with respect to a number of concepts. For example, he noted that in SAE we apply plurals both to real and imaginary things. Thus we say 'ten men' and also 'ten days'; ten men can be objectively perceived and is in this sense a real plural, but ten days cannot be objectively experienced, for we experience only one day and the other nine are conjured up from memory or imagination. In this way we come to regard ten days as a group, just as we regard ten men as a group, and we perform this same operation when we speak of 'ten steps forward' or 'ten strokes of a bell'. Now, according to Whorf, our basic awareness of time does contain something immediate and subjective, namely the sense of 'becoming later', but in SAE communities concepts of time lose contact with this subjective experience and are, instead, objectified as counted qualities, especially as lengths made up of units. A 'length' of time is thus envisaged as a row of similar units. In Hopi, on the other hand, there are no imaginary plurals and such an expression as 'ten days' is not used. The equivalent statement is an operational one which preserves the subjective experience of time as 'becoming later'. 'They stayed ten days' becomes 'They stayed until the eleventh day' or 'They left after the tenth day'. 'Ten days is greater than nine days' becomes 'The tenth day is later than the ninth'. Whorf interprets these differences by arguing that instead of our linguistically promoted objectification of that datum of consciousness we call time, the Hopi language has not laid down any pattern that cloaks the subjective 'becoming later' that is the essence of time.

Among other differences noted by Whorf the use of nouns of physical quantity is perhaps particularly illuminating. SAE has two kinds of nouns denoting physical things – individual nouns and mass nouns. Individual nouns denote bodies with definite outlines: a tree, a stick, a man, etc. Mass nouns denote homogeneous continua without implied boundaries, e.g. water, milk, meat, etc. Whorf observed that the distinction between the two types of nouns is more widespread in language than in the observable appearance of things, for rather few natural occurrences present themselves as unbounded extents: air, and often water, snow and grass do, but we do not encounter butter, meat, glass or most materials in this manifestation, but in bodies with definite outlines. This fact is so inconvenient that in many cases we need some way of individualizing the mass noun by further linguistic devices. So we talk of 'a stick of wood' or a 'pane of glass' and even introduce names of containers, e.g. 'glass of water' or 'bottle of beer', though it is with the contents that we are really concerned. According to Whorf, these common container formulas influence our thinking. We come to assume that the containers or the 'lumps, blocks, pieces . . . of' contain something, a stuff, substance or matter that answers to the water, coffee, etc., in the container formulas. Hopi language, on the other hand, does not make this distinction. In specific statements 'water' means one certain mass of water, not what we call the substance, water. Since nouns are individual already, they do not have to be individualized by names of containers. The noun itself implies a suitable container, so that one says, not 'a glass of water', but 'a water', not 'a piece of meat', but 'a meat'.

On the basis of differences such as these, Whorf argued that the two language systems of SAE and Hopi condition their users to experience reality in different ways. Whilst SAE people see reality in terms of things and substances, the Hopi seem to have analysed reality in terms of events, of what becomes of things as they grow and decline. Concomitantly, Hopi culture lays great emphasis on preparation; this includes announcing and getting ready for events well beforehand and taking elaborate precautions to ensure the persistence of desired conditions. SAE, on the contrary, with its distinction between formless substances and forms, fosters dualistic conceptions and objectifies time.

Granted that there is a relationship between language, culture and behaviour, there is still the question: which was first – the language patterns or the cultural norms? Whorf replies that, in the main, language and culture develop together, constantly influencing each other, but in this partnership the nature of language is the factor that limits free plasticity and rigidifies development in a more autocratic way. This is so, he says, because language is a system, not just an assemblage of norms. Consequently, linguistic changes can only occur very slowly while many cultural innovations are made with comparative quickness. He thus concluded, in answer to his first question, that concepts of time, space and matter are not given in substantially the same form by experience to all men but depend upon the nature of the languages, through the use of which they have been developed, and, in answer to his second question, that there are connections between cultural norms and linguistic patterns.

However, Whorf's evidence for the linguistic relativity hypothesis is open to question. Lenneberg (1961) has criticized Whorf's work on two counts. First, he criticizes the technique of translation which Whorf so often employed to demonstrate differences in languages, arguing that large differences in the linguistic handling of an event do not necessarily imply corresponding differences in the perception of that event and may merely result from metaphorical developments in the language, about which the speakers may not ordinarily be aware. Secondly, Lenneberg argues that linguistic and non-linguistic events must be separately observed and described before they can be correlated, otherwise the linguistic relativity principle becomes circular or tautological, in that the only evidence for differences in 'world view' turns out to be linguistic differences. Consequently, certain kinds of evidence which may appear to support the hypothesis do not. For example, it is well known that

Eskimos have many more words for snow than we have and that Arabs have many more words for camels, but it cannot be concluded from this evidence that we perceive the world (in this case, of snow or camels) any differently than those who speak Eskimo or Arabic. We have got to go beyond purely linguistic analysis and examine the relationship between verbal usage on the one hand and perception, recall and thought on the other.

It has long been recognized that the colour continuum provides a suitable modality for investigating the effects of naming or labelling upon perceptual recognition. Rivers (1905) observed that the Todas of the Torres Strait have a tendency to discriminate greens, blues and violets less definitely than reds and yellows and that this deficiency was paralleled by a deficiency in the nomenclature for the former group of colours. He believed, however, that this was evidence of genetic differences in perception producing differences in linguistic usage. It is true that some evidence exists for genetic differences in various types of defects in colour vision (e.g. the higher proportion of men suffering from red-green deficiency) but it is hardly possible that genetic factors could account for the extensive differences in nomenclature that are found to exist between languages which cannot be considered as genetically isolated from one another.

The first experiment explicitly addressed to the problem of the effect of colour naming on perceptual recognition was conducted by Brown and Lenneberg (1954). These authors began by determining the 'codability' of each of 25 colours. Codability was defined as the consistency with which a name was applied to a stimulus. By measuring the amount of agreement among subjects, a rank order of codability was established for this series of colours. The next task was to correlate codability with efficiency of recognition. This was done with a new group of subjects who were first shown some of the original stimuli and then asked to recognize them on a chart containing 120 different colours. There were several experimental conditions: the number of colours originally exposed was either one or four; the time interval between the inspection of the original stimuli and their presentation on the chart varied between 7 seconds and 3 minutes. Significant, positive correlations between the degree of codability and correct recognition were found in all the experimental conditions except the easiest, that is, one colour after 7 seconds. As the task of recognition became progressively more difficult, the degree of direct relationship between codability and recognition increased. Now, these results would not by themselves justify the conclusion that codability is a

H

causal factor in perceptual recognition, since the colours may also have differed in their degree of discriminability, which could have related both to recognition and to codability. However, an earlier experiment had determined the discriminability of each of the colours used in the Brown and Lenneberg study. Consequently, the latter could hold the factor of discriminability constant (by the method of partial correlation) and, when they did this, they got much the same results. They concluded, therefore, that codability is a causal factor in perception.

The technical terms given to the process which is assumed to occur in situations like that described by Brown and Lenneberg are 'encoding' and 'decoding'. Encoding means 'giving a stimulus a name' while decoding refers to the process by which we translate that name back on to the stimulus. This distinction is perhaps most readily understood if one thinks of the process of taking down a message in morse code (encoding) and subsequently translating the morse back into language (decoding). The findings of Brown and Lenneberg imply that the effects of labelling on perceptual recognition are due to a process of verbal encoding of a stimulus followed by a decoding when an array of stimuli, including those previously seen, is subsequently presented. The more consistent is the linguistic usage applying to a stimulus, the more efficient is the process of encoding assumed to be.

However, there have been contradictory findings with this method. Lenneberg (1961) himself found in other experiments that recognition was negatively related to codability. An alternative approach, reported by Brown (1965), has been developed by Lantz (1963). She reasoned that the most obvious characteristic of linguistic codability should be the correspondence between encoding and decoding. A measure of codability could then be established empirically by asking if someone refers by name to a specific colour, with what degree of efficiency can someone else identify that colour among a number of others when he is given that name? Lantz, accordingly, determined the codability of a set of colours by using two groups of subjects: the first group assigned a name to each stimulus; the second was asked to identify, on the basis of these names, each of the original colours included in a larger array. She found that the rank order of codability determined in this fashion correlated with the scores for subsequent recognition obtained for further groups of subjects and that these correlations were substantially higher than those reported by Brown and Lenneberg. In addition, Lantz taught subjects new names for poorly communicated colours and was able to increase the accuracy with which they were recognized.

The evidence that language influences recognition suggests that it plays a formative role in concept formation: as Brown and Lenneberg say, the word 'spotlights' a moment of consciousness and puts it in connection with other events similarly spotlighted. But do the structural characteristics of a language exert a similar influence? One answer to this question has been the proposal that there are two major types of linguistic code, restricted and elaborated, and that exposure to a restricted code alone leads to restrictions upon thinking.

Restricted and Elaborated Codes

According to Bernstein (1961, 1964), the primary function of the restricted code is to maintain or change the nature of an immediate social relationship. It is the language of the *status quo*, serving to define existing role relationships. A restricted code is thus stereotyped and condensed and it lacks specificity and exactness. On the other hand, the primary function of the elaborated code is to communicate information about the physical and social world, so that possession of such a code enhances the capacity for appreciating the uniqueness of individual experience. Elaborated codes are those in which communication is individualized and the message is specific to a particular situation. Bernstein believes that, whilst middle-class children are exposed to both restricted and elaborated codes, the working-class child has access only to restricted codes. In the middle-class child there is a progressive development towards verbalization and making explicit subjective intent, but this is not the case for the working-class child. This failure of development comes about as a consequence of the social relationship acting through the medium of language; lower working-class society is limited to forms of expression which are general and vague because it is founded upon a system of non-verbal, shared identifications. Consequently, the working-class person has difficulty in communicating his own thoughts, in understanding the fine discriminations which normal social intercourse demands, and in developing his thinking in the direction of greater discrimination and generalization.

A study which anticipated Bernstein's theory is Milner's (1951) investigation of the relationship between reading readiness and patterns of parent-child interaction. She gave some reading tests to children from three different schools – a school attended almost entirely by the children of professional and business men, a school attended mainly by children of middle-income families, and a school in a slum area of the city. The 21 children obtaining the highest scores on the reading tests were then compared with the 21 children with the lowest scores. As expected, there was a significant relationship between reading readiness and status. The high scorers were surrounded by a much richer verbal environment than were the low scorers: they had more books and were read to more by important adults and were encouraged to talk. Milner also found that the parents of high-scoring children tended to express their affection for their children in an overt manner, while parents of low scorers did not consistently give their children overt signs of affection. Milner concluded that the lower-class child lacks two facilities: a warm family atmosphere (which she saw as a prerequisite for any kind of adult-controlled learning) and the opportunity to interact verbally with adults of high personal value to the child who possess adequate speech patterns.

These conclusions regarding social class differences in the use of language are supported by later studies (e.g. Douglas, 1964; Newson and Newson, 1968), although there is no support for the suggestion that working-class mothers are less warm than middle-class mothers. A study which specifically links the dimension of restricted versus elaborated language to cognitive behaviour is that by Hess and Shipman (1965), in which two principal hypotheses were tested. It was suggested, firstly, that the interrelationship between social interaction and language is illustrated by the distinction between two types of family control: the one, favoured by restricted codes, is oriented toward control by status appeal or ascribed role norms, the other, fostered by elaborated codes, is oriented towards persons and the unique characteristics of the person and the situation are taken into account. The second hypothesis was that the use of elaborated codes would be associated with a more advanced way of responding on an object-sorting task. As predicted, there were significant differences in language behaviour between the classes, with the higher social classes using elaborated codes more than the lower classes. Middle-class mothers tended to use person-oriented modes of control significantly more than working-class mothers and children in the lower-status groups tended to sort objects according to subjective and personal criteria, whereas the higher-status groups produced more objective, general, and abstract classifications. Hess and Shipman concluded that the teaching styles of mothers shape the learning styles of their children.

The picture that is beginning to emerge is that the meaning of deprivation is a deprivation of meaning – a cognitive environment in which behaviour is controlled by status rules rather than by attention to the individual characteristics of a specific situation and one in which behaviour is not mediated by verbal cues or by teaching that relates events to one another and the present to the future. (p. 885).

Further evidence for the existence of class and ethnic differences in the relationship between parental teaching styles and children's cognitive style comes from studies by Smilansky (1968) and Hertzig *et al.* (1968). The issue is, of course, of great educational concern, since, once the deficiencies have been analysed, the next step is to devise teaching programmes for disadvantaged children. Such a programme was designed by Blank and Solomon (1969). This consists of a series of dialogues focused around simple problem-solving tasks. Through these dialogues the child is taught to attend to instructions, to think about specific situations and to relate to future events. However, although differences in the use of language between social classes appear to be a major influence on the development of cognitive style, there are other variables which differentiate between these groups, for example, material benefits and parents' expectations for their children, so that we need more sophisticated analyses to determine the relative importance of all these interacting variables. Moreover, future studies would be advised to note the criticisms of Houston (1970) and, in particular, the thesis that the disadvantaged child has both a restricted language which he uses at school and a highly elaborate language which he uses out of school.

Development of Linguistic Control over Behaviour

In his early work on the language and thought of the child Piaget (1926) had argued that the Freudian distinction between primary and secondary processes could be conceptualized as a distinction between individual and socialized thought. He hypothesized that there exists a form of thought, which he termed egocentric, which stands midway between autism and socialized thought, that is, between that form of thought which merely hallucinates reality and that which is adapted to it. It is intermediate in the sense that it exhibits the qualities of both types of thought; in the first place, its basic function is self-gratification, for the child sees things from his own perspective and is unable to decentre or shift his perspective to encompass that of others; but, secondly, it is not fully autistic, for it does include some kind of reality orientation. Thus, essentially, Piaget was trying to study the relationship between language and thought from the standpoint of cognitive centring and decentring, and his object was to discover if there was a special kind of egocentric speech that could be distinguished from socialized speech. His own analyses of children's speech led him to believe that this was, in fact, possible, that up to the age of seven the child's speech was predominantly egocentric, but that after that age speech was adapted to the points of view of others.

These early studies aroused some controversy and stimulated a number of validation studies. These, which are reviewed by McCarthy (1954), found little support for Piaget's conclusions. McCarthy herself, for example, found a much smaller ratio of egocentric speech in American children, while Johnson and Josey (1931) found 'all our children to be socially minded and in no manner dominated by an egocentric attitude'. More recently, Piaget (1962) has commented that these studies have been widely misinterpreted. They do, he grants, demonstrate that it is extremely difficult to categorize children's speech on an egocentrism-adaptation dimension, but they do not disprove the notion of ego-centrism, since they were not designed to test it. In fact, he says, the study of actual (as against verbal) behaviour has proved a better guide to what egocentrism means.

The notion of egocentric speech was also taken up by the Russian psychologist, Vygotsky (1962). His own studies led him to accept the existence of egocentric speech, but, whereas Piaget had assumed that it simply disappears with advancing age, Vygotsky argues that it fulfils a useful function in the child's development. What he did was to introduce a series of frustrations and difficulties into the child's activities. For example, if a child was getting ready to draw, he would suddenly find that there was no paper or no pencil of the appropriate colour. In short, he was made to face problems. Vygotsky found that in such situations egocentric speech almost doubled. The child would try to grasp and remedy the situation by talking to himself. He might say, for example, 'Where's the pencil? I need a blue pencil. Never mind, I'll draw with the red one and wet it with water; it will become dark and look like blue.' As a result of these observations, Vygotsky reasoned that egocentric speech is not merely an accompaniment to the child's activity but an instrument of thought which helps him to plan the solution of a problem. The evidence presented is rather scanty, but he concludes: 'We observed how egocentric speech at first marked the end-result of an activity, then was gradually shifted toward the middle and finally to the beginning of the activity, taking on a directing, planning function and raising the child's acts to the level of purposeful behaviour' (p. 17). After the age of seven egocentric speech becomes 'inner speech', while still maintaining the function of controlling thought and behaviour. Thus, whilst for Piaget egocentric speech is midway between autistic and socialized speech, for Vygotsky it is midway between speech directed to others and speech which has been internalized as thought.

Although Vygotsky believed that language plays a crucial role in the development of thinking, he did not believe that thinking is reducible to the manipulation of words. Since there is evidence of problem-solving capacity in the pre-linguistic organism (e.g. Köhler's (1925) apes), he maintained that thought and language originate independently but join together at a certain point in development, so that, as Diebold (1965) puts it, thought becomes verbal and speech rational. Nevertheless, Vygotsky's work has contributed to the special emphasis placed in Soviet psychology on what Pavlov (1932) termed the 'second signal system'. According to Pavlov, man is not only governed by the first signal system of conditioned reflex mechanisms but can also use words as signals of signals. Thus, just as a light stimulus may come to act as a signal for the coming of food, so the word 'light' can become a signal for the light. The development of this second system allows man to detach himself from the influence of immediate stimulation, to form classes of non-verbal stimuli with a certain property or set of properties in common, to form associations very rapidly, and to achieve a flexibility of behaviour far above that of non-linguistic organisms.

Luria (1961), working within this tradition, has shown how language comes to have an increasing influence upon voluntary behaviour. In the young child of one-and-a-half to two years, the language of an adult does not have much effect other than that of producing an orienting response. If the experimenter says something to the child, the latter may stop whatever he is doing and look at the adult or he may look at the object the adult names, but he is not capable of following instructions; thus, if the experimenter says, 'Give me the ball', the child of this age will just look at the ball. At a somewhat later age, language has an impulsive or releasing function, so that the effect of a verbal instruction is to make the child do whatever he is ready to do. Consequently, if the child is ready to give an adult a ball and the adult says, 'Give me the doll', he will give the adult the ball, for this is what he was ready to do and the language of the other merely releases the response. Subsequently, language acquires a selective function: the child is told, for example, to press a bulb and he does so immediately, showing that he can now obey simple orders. Finally, when language is internalized so that the child can instruct himself as well as receive instructions from others, language acquires the function of pre-selection. Luria devised a number of situations to test this function. A simple test is to ask the child to press a bulb when a red light comes on; a harder test is for the experimenter to say, 'Press the bulb if the red light comes on, but do not press it if a green light comes on'. A child of two-and-a-half years will fail both these tests, since he will start pressing the bulb immediately and stop when the red light comes on; the 3-year-old can solve the simpler problem, but will also press when the green light comes on; finally, the 6-year-old can solve both parts of the discrimination and shows a general capacity to perform or to withhold action according to the instructions. The work of Zaporozhets (reviewed by Berlyne, 1970) may be regarded as an extension of Luria's investigations since it, too, shows how inner speech comes to function in the voluntary control of behaviour. The Soviet view is well stated by Leontiev (1971) when he claims that language does not simply facilitate conceptualization; it forms categories and imparts a new element to it. However, it should be noted that attempts to replicate Luria's findings have not always been successful. Miller, Shelton and Flavell (1970), for instance, concluded that, far from being a useful mediator of motor performance, verbal responding appeared to be only an additional task for the child.

Thinking in the Deaf

However, there is one body of evidence which it is difficult to reconcile with the emphasis placed by Whorf, Bernstein and Soviet psychologists on the role of language in the development of thinking, namely, that from studies which have compared deaf and hearing subjects. Reviews of this literature by Rosenstein (1961), Vernon (1967) and Furth (1971) concur in the conclusion that there is no relationship between level of language development and a great many measures of thinking, for example, problem-solving, rule-learning, concept formation, and Piagetian tasks. Those tasks on which the deaf do perform badly are frequently those in relation to which one can establish that verbal habits are of direct help. Furth (1966) argues that these tests are rather specific, as is a digit recall test or a non-verbal discovery test of opposition, but that, apart from such effects, the basic development and structure of intelligence of the deaf is unaffected by the absence of verbal language. He states that logical, intelligent thinking does not need the support of a symbolic system, as it exists in the living language of society.

However, Furth seems to believe that, because deaf subjects are not familiar with verbal language, they lack any form of symbolic system. Thus, he writes:

> One would not be justified in asserting that the deaf children who were tested in this study had a symbolic system available to them. Most of them were unfamiliar with the verbal language of society and only poorly acquainted with the manual sign language. Yet they succeeded in tasks of thinking and quite likely produced symbols if and when they were needed. Whatever system of intellectual ordering of experience was manifest in their behaviour was entirely due to their internal structure of thinking and could not conceivably be ascribed to a non-existing symbolic system. (p. 228)

Furth maintains that these opinions are in accord with Piagetian theory which regards thinking as deriving from actions which are internalized as systems of operations. But it may be pointed out that Piaget himself has talked of the relationship between language and thought as being 'naturally reciprocal' (Piaget, 1951, p. 221) and has agreed that, although speech is not the cause of the formation of operational co-ordinations, it nevertheless extends their power indefinitely and imparts a mobility and a generality to them which they would not possess without speech (Piaget, 1954a). Moreover, Ausubel (1968) has argued that one cannot rule out the possibility that Furth's subjects had access to other kinds of symbolism, of imagery or of gesture, for instance. Particularly dramatic cases of these other forms of symbolism are evident in the development of Helen Keller and Laura Bridgman, two blind, deaf-mute children who learned to use symbols by being able to give to themselves the same sorts of tactile impressions they could give to others. Cassirer (1945) has suggested that a major advance in the development of these girls occurred when they realized that everything has a name, in other words, that the symbolic function is not restricted to particular cases but is a principle of universal applicability. Henceforth, Cassirer says, the child can use symbols, not merely as mechanical signs, but as an instrument of thought.

'LANGUAGE ACCOMPLISHES THOUGHT'

Goldstein's (1948) work on language disturbances associated with brain lesions has been the stimulus for many discussions on the relationship between language and thought, notably Cassirer (1953b), Merleau-Ponty (1962) and Schutz (1967). Goldstein endorsed Vygotsky's

H*

criticism of Piaget's theory of egocentric speech, maintaining that although the language of the child corresponds to the primitive way in which he understands his environment, it is an instrument in enabling the child to overcome these limitations. The major developmental change, according to Goldstein, is the change from a concrete attitude, in which we are passively bound to the immediate situation, to an abstract attitude, possession of which involves the ability to take a certain point of view, to assess a situation and to think in terms of possible alternatives. Corresponding to this distinction, there is a distinction between concrete and abstract language: the former is involved in our understanding of language in familiar situations and of emotional utterances, whilst the latter is volitional, propositional and rational. When a subject's ability to use abstract language is impaired through brain damage, he may be able to utter words but lack the capacity to use them as symbols of general categories of experience. This feature is apparent with regard to the activity of naming objects. When a person truly names an object, he considers the object as representing a category, but patients who have lost the abstract attitude may use words to name objects in a much more specific way. For example, a patient offered a knife together with a pencil called the knife a pencil sharpener; when the knife was offered together with an apple, it was an 'apple parer', and so forth. From his observation that changes in the use of words are often paralleled by disturbances of abstract behaviour in general, and also of non-linguistic performance, Goldstein concluded that we should consider changes in language and thought as expressions of the same basic disturbance: to approach the world with an abstract attitude involves the capacity to use words as symbols for general ideas.

Merleau-Ponty (1962), however, believes that many of the failures of Goldstein's patients are not failures of the abstract attitude, defined as the ability to group elements under abstract categories, but arise from the fact that these subjects can only relate elements by explicit subsumption. Thus, a patient, given the task of understanding the analogy, 'eye is to light and colours as ear is to sounds', does not understand until he has made the analogy explicit by recourse to conceptual analysis. He looks for a common material characteristic from which he can infer the identity of the two relationships, stating, 'the eye and the ear are both sense organs, therefore, they must give rise to something similar'. But, says Merleau-Ponty, normal thought does not proceed by subsuming under some explicitly defined category. The normal subject grasps the meaning of the analogy immediately, *before* he formulates an explicit argument: the relationship is lived before being conceived. The efforts of Goldstein's patients to name objects and to solve problems are reminiscent of the procedures by which the scientist refers to sense-data in the light of hypotheses which remain to be verified; these procedures contrast sharply with the spontaneous methods of normal cognition, which rests implicitly upon systems of meaning that the subject can take up without such explicit interpretation. For Merleau-Ponty, then, the linguistic and intellectual difficulties of these subjects are due, not to a failure of the abstract attitude, but to a failure in that level of awareness which is prior to abstract thought:

> Let us, therefore, say . . . that the life of consciousness – cognitive life, the life of desire or perceptual life – is subtended by an 'intentional arc' which projects round about us our past, our future, our human setting, our physical, ideological and moral situation, or rather which results in our being situated in all these respects. It is this intentional arc which brings about the unity of the senses, of intelligence, of sensibility and motility. And it is this which 'goes limp' in illness. (p. 136)

Moreover, language fulfils an essential function in this intentional arc of experience. For if speech were simply the expression of insights already attained in pure thought, we could not understand why thinking is motivated towards expression as a means of completion, why, for example, in order to recognize an object completely, we should need to name it. Merleau-Ponty says, then, that it is through speech and other forms of symbolism that meaning is attained and the transition from the implicit to the explicit accomplished. One implication of this view is that there must be a sense in which it can be said that the listener receives thought from speech itself. The notion is a strange one, since it is commonly assumed that the subject gives meaning to speech, but it seems unavoidable if it is to be conceded that the subject learns something from expression and communication instead of knowing everything in advance. Merleau-Ponty's solution to this paradox is to argue that there is a 'gestural meaning' inherent in speech. When I communicate with another, it is true that there must be a shared vocabulary and syntax, but this could not be taken to mean that words are effective by arousing in me 'representations' which match the representations of the other. Rather, I communicate primarily with a speaking subject who has a certain style of approaching the world. Just as the other person in speaking does not merely translate an already accomplished and therefore explicit thought, so my comprehension of his meaning is, fundamentally, not a process of reflective thinking, but one of taking up the other's intentions. In the same way, I understand the meaning of a gesture, not by an act of intellectual interpretation, but by 'a kind of blind recognition which precedes the intellectual working out and clarification of the meaning' (p. 185).

In conclusion, it is interesting to note that the results of these phenomenological analyses are in accord with the widely held view that the relationship between language and thought is naturally reciprocal and, indeed, help us to understand how such reciprocity is effected. For it is evident that Merleau-Ponty refers, as does Ehrenzweig in commenting upon the paradox noted by Wittgenstein, to that pre-reflective level of experience, at which the meaning of a word or an idea is grasped implicitly before it is conceptualized explicitly. But this level of experience has so far – in these discussions of creative thinking and of the creative use of language – only been hinted at and has not yet been articulated. It is the task of the final chapter to draw further upon the insights gained from phenomenological analysis in order to understand the function of pre-reflective thinking and its relation to abstract thought. Since, if the phenomenologists are correct, abstract thinking assumes and rests upon pre-reflective awareness, the psychology of thinking would remain incomplete without this exposition.

The phenomenology of thinking

PHENOMENOLOGY AND PSYCHOLOGY

We have seen that a number of authors have argued for the existence of two forms of awareness in order to explain creative thinking and the creative use of language. However, it is doubtful whether the conceptions considered so far amount to a very thorough description of the psychological processes involved in such thinking. In particular, the relationship between these two forms will remain obscure unless an account of conscious activity may be framed which permits an understanding of the two as aspects of a single process, during which ideas, which are initially obscure and tentative, become clear and particular. Such an explanation – the doctrine of the intentional nature of conscious activity – has been proposed by Husserl (1900, 1901) and has been elaborated by other phenomenologists, notably by Merleau-Ponty (1962). The task of this final chapter, then, is to examine this doctrine and to assess its implications for the psychology of thinking. The pursuit of this aim is likely to raise criticisms from two principal sources – from phenomenologists who resist 'psychologism', the reduction of knowing to merely psychological processes (thinking) which do not themselves allow any distinction to be made between genuine knowledge and sheer illusion, and from behaviourists who regard analyses of consciousness as regressions to an outdated 'mentalism'. My own opinion is that both criticisms may be met and that a psychology which can account for the means by which subjects come to know and understand is precisely one which avoids the fallacy of 'the ghost in the machine'.

We must begin, again, with the crucial distinction between reflective thinking, which leads to objective knowledge, and pre-reflective awareness, which leads to tacit knowledge in which our actions and perceptions are grounded. Merleau-Ponty (1962) provides many examples of the impossibility of explaining perception solely in terms of objective relations. Thus, he says, there is no *reason* why a steeple should appear to be smaller and further away when the subject is better able to see the details of the landscape between, since the intervening objects do not act on the apparent distance in the relation of cause to effect. Rather, they provide a *motive* that is tacitly adopted by the perceiver, a meaning that is grasped as it is lived. This concept of motivation is necessary in order to describe how one phenomenon releases another, 'not by means of some objective, efficient cause, like those which link together natural events, but by the meaning which it holds out – there is an underlying reason for a thing which guides the flow of phenomena without being explicitly laid down in any one of them, a sort of operative reason' (p. 50). Thus, traditional empiricism is in error when it accepts the results of the objective attitude un-questioningly and distinguishes sharply between 'sensations' and thought: pure sensations would only exist if the world were a spectacle and one's own body a mechanism for copying it. But this is not the case, for things assume their meanings in relation to attitudes and intentions towards them; thus, the light of a candle changes its appear-ance for a child after he has been burned, a wheel lying on the ground is not, for sight, the same thing as a wheel bearing a load, and so forth. Similarly, if things have a meaning prior to the operation of reflective intelligence which relates them explicitly, thought ceases to be sharply distinguishable from sensory experience and we have to re-examine the relationship between pre-reflective and reflective modes.

One major implication of this reasoning is that any psychology which accepts without qualification the naturalism of the physical sciences will inevitably distort the meaning of phenomena. A thing, Husserl (1911) says, is what it is, and it remains in its identity for ever. The properties of a thing can be determined with objective validity and confirmed or modified in new experiences, but the psychological, the 'phenomenon', comes and goes, retaining no enduring, identical being that is objectively determinable in the sense of natural science. To be sure, there is an order and a unity in the appearance of phenomena but this unity is not that of things but of the 'flow' of consciousness in which phenomena emerge into the present and constantly sink back into a 'having been'. Thus, an empirical psychology which objectifies phenomena and seeks to account for their interrelationships in the manner of the physical sciences is bound to misinterpret the essential nature of psychological processes. To the assertion that psychologists must imitate the procedures of the natural sciences in order to establish their discipline on a sound, scientific basis, Husserl replies that a true science follows the nature of what has to be investigated and not our prejudices and preconceptions.

These phenomenological analyses do not, therefore, signify a rejection of the possibility of a scientific psychology, but they do suggest that an analysis of phenomena that is not constrained by traditional naturalism will play a fundamental role in such a discipline. Although Husserl was consistently severe in his attacks on 'psychologism', especially, as we saw in the first chapter, on the reduction of logical implications to psychological processes, he himself realized (e.g. Husserl, 1954) that nothing is accomplished by rejecting a psychological grounding of norms and that a psychology must be devised which can accomplish this task. 'The only radical reform of psychology', he wrote (1960), 'is the pure development of an intentional psychology' (p. 49). Only when consciousness is regarded as a network of intentions and when we know more of the nature of these intentions will a science of psychological processes be established, since it is these which provide for the order and unity of phenomena. These views are directly opposed to the doctrine that consciousness consists of a passive reception of sensations. It is true that other thinkers had, before Husserl, outlined their opposition to the traditional analysis. Brentano (1874) had proposed that the essential feature of conscious activity is the reference to an object, so that to be conscious is to be 'conscious of' something: to hear is to hear something, to feel elation is to be elated about something and to think is to think of something. And there are certain affinities between Husserl and William James; in the *Principles of Psychology*, James (1890) discusses the 'flow of consciousness' and talks of the activity of the mind as 'intending', not copying, reality. However, Husserl did far more than merely accept these earlier discussions. The reference by James to the activity of intending was somewhat casual and not given systematic importance, whereas for Husserl it was a fundamental idea. There are, moreover, important differences between Brentano's and Husserl's use of the concept of intentionality. Whereas the former was content to define consciousness in terms of relatedness to an object, Husserl employed the concept of intention to refer to an active and creative capacity of the mind.

INTENTIONALITY

He distinguished between meaning-giving and meaning-fulfilling acts. An expression, as distinct from a mark which relates to something simply by association, acquires a meaning as a result of a meaning-giving act, an intention towards something. All genuine expressions have this characteristic. Thus, as Mohanty (1969) says, the expressions, 'The present King of France', 'The other side of the moon', and 'The white wall before me' are alike in being animated by a meaning-intention, whilst 'Abcaderaf' lacks this quality. This distinction cannot be understood from the standpoint of a completely detached observer, for it can only be grasped as subjectively evident whether a sign embodies an intention and thus expresses something or whether it is merely a mark which does not. Now, meaning-intentions differ in the extent to which they are capable of fulfilment and in the manner in which they may be fulfilled. Many expressions do not refer to actually existing objects. Husserl would say of these that they have meaning but that this cannot be completely fulfilled; 'The present King of France', for example, was at one time capable of actual fulfilment but, as used by anyone now, the meaning-intention of this expression is incapable of fulfilment. Another way of expressing this state of affairs would be to say that one can *think* of 'The present King of France' but one cannot have *knowledge* of him. The distinction between thought and knowledge is that the latter consists of the fulfilment of an intention accompanied by an awareness of the identity of the fulfilment with the intention. To know something is to recognize that an intention has been fulfilled.

In understanding the precise meaning of the assertion that consciousness is intentional, we must bear in mind the important distinction between the kind of directedness evident in the relationship between a desire (say, for food) and its fulfilment and that in evidence in what Husserl called 'operative intentionality'. The former refers to an intention that may be termed an expectation, whilst with the latter there is not an expectation in the usual psychological sense, although there is a meaning-intention which seeks completion. Many of Merleau-Ponty's (1962) analyses of the phenomenology of perception are explorations of this operative intentionality. Consider the following description, for example:

> If I walk along a shore towards a ship which has run aground, and the funnel or masts merge into the forest bordering on the sand dune, there will be a moment when these details suddenly become part of the ship, and indissolubly fused with it. As I approached, I did not perceive resemblances or proximities which finally came together to form a continuous picture of the upper part of the ship.

I merely felt that the look of the object was on the point of altering, that something was imminent in this tension, as a storm is imminent in storm clouds. Suddenly the sight before me was recast in a manner satisfying to my vague expectation. Only afterwards did I recognize, as justifications for the change, the resemblance and contiguity of what I call 'stimuli' – namely the most determinate phenomena, seen at close quarters and with which I compose the 'true' world. 'How could I have failed to see that these pieces of wood were an integral part of the ship? For they were of the same colour as the ship, and fitted well enough into its superstructure.' But these reasons for correct perception were not given as reasons beforehand. The unity of the object is based on the foreshadowing of an imminent order which is about to spring upon us a reply to questions merely latent in the landscape. It solves a problem set only in the form of a vague feeling of uneasiness, it organizes elements which up to that moment did not belong to the same universe and which, for that reason as Kant said with profound insight, could not be associated. By placing them on the same footing, that of the unique object, synopsis makes continuity and resemblance between them possible. An impression can never by itself be associated with another impression. (p. 17)

Through such analyses Merleau-Ponty arrives at a theory of cognition whose central point of reference is the motility of the body. Phenomenology returns to the world of actual experience, which is prior to the objective world, to reveal the existence of a 'motor intentionality' (p. 110) in our perception, habit and thinking. Consciousness is in the first place not a matter of 'I think that' but of an 'I can'. This fact emerges clearly from the descriptions of Goldstein's brain-damaged patients. If one subject, Schneider, is asked to trace a square or a circle in the air, he first 'finds' his arm, then lifts it up in front of him and finally makes a few rough movements in a straight line or describing various curves; if one of these happens to be circular, he promptly completes the circle. Merleau-Ponty comments that in this case the patient does not intend or fulfil the figure in the normal manner, but moves his body about until the correct movement is approximated. The instruction to draw a circle is not meaningless to the subject, since he is aware of the inadequacy of his first attempts and he is capable of making correct use of a gesture produced fortuitously. The cognitive deficiency of this patient lies in the fact that the instruction has only an *intellectual* significance and not a *motor* one.

What he lacks is neither motility nor thought, and we are brought to the recognition of something between movement as a third person process and thought as a representation of movement – something which is an anticipation of, or arrival at, the objective and is ensured by the body itself as a motor power, a 'motor project' ('*Bewegungsentwurf*'), a 'motor intentionality' in the absence of which the order remains a dead letter. (p. 110)

There are other patients who are unable to trace in objects the directions which are useful from the point of view of action or, generally, to assign to the spatial scene delimitations in human terms which make it the field of our action. For instance, patients faced with a dead end in a labyrinth have difficulty in finding 'the opposite direction'; they are very inaccurate in pointing out on another person's arm the point corresponding to the one stimulated on their own; they are incapable of comparing the number of units contained in two sets of sticks placed in front of them – they may count the same stick twice or include in one set of sticks some which belong to the other. These subjects are unable, then, to keep perspectives in view and to organize the given world in accordance with the projects of the present moment; they cannot build into the geographical setting a behavioural one, a system of meanings in which intentions are fulfilled through actions. For these patients, therefore, the world exists 'ready-made', whereas for the normal person his projects polarize the world, thus producing the signs which guide thinking and behaviour.

In a passage that is strikingly similar to Polanyi's analysis of knowing (e.g. Polanyi, 1967), Merleau-Ponty describes how a sighted subject might become accustomed to using a stick in the manner of a blind man. In order to get used to the stick, he has to use it as an instrument, as an extension of his body. There is no question of an explicit comparison between the objective length of the stick and the objective distance of things. The points in space do not stand out as objective positions in relation to the objective position occupied by our body. Rather, they mark the varying range of our aims and gestures. To get used to the stick is thus to be 'transplanted' into it or to incorporate it into our own body. If consciousness is in the first instance a matter of 'I can', it is the body, as the medium for motor intentionality, which is the origin of the worlds which we construct. 'The body is our general medium for having a world' (p. 146). Sometimes it is restricted to the actions necessary for survival and accordingly it posits around us a biological world; at other times, it elaborates upon these primary actions and derives a figurative meaning from them as in dancing. Sometimes, finally, the meaning aimed at cannot be achieved by the body's natural means; it must then build itself an instrument, and it projects around itself a cultural world.

Langan (1966) emphasizes that the key to understanding the role of the body in Merleau-Ponty's theory is to understand the reciprocal relationship between motor intentionality and environment. The subject's perception is not a *de facto* effect of environmental stimulation but represents the way in which the organism meets stimulation. 'The function of the organism in receiving stimuli is, so to speak, to "conceive" a certain form of excitation' (p. 75). The body then, gives the world a meaning but not, arbitrarily, any meaning but a meaning grounded in the very things which appear in its field. The active processes in perception and thinking re-work or take up again a sense that is already latent in the environmental events because the body originally animates these in its own way. But this animation is itself dependent upon the texture and field of the world in which it takes place. Consequently, far from positing the 'mental' as that which is interior and thus, somehow, distinct from behaviour, this theory unites the study of consciousness with the study of the behaving subject. As Merleau-Ponty (1965) argues, this conception links consciousness with action by enlarging our idea of action. We can no longer be content to study behaviour from a merely external, objective point of view, since such an attitude fails to encompass the intentions which animate behaviour; conversely, we can no longer analyse mental processes, such as perception, feeling or thinking, as though they took place in a self-contained and interior realm, for then we would fail to understand how such phenomena can ever relate to the subject's involvement in a real environment.

PERSONAL KNOWLEDGE

Knowing, it has been asserted, consists of the fulfilment of an intention accompanied by an awareness of the identity of the fulfilment with the intention. There are a number of ideas about the nature of thinking and knowing contained in this definition and it is necessary to elaborate them in order to understand how this definition is consistent with a theory of personal knowledge.

It is motor intentionality which provides a direction for thinking and which motivates us to the attainment of concepts which 'complete' our thought. Thus, Merleau-Ponty (1962) argues that the construction of a triangle is the outward and explicit expression of the motor intentions of a subject who is able to place himself at a certain point and to project lines to other spatial positions. 'Thus do I grasp the concrete essence of the triangle, which is not a collection of objective "characteristics", but the formula of an attitude, a certain modality of my hold on the world, a structure, in short' (p. 386). To form a concept, then, is not, fundamentally, to subsume resemblances under explicit categories, but to synthesize things through the intentions which we have towards them. That the act of explicit subsumption is a secondary development and not the fundamental mode of cognition has been noted in connection with the deficiencies of certain brain-damaged patients who have lost their 'intentional hold' upon things. The fundamental form of cognition is personal, therefore, in the sense that intentionality implies an involvement in an environmental and not a detached attitude.

This capacity itself presupposes the ability of the subject to retain an overall view of his successive acts. When he constructs a triangle, the subject does not arbitrarily add one line to the next in such a way that the meaning of the drawing is changed at each stroke. On the contrary, the process from start to finish has a triangle in view, albeit tacitly and intuitively to begin with, and not explicitly and formally. It is not a question of the draughtsman being guided by a definite image, his construction being merely a copy of this completed figure, for the unity is the unity of one's actions. One would not, however, be capable of recognizing the finished construction as the fulfilment of an intention unless the whole series of acts had been experienced as a unity in the 'flow' of consciousness. Again, we may speak of personal knowledge since it is the individual who prevails over the dispersion of his thoughts in time.

Because this ability to maintain an intentional unity, this 'self-possession', as Merleau-Ponty calls it, is not a matter of arranging elements under an established category, it must refer to an attitude which, in a sense, is open and necessarily incomplete in so far as the individual is genuinely capable of establishing new truths for himself. This is true in two ways. In the first place, to be able to acquire greater knowledge is possible because there is a sense in which we can intuitively know what we are seeking and thus recognize something as the fulfilment of an intention; progress in knowledge occurs, then, because the thinking subject is able to project a series of developments, some of which are actualized. But, secondly, this attitude is an open-ended one because these projected, possible developments inevitably rest upon presuppositions which can never be made fully explicit. 'Once launched, and committed to a certain set of thoughts, Euclidean space, for example, or the conditions governing the existence of a certain society, I discover evident truths, but these are not unchallengeable, since perhaps this space or this society are not the only ones possible' (Merleau-Ponty, 1962, p. 396). This does not imply, of course, that the discovery of other kinds of space or social rules invalidates the earlier ones, for in many cases a perspective is attained which incorporates past conceptions in a broader framework. But it does mean, for Merleau-Ponty and other existential philosophers, that there is no question of this process ever being finalized in a formal system. It is of the essence of creative thinking to outrun its products and there is no end to what Valéry called its 'permanent dissonance'. It is this capacity of going beyond created structures to create others, of varying points of view and of orienting oneself in relation to the possible, which constitutes the very nature of human existence. We must speak of personal knowledge, therefore, in the sense that there is no system or set of formulae which will enable us to comprehend the world completely in a detached and objective manner; we come to know by acts of personal involvement whose presuppositions can never be fully known and whose fulfilments are always uncertain.

However, an attempt can be made to understand systematically the many forms which the interpretation of reality can assume. James (1890) pointed out that there are many categories of reality and illusion; there is the world of sensory experience, the world of science, the world of 'ideal relations', as in logic, mathematics and other formal disciplines, the worlds of superstition and the supernatural. All these are sub-universes of reality with their own special styles of existence. He maintained that in all cases the distinction between the real and the unreal is based upon two fundamental, psychological facts – 'first that we are liable to think differently of the same, and second that, when we have done so, we can choose which way of thinking to adhere to and which to disregard' (Vol. II, p. 290). Schutz (1967), in elaborating upon this insight, refers to these worlds as 'finite provinces of meaning' (Vol. I, p. 232), indicating that the experiences relating to any one province may be consistent within that province but may appear merely fictitious, inconsistent or incompatible from the viewpoint of others. But this immediately raises the question of how it is possible for the individual to pass from one mode of thought to the next if there are distinct provinces of meaning. Schutz reasons that these provinces of meaning are not separated states of mental life but are merely names for different 'tensions' of one and the same consciousness. He attaches particular importance to the province of 'working acts', which he defines as the realm of bodily operations and of motor intentions. This mode is fundamental in that it is the one I share with others; it is the reality within which communication and the interaction of mutual motivations become effective. When a number of people agree upon the criteria for interpreting and judging reality, we can speak of an epistemic community. For example, the scientific community is founded upon the requirement of the intersubjective verification of observations: experiences which are in principle only accessible to one person are outside the province of science. The investigation of epistemic communities is the province of the sociology of knowledge.

THEORIES OF THINKING: SOME COMPARISONS

Finally, it is illuminating to consider the relationship of these views to the other major perspectives on the psychology of thinking together with the conclusions from empirical studies which have derived from these perspectives. To what extent are these perspectives complementary? Are there grounds for establishing generalizations from the convergence of theories and lines of research?

There appears to be a good deal of agreement concerning that issue which is, perhaps, the most fundamental of all. Any major psychological theory cannot avoid the question of defining, either implicitly or explicitly, the manner in which subject and environment are related. In the present cases, the definitions are explicit and virtually identical; it seems, in effect, as if the same idea is present in all the theories and only the language in which it is stated is different. For Piaget, the concept of adaptation provides the language in which this idea is defined. This concept implies that the organism neither suffers passively the influence of environmental events, since it is equipped with schemes for the assimilation of these events, nor produces whatever results it desires on an indifferent environment, since in order to adapt and act effectively it must accommodate to the demands of the environment. The relationship between the organism and its environment is thus a reciprocal one and this can only mean that the organization of reality develops concurrently with the elaboration of cognitive structures. In the language of differentiation theory, this same idea takes the form of the assertion that the organism develops its repertoire of responses as it discriminates among environmental stimuli, so that development must be conceptualized as a process which brings about the parallel and progressive differentiation of stimulation and responses. This fact was stated clearly by Dewey, whose ideas anticipated by many years the concept of the feedback-loop which is central to the cybernetic hypothesis and to the approach to thinking in terms of information-processing. He argued that stimulus and response are not distinctions of existence but of function: a stimulus becomes a stimulus because of the intentions and actions of the subject towards it and must, therefore, be regarded, not as an independent existent which leads to a response, but as one aspect of a co-ordinating action. It is evident that each of these analyses states in a different form exactly the conception which underlies Merleau-Ponty's phenomenology, that it is our motor intentions which give the world a meaning, although this meaning does not derive from those intentions alone, but from the interaction of intentions and the nature of the things experienced.

In Piagetian theory the necessity and universality of logical and mathematical laws are accounted for by saying that they are operations, which are internalized systems of co-ordinated actions. These actions are assumed to be universal and hence one can talk of the epistemic subject. On this reasoning, it is productive and non-circular to apply logical models to the study of actual cases, since the former are derived by deductive methods whose results may be tested empirically. The empirical evidence which has accumulated to date tends to support the major features of Piaget's theory, but it is equally clear that the adaptation of the subject to the characteristics of his environment assures that his logical competence is not solely describable in terms of a deductive model. The subject's competence is not absolute; given that he possesses the operations necessary for solution of one task with one set of material, it cannot be concluded that he can apply these operations equally successfully to all kinds of material. Consequently, competence can only be defined by reference to the environmental conditions in which that competence is manifested. In this way, we may reconcile the attempt to employ formal, deductive models to describe thinking with the attempt to understand the subject as he adapts to his environment.

However, this reconciliation is only possible if the concept of adaptation is given a certain meaning. Merleau-Ponty (1965) points out that, although it may be asserted that the adaptive function of clothing is to protect us from the cold and that of language is to facilitate social communication and co-operation, these activities also reveal values which are characteristically human, for example, the capacity to utilize materials to express values or the capacity to represent reality by means of systems of symbols. Human adaptation is, then, to be defined properly, not only in terms of survival in an environment, but also in terms of the construction of points of view, which, by going beyond the here-and-now, enable man to achieve a greater understanding of his environment. This adaptation is progressive and creative. Our increased understanding may, indeed, be called adaptive, but it is so in the special sense that we are capable of adapting to an environment which we ourselves have created and which we recognize to be but one of many possible environments.

The traditional theory of abstraction fails to explain concept formation since it assumes that the subject has only to recognize resemblances among elements in order to group them into categories. We know now, however, that it is through the adoption of points of view, in short, through the subject's intentions towards things, that concepts are formed. Moreover, because of this fact, the generality of the concept is grasped tacitly prior to the act of subsuming elements under an explicit category. We might say, mixing the language of *S-R* theory and phenomenology, that the stimulus and the response become clearer and more definite as the intention which animates them is fulfilled. Concept formation, as all cognitive development, is to be regarded as that process which gives rise to the increasing differentiation of stimulation and responses together with an increasing correspondence between them. The experimental evidence pertaining to the development of behaviour in concept-shift problems provides some support for this thesis. According to this conception, the task of psychological analysis is to describe the relationships between stimulation and patterns of response at different phases of development. Now, Merleau-Ponty has commented upon this kind of analysis on a number of occasions (e.g. 1962, p. 311; 1968, p. 21), maintaining that the relationship between subject and environment can be described in the language of objective, functional relations, as the Gestalt psychologists claimed, but this description will always be '*post hoc*', since it does no more than describe the end-results of the subject's involvement in the world through the medium of motor intentionality. This follows from a proper understanding of the terms, stimulus and response, which, as we have already noted, are to be conceived as aspects of a process rather than as independent existents. Thus, in describing the activity of forming a concept or making a depth discrimination or constructing a sentence, no causal priority can be given to what exists in the environment or to the subject's activity – that is, to what is 'out there' or what is 'in here' – although looking back, when the process is completed, it is possible to identify the external conditions for each of these, differentiate these from the 'responses' and note their correspondence.

But it is only on 'looking back' that we do this. The well-defined stimulus and response are the end-products of a process which has led to their differentiation and correspondence. At the moment of forming a depth discrimination, a sentence or an arithmetical relation, the subject's behaviour cannot be described as a response to a stimulus, since stimulus and response are in the process of being formed. Two terms which refer to the end-products of a process can hardly provide an adequate description of that process, so that it would be a mistaken ideal for a functional analysis to attempt to remain entirely on the level of objective relationships between explicitly defined stimuli and responses.

The distinction between inductive and deductive reasoning is a customary point of departure for studies of human problem-solving, but the evidence suggests that there are not two distinct psychological processes. The subject thinks neither purely deductively, since he is open to the influence of other variables, for example, attitudes and linguistic habits, nor purely inductively, since, as experiments on concept attainment demonstrate, he is guided by hypotheses and, to some extent at least, by deductive rules. The failure of both deductive and inductive models lies in their not being able to express the interplay of thinking and experience. If a man thought and expressed himself in either of these modes, one would not know, as Kierkegaard (1846) puts it, whether it was a human being who was speaking or an artificial product, 'a cunningly contrived walking stick in which a talking machine had been concealed' (p. 175). There is a clear parallel between these theories of thinking and the workings of present-day computers which are programmed to simulate human thinking. Their characteristic limitation, too, is that they have no means of interacting creatively with their environment, for this is already defined for them by the programmer and we do not yet know how to programme a machine so that it can enter and define problem-spaces for itself in the flexible and creative way in which humans do.

The capacity for defining problems, as well as solving them, must be encompassed by a psychology of creative thinking which is to avoid the paradox described first by Plato with respect to the acquisition of knowledge and later by Wittgenstein in relation to the problem of the acquisition of the meaning of words. The paradox states that we must be ignorant of a thing before we can be said to acquire knowledge of it, but, if we were ignorant of it, we would not be able to recognize it as that which we were seeking. Bearing in mind Polanyi's distinction between tacit and explicit knowledge, we are able to account for this paradox: the inquiring subject knows tacitly the meaning he seeks when he defines the problem but knows the meaning explicitly when the problem is solved. Psychological studies of creative thinking provide convincing support for the existence of these two types of attention. However, the very possibility of a transition from tacit to explicit knowledge presupposes that these forms of awareness are but different aspects of the same process. Consequently, it is maintained, following Husserl, that thinking and knowing must be interpreted in terms of the intentional nature of consciousness. Knowing is the fulfilment of an intention accompanied by an awareness of the identity of the fulfilment with the intention.

From the point of view of human existence, thinking cannot be described exclusively by a deductive model or as a series of responses to environmental stimuli (however stimulus and response are defined), because these orientations fail to make clear that it is the active, intentional subject who learns more about things through acts of personal involvement. Jaspers (1963), in defining phenomenology as a method, argued that the attempt to attend to phenomena without prior interpretation is an attitude of mind which we have to achieve again and again for it involves a continual onslaught on our prejudices. If existential phenomenology were to be similarly characterized, one would have to say that its purpose is to serve as a constant reminder of the adventure of existence, that ambiguous condition which succeeds in eluding the grasp of both formal necessity and empirical predictability.

References

ADAMSON, R. E. (1952) Functional fixedness as related to problem solving: a repetition of three experiments. *J. Exp. Psychol.*, **44**, 288-91.

ALLEN, M. A. (1962) A concept attainment program that simulates a simultaneous learning strategy. *Behav. Sci.*, **7**, 247-50.

ALLPORT, G. W. (1937) *Personality*. London: Constable.

AMPÈRE, A. (1834) *Essai sur la philosophie des Sciences*. Paris.

ANDRÉ, J. (1969) Reversal shift behaviour and verbalisation in two age groups of hearing and deaf children. *J. Exp. Child Psychol.*, **7**, 407-18.

ANSCHUTZ, R. P. (1949) The logic of J. S. Mill. *Mind*, **58**, 277-305.

ARISTOTLE (1952) *Complete Works of Aristotle*. London: Oxford Univ. Press.

ASHBY, W. R. (1952) *Design for a Brain*. London: Chapman & Hall.

AUSUBEL, D. P. (1968) Symbolization and symbolic thought: response to Furth. *Child Devel.*, **39**, 997-1001.

AVELING, F. (1912) *On the Consciousness of the Universal and the Individual*. London: Macmillan.

AYER, A. J. (1946) *Language, Truth and Logic*, 2nd ed. London: Gollancz.

BANDURA, A. and WALTERS, R. H. (1965) *Social Learning and Personality Development*. New York: Holt, Rinehart & Winston.

BARRON, F. (1953) *Creativity and Personal Freedom*. Princeton, N.J.: Van Nostrand.

BARRON, F. and WELSH, G. S. (1952) Artistic perception as a factor in personality style: its measurement by a figure preference test. *J. Psychol.*, **33**, 199-203.

BARTLETT, F. C. (1958) *Thinking: an Experimental and Social Study*. London: Allen & Unwin.

BEARD, R. M. (1961) A study of number concepts in the infants' school. *A.T.C.D.E. Maths Section*.

BEARD, R. M. (1963) The order of concept development studied in two fields. I. Number concepts in the infant school. *Educ. Rev.*, **15**, 105-17.

BEILIN, H. (1965) Learning and operational convergence in logical thought and development. *J. Exp. Child Psychol.*, **2**, 317-39.

BEILIN, H. (1968a) Cognitive capacities of young children: a replication. *Science*, **162**, 920-1.

BEILIN, H. (1968b) What children do in spite of what they know. *Science*, **162**, 924-5.

BEILIN, H. (1969) Stimulus and cognitive transformation in conservation. In ELKIND, D. and FLAVELL, J. H. (eds.) *Studies in Cognitive Development*. New York: Oxford Univ. Press. pp. 409-37.

BELL, S. M. (1970) The development of the concept of object as related to infant mother attachment. *Child Devel.*, **41**, 291-311.

BELLAK, L. (1958) Creativity: some random notes to a systematic consideration. *J. Proj. Techniq.*, **22**, 363-80.

BELOFF, J. R. (1962) *The Existence of Mind*. London: MacGibbon and Kee.

BERKELEY, G. (1708) *Treatise Concerning the Principles of Human Knowledge*. London: Nelson (1945).

BERKO, J. and BROWN, R. (1960) Psycholinguistic research methods. In MUSSEN, P. H. (ed.), *Handbook of Research Methods in Child Development*. New York: Wiley. pp. 517-57.

BERLYNE, D. E. (1970) Children's reasoning and thinking. In MUSSEN, P. H. (ed.), *Carmichael's Manual of Child Psychology*, Vol. I. New York: Wiley. pp. 939-81.

BERNSTEIN, B. (1961) Social structure, language, and learning. *Educ. Res.*, **3**, 163-76.

BERNSTEIN, B. (1964). Elaborated and restricted codes: their social origins and some consequences. *Amer. Anthrop.*, **66**, 55-69.

BETH, E. W. and PIAGET, J. (1966) *Mathematical Epistemology and Psychology*. Dordrecht: Reidel.

BEVER, T. G. (1970) The cognitive basis for linguistic structures. In HAYES, J. R. (ed.), *Cognition and the Development of Language*. New York: Wiley. pp. 279-362.

BEVER, T. G., MEHLER, J. and EPSTEIN, J. (1968) What children do in spite of what they know. *Science*, **162**, 921-4.

BIERI, J., BRADBURN, W. M. and GALINSKY, M. D. (1958) Sex differences in perceptual behaviour. *J. Pers.*, **26**, 1-12.

BIRCH, H. G. and RABINOWITZ, H. S. (1951) The negative effect of previous experience on productive thinking. *J. Exp. Psychol.*, **41**, 121-5.

BLACK, M. (1962) *The Importance of Language*. Englewood Cliffs, N. J.: Prentice-Hall.

BLANK, M. (1966) The effects of training and verbalization on reversal and extradimensional learning. *J. Exp. Child Psychol.*, 4, 50-7.

BLANK, M. (1967) Effect of stimulus characteristics on dimensional shifting in kindergarten children. *J. Comp. Physiol. Psychol.*, 64, 522-5.

BLANK, M. and KLIG, S. (1970) Dimensional learning across sensory modalities in nursery school children. *J. Exp. Child Psychol.*, 9, 166-73.

BLANK, M. and SOLOMON, F. (1969) How shall the disadvantaged child be taught? *Child Devel.*, 40, 47-61.

BLANSHARD, B. (1939) *The Nature of Thought* (2 Vols.). London: Allen & Unwin.

BLOOMBERG, M. (1967) An inquiry into the relationship between field-independence-dependence and creativity. *J. Psychol.*, 67, 127-40.

BLOOMBERG, M. (1971) Creativity as related to field-independence and motility. *J. Genet. Psychol.*, 118, 3-12.

BOERSMA, F. J. and O'BRIEN, K. (1968) An investigation of the relationship between creativity and intelligence under two conditions of testing. *J. Pers.*, 36, 341-8.

BOGARTZ, W. (1965) Effects of reversal and nonreversal shifts with CVC stimuli. *J. Verb. Learn. Verb. Behav.*, 4, 484-8.

BOOLE, G. (1854) *An Investigation of the Laws of Thought*. London: Macmillan.

BOURNE, L. E. (1966) *Human Conceptual Behaviour*. Boston: Allyn & Bacon.

BOURNE, L. E. (1970) Knowing and using concepts. *Psychol. Rev.*, 77, 546-56.

BOURNE, L. E. and BUNDERSON, C. U. (1963) Effects of delay of informative feedback and length of feedback interval on concept identification. *J. Exp. Psychol.*, 65, 1-5.

BOURNE, L. E. and RESTLE, F. (1959) Mathematical theory of concept identification. *Psychol. Rev.*, 66, 278-96.

BOWER, T. G. R. (1967) The development of object permanence: some studies of existence constancy. *Percep. and Psychophysics*, 2, 411-18.

BOWER, T. G. R. (1971) The object in the world of the infant. *Sci. Amer.*, 225, 4, 30-8.

BOWER, T. G. R. and TRABASSO, T. R. (1964) Concept identification. In ATKINSON, R. C. (ed.), *Studies in Mathematical Psychology*. Stanford: Stanford Univ. Press. pp. 32-95.

BOYLE, D. G. (1969) *A Student's Guide to Piaget*. London: Pergamon.

BRAINE, M. D. S. (1959) The ontogeny of certain logical operations: Piaget's formulation examined by non-verbal methods. *Psychol. Monogr.*, **73**, No. 5 (Whole No. 475).

BRAINE, M. D. S. (1964) Development of a grasp of transitivity of length. *Child Devel.*, **35**, 799-810.

BRAINE, M. D. S. and SHANKS, B. L. (1965) Development of conservation of size. *J. Verb. Learn. Verb. Behav.*, **4**, 227-42.

BRENTANO, F. (1874) *Psychologie vom Empirischen Standpunkt*. Leipzig: F. Meier (1924).

BRIDGMAN, P. W. (1927) *The Logic of Modern Physics*. New York: Macmillan (1960).

BROOKSHIRE, K. H., WARREN, J. M. and BALL, C. G. (1961) Reversal and transfer learning following overtraining in rat and chicken. *J. Comp. Physiol. Psychol.*, **54**, 98-102.

BROWN, A. L. (1970) Transfer performance in children's oddity learning as a function of dimensional preference, shift paradigm and overtraining. *J. Exp. Child Psychol.*, **9**, 307-19.

BROWN, R. (1965) *Social Psychology*. London: Crowell Collier and Macmillan.

BROWN, R. and LENNEBERG, E. H. (1954) A study in language and cognition. *J. Abnorm. Soc. Psychol.*, **49**, 454-62.

BRUNER, J. S. (1959) Inhelder and Piaget's *The Growth of Logical Thinking*. I – A psychologist's viewpoint. *Brit. J. Psychol.*, **50**, 363-71.

BRUNER, J. S., GOODNOW, J. L. and AUSTIN, G. A. (1956) *A Study of Thinking*. New York: Wiley.

BRUNER, J. S., OLVER, R. R. and GREENFIELD, P. M. (1966) *Studies in Cognitive Growth*. New York: Wiley.

BURT, C. (1940) *The Factors of the Mind*. London: Univ. London Press.

BUSH, M. (1969) Psychoanalysis and scientific creativity: with special reference to regression in the service of the ego. *J. Amer. Psychoanal. Assoc.*, **17**, 136-90.

BUSS, A. H. (1953) Rigidity as a function of reversal and non-reversal shifts in the learning of successive discriminations. *J. Exp. Psychol.*, **45**, 75-81.

BUTCHER, H. J. (1968) *Human Intelligence. Its Nature and Assessment*. London: Methuen.

CAMPBELL, D. T. (1960) Blind variation and selective retention in creative thought as in other knowledge processes. *Psychol. Rev.*, **67**, 380-400.

CANNON, W. B. (1932) *The Wisdom of the Body*. New York: Norton.

CARON, A. J. (1968) Conceptual transfer in preverbal children as a consequence of dimensional training. *J. Exp. Child Psychol.*, **6**, 522-42.

CASE, D. and COLLINSON, J. M. (1962) The development of formal thinking and verbal comprehension. *Brit. J. Ed. Psychol.*, **32**, 103-12.

CASSIRER, E. (1945) *An Essay on Man*. New Haven: Yale Univ. Press.

CASSIRER, E. (1950) *The Problem of Knowledge*. New Haven: Yale Univ. Press.

CASSIRER, E. (1953a) *Substance and Function and Einstein's Theory of Relativity*. London: Constable. (Originally published by Open Court: Chicago, 1923.)

CASSIRER, E. (1953b) *The Philosophy of Symbolic Forms. Vol. 3. Phenomenology of Knowledge*. New Haven: Yale Univ. Press.

CATTELL, R. B. and BUTCHER, H. J. (1968) *The Prediction of Achievement and Creativity*. New York: Bobbs-Merrill.

CHAPMAN, L. J. and CHAPMAN, J. D. (1959) Atmosphere effect re-examined. *J. Exp. Psychol.*, **58**, 220-6.

CHARLESWORTH, W. R. (1966) Development of the object concept in infancy: a methodological study. *Amer. Psychologist*, **21**, 623 (Abstract).

CHOMSKY, N. (1965) *Aspects of the Theory of Syntax*. Cambridge: M.I.T. Press.

CHOMSKY, N. (1968) *Language and Mind*. New York: Harcourt, Brace.

CLARK, H. H. (1969) Linguistic processes in deductive reasoning. *Psychol. Rev.*, **76**, 387-404.

COBB, N. J. (1965) *Reversal and nonreversal shift learning in children as a function of two types of pretraining*. Unpub. Ph.D. thesis, Univ. of Massachusetts.

COFER, C. N. (1957) Reasoning as associative process. 3 – The role of verbal responses in problem-solving. *J. Gen. Psychol.*, **57**, 55-68.

COHEN, G. M. (1967) Conservation of quantity in children: the effect of vocabulary and participation. *Quart. J. Exp. Psychol.*, **19**, 150-4.

COHEN, J. (1954) Thought and language. *Acta Psychol.*, **10**, 111-24.

COHEN, M. R. and NAGEL, E. (1934) *An Introduction to Logic and Scientific Method*. New York: Harcourt, Brace.

COLBY, M. G. and ROBERTSON, J. B. (1942) Genetic studies in abstraction. *J. Comp. Psychol.*, **33**, 385-401.

COLE, M., GAY, J. and GLICK, J. (1968) Reversal and nonreversal shifts among Liberian tribal people. *J. Exp. Psychol.*, **76**, 323-4.

COWAN, J. L. (1970) (ed.) *Studies in Thought and Language*. Tucson, Arizona: Univ. Arizona Press.

CRAIK, K. J. W. (1943) *The Nature of Explanation*. London: Cambridge Univ. Press.

CROMER, R. F. (1968) *The development of temporal reference during the acquisition of language*. Unpub. Ph.D. thesis. Harvard Univ.

CROPLEY, A. J. (1967) *Creativity*. London: Longmans.

CROPLEY, A. J. (1968) A note on the Wallach-Kogan test of creativity. *Brit. J. Psychol.*, **38**, 197-201.

CROPLEY, A. J. and MASLANY, G. W. (1969) Reliability and factorial validity of the Wallach-Kogan creativity tests. *Brit. J. Psychol.*, **60**, 395-8.

DACEY, J., MADAUS, G. and ALLEN, A. (1969) The relationship of creativity and intelligence in Irish adolescents. *Brit. J. Ed. Psychol.*, **39**, 261-6.

DÉCARIE, T. G. (1965) *Intelligence and Affectivity in Early Childhood*. New York: Int. Univ. Press.

DE GROOT, A. D. (1965) *Thought and Choice in Chess*. The Hague: Mouton.

DESIDERATO, O. and SIGAL, S. (1970) Associative productivity as a function of creativity level and type of verbal stimulus. *Psychonom. Science*, **18**, 357-8.

DE SOTO, C., LONDON, M. and HANDEL, S. (1965) Social reasoning and spatial paralogic. *J. Pers. Soc. Psychol.*, **2**, 513-21.

DEWEY, J. (1896) The reflex arc concept in psychology. *Psychol. Rev.*, **3**, 357-70.

DEWEY, J. (1910) *How We Think*. London: D. C. Heath & Co.

DEWEY, J. (1921) *Reconstruction in Philosophy*. London: Univ. of London Press.

DEWEY, J. (1930) *The Quest for Certainty*. London: Allen & Unwin.

DEWEY, J. (1938) *Logic: The Theory of Inquiry*. New York: Holt.

DICKERSON, D. J. (1966) Performance of preschool children on three discrimination shifts. *Psychon. Sci.*, **4**, 417-18.

DICKERSON, D. J. (1967) Irrelevant stimulus dimensions and dimensional transfer in the discrimination learning of children. *J. Exp. Child Psychol.*, **5**, 228-36.

DIEBOLD, A. R. (1965) A survey of psycholinguistic research, 1954-1964. In OSGOOD, C. E. and SEBEOK, T. A. (eds.) *Psycholinguistics: a Survey of Theory and Research Problems*. Bloomington: Univ. Indiana Press.

DODWELL, P. C. (1960) Children's understanding of number and related concepts. *Canad. J. Psychol.*, **14**, 191-205.

DODWELL, P. C. (1961) Children's understanding of number concepts: characteristics of an individual and a group test. *Canad. J. Psychol.*, **15**, 29-36.

DODWELL, P. C. (1962) Relationship between the understanding of the logic of classes and of cardinal number in children. *Canad. J. Psychol.*, **16**, 152-60.

DONALDSON, M. (1959) Positive and negative information in matching problems. *Brit. J. Psychol.*, **50**, 235-62.

DONALDSON, M. and WALES, R. J. (1970) On the acquisition of some relational terms. In HAYES, J. R. (ed.), *Cognition and the Development of Language*. New York: Wiley. pp. 235-68.

DOUGLAS, J. W. B. (1964) *The Home and the School*. London: MacGibbon & Kee.

DREISTADT, R. (1969) The use of analogies and incubation in obtaining insights in creative problem solving. *J. Psychol.*, **71**, 159-75.

DUNCKER, K. (1945) On problem solving. *Psychol. Monogr.*, **58**, No. 270.

DUVALL, A. N. (1965) Functional fixedness: a replication study. *Psychol. Rec.*, **15**, 497-9.

EDWARDS, M. P. and TYLER, L. E. (1965) Intelligence, creativity, and achievement in a nonselective public junior high school. *J. Educ. Psychol.*, **56**, 96-9.

EHRENZWEIG, A. (1967) *The Hidden Order of Art: a Study in the Psychology of Artistic Imagination*. Berkeley, Calif.: Univ. Calif. Press.

EIFERMAN, R. R. (1961) Negation: a linguistic variable. *Acta Psychol.*, **18**, 258-73.

EIMAS, P. D. (1965) Comment: comparisons of reversal and nonreversal shifts. *Psychon. Sci.*, **3**, 445-6.

EIMAS, P. D. (1966) Effects of overtraining and age on intradimensional and extradimensional shifts in children. *J. Exp. Child Psychol.*, **3**, 348-55.

EIMAS, P. D. (1967) Optional shift behaviour in children as a function of overtraining, irrelevant stimuli, and age. *J. Exp. Child Psychol.*, **5**, 332-40.

EIMAS, P. D. (1969) Observing responses, attention, and the overtraining reversal effect. *J. Exp. Psychol.*, **82**, 499-502.

EISENMAN, R. (1969) Creativity, awareness and liking. *J. Cons. Clin. Psychol.*, **33**, 157-60.

I

EISENMAN, R. and CHERRY, H. O. (1970) Creativity, authoritarianism and birth order. *J. Soc. Psychol.*, **80**, 233-5.

EISENMAN, R. and SCHUSSEL, N. R. (1970) Creativity, birth order, and preference for symmetry. *J. Cons. Clin. Psychol.*, **34**, 275-80.

ELKIND, D. (1961a) The development of quantitative thinking: a systematic replication of Piaget's studies. *J. Genet. Psychol.*, **98**, 37-46.

ELKIND, D. (1961b) Children's discovery of the conservation of mass, weight and volume: Piaget replication study 2. *J. Genet. Psychol.*, **98**, 219-27.

ELKIND, D. (1961c) The development of the additive composition of classes in the child: Piaget replication study 3. *J. Genet. Psychol.*, **99**, 51-7.

ELKIND, D. (1961d) Children's conceptions of right and left: Piaget replication study 4. *J. Genet. Psychol.*, **99**, 269-76.

ELKIND, D. (1962) Children's conceptions of brother and sister: Piaget replication study 5. *J. Genet. Psychol.*, **100**, 129-36.

ELKIND, D. (1967a) Piaget's conservation problems. *Child Devel.*, **38**, 15-27.

ELKIND, D. (1967b) Egocentrism in adolescence. *Child Devel.*, **38**, 1025-34.

EYSENCK, H. J. (1967) Intelligence assessment: a theoretical and experimental approach. *Brit. J. Ed. Psychol.*, **37**, 81-98.

FARBER, M. (1943) *The Foundation of Phenomenology.* Cambridge, Mass: Harvard Univ. Press.

FEE, F. (1968) An alternative to Ward's factor analysis of Wallach and Kogan's 'creativity' correlations. *Brit. J. Ed. Psychol.*, **38**, 319-21.

FEIGENBAUM, K. (1963) Task complexity and I.Q. as variables in Piaget's problem of conservation. *Child Devel.*, **34**, 423-32.

FEIGENBAUM, K. and SULKIN, H. (1964) Piaget's problem of conservation of discontinuous quantities: a teaching experience. *J. Genet. Psychol.*, **105**, 91-7.

FIELDS, P. E. (1932) Studies in concept formation, 1. *Comp. Psychol. Monogr.*, **9**, No. 2.

FISHER, S. C. (1916) The process of generalizing abstraction and its product, the general concept. *Psychol. Monogr.*, **21**, No. 2 (Whole No. 90).

FLAVELL, J. H. (1963) *The Developmental Psychology of Jean Piaget.* Princeton, N. J.: Van Nostrand.

FLAVELL, J. H. (1968) *The Development of Role-taking and Communication Skills in Children.* New York: Wiley.

FLAVELL, J. H. and WOHLWILL, J. F. (1969) Formal and functional aspects of cognitive development. In ELKIND, D. and FLAVELL, J. H. (eds.) *Studies in Cognitive Development*. New York: Oxford Univ. Press. pp. 67-120.

FLAVELL, J. H., BEACH, D. H. and CHINSKY, J. M. (1965) Spontaneous verbal rehearsal in a memory task as a function of age. *Child Devel.*, **37**, 283-99.

FLAVELL, J. H., COOPER, A. and LOISELLE, R. H. (1958) Effect of the number of pre-utilization functions on functional fixedness in problem solving. *Psychol. Rep.*, **4**, 343-50.

FOWLER, W. (1962) Cognitive learning in infancy and early childhood. *Psychol. Bull.*, **59**, 116-52.

FREEDMAN, J. L. (1965) Increasing creativity by free-association training. *J. Exp. Psychol.*, **69**, 89-91.

FREGE, G. (1884) *Die Grundlagen der Arithmetik*. Breslau: W. Koebner.

FREIBERGS, V. and TULVING, E. (1961) The effect of practice on utilization of information from positive and negative instances in concept identification. *Can. J. Psychol.*, **15**, 101-6.

FREUD, S. (1900) *The Interpretation of Dreams*. Standard Edition of the Complete Works. Vols. 4 and 5. London: Hogarth.

FREUD, S. (1905) *Wit and its Relation to the Unconscious*. Standard Edition of the Complete Works. Vol. 8. London: Hogarth.

FREUD, S. (1910) Leonardo da Vinci and a memory of his childhood. In Vol. 11. The Standard Edition of the Complete Works. London: Hogarth.

FREUD, S. (1915) The unconscious. In Vol. 14 of the Standard Edition of the Complete Works. London: Hogarth.

FREUD, S. (1929) *Introductory Lectures on Psycho-analysis*. London: Allen & Unwin.

FREYBERG, P. S. (1966) Stages in cognitive development – general or specific? *New Zeal. J. Ed. Studies*, **1**, 64-77.

FRIJDA, N. H. (1967) Problems of computer simulation. *Behav. Sci.*, **12**, 59-67.

FRITZ, B. and BLANK, M. (1968) Role of the irrelevant cue in rapid reversal learning in nursery school children. *J. Comp. Physiol. Psychol.*, **65**, 375-8.

FULGOSI, A. and GUILFORD, J. P. (1968) Short-term incubation in divergent production. *Amer. J. Psychol.*, **81**, 241-6.

FURTH, H. G. (1964) Research with the deaf: implications for language and cognition. *Psychol. Bull.*, **62**, 145-64.

FURTH, H. G. (1966) *Thinking without Language: the Psychological Implications of Deafness.* New York: Free Press.

FURTH, H. G. (1968) Piaget's theory of knowledge: the nature of representation and interiorization. *Psychol. Rev.,* **75**, 143-54.

FURTH, H. G. (1969) *Piaget and Knowledge.* Englewood Cliffs, N.J.: Prentice-Hall.

FURTH, H. G. (1971) Linguistic deficiency and thinking: research with deaf subjects 1964-1969. *Psychol. Bull.,* **76**, 58-72.

FURTH, H. G. and YOUNISS, J. (1964) Effect of overtraining of three discrimination shifts in children. *J. Comp. Physiol. Psychol.,* **57**, 290-3.

GAGNÉ, R. M. (1966) The learning of principles. In KLAUSMEIER, H. J. and HARRIS, C. W. (eds.) *Analyses of Concept Learning.* New York: Academic Press. pp. 81-95.

GALANTER, E. and GESTENHABER, M. (1956) On thought: the extrinsic theory. *Psychol. Rev.,* **63**, 218-27.

GAMBLE, K. R. and KELLNER, H. (1968) Creative functioning and cognitive regression. *J. Pers. Soc. Psychol.,* **9**, 266-71.

GARDNER, R. W. (1961) Cognitive controls of attention deployment as determinants of visual illusions. *J. Abnorm. Soc. Psychol.,* **62**, 120-7.

GARDNER, R. W. and LONG, R. (1962a) Control, defence, and centration effect: a study of scanning behaviour. *Brit. J. Psychol.,* **53**, 129-40.

GARDNER, R. W. and LONG, R. (1962b) Cognitive controls of attention and inhibition: a study of individual consistencies. *Brit. J. Psychol.,* **53**, 381-8.

GARDNER, R. W. *et al.* (1959) *Cognitive Control.* Psychol. Issues, Vol. 4. New York: Int. Univ. Press.

GEACH, P. T. (1957) *Mental Acts.* London: Routledge & Kegan Paul.

GELMAN, R. (1969) Conservation acquisition: a problem of learning to attend to relevant attributes. *J. Exp. Child Psychol.,* **7**, 167-87.

GETZELS, J. W. and JACKSON, P. W. (1962) *Creativity and Intelligence: Explorations with Gifted Students.* New York: Wiley.

GHISELIN, B. (1952) *The Creative Process: a Symposium.* Calif: Univ. Calif. Press.

GIBSON, E. J. (1960) *Association and differentiation in perceptual learning.* Paper read at the International Congress of Psychology, Bonn.

GIBSON, J. J. (1968) *The Senses Considered as Perceptual Systems.* London: Allen & Unwin.

GIBSON, J. J. and GIBSON, E. J. (1955a) Perceptual learning – differentiation or enrichment? *Psychol. Rev.,* **62**, 32-41.

GIBSON, J. J. and GIBSON, E. J. (1955b) What is learned in perceptual learning? A reply to Professor Postman. *Psychol. Rev.,* **62**, 447-50.

GILL, M. M. (1963) *Topography and Systems in Psychoanalytic Theory*. Psychol. Issues, Vol. 10. New York: Int. Univ. Press.

GILL, M. M. (1967) The Primary Process. In HOLT, R. R. *Psychological Issues: Motives and Thought*. New York: Int. Univ. Press. pp. 260-98.

GINSBURG, G. P. and WHITTEMORE, R. G. (1968) Creativity and verbal ability: a direct examination of their relationship. *Brit. J. Psychol.*, **38**, 133-9.

GOLDSCHMID, M. L. and BENTLER, P. M. (1968) The dimensions and measurement of conservation. *Child Devel.*, **39**, 787-802.

GOLDSTEIN, K. (1948) *Language and Language Disturbances*. New York: Grune & Stratton.

GOODNOW, J. J. (1969a) Cultural variations in cognitive skills. In PRICE-WILLIAMS, D. R. (ed.) *Cross-cultural Studies*. Harmondsworth: Penguin. pp. 246-64.

GOODNOW, J. J. (1969b) Problems in research on culture and thought. In ELKIND, D. and FLAVELL, J. H. (eds.) *Studies in Cognitive Development*. New York: Oxford Univ. Press. pp. 439-62.

GOODNOW, J. J. and BETHON, G. (1966) Piaget's tasks: the effects of schooling and intelligence. *Child Devel.*, **37**, 573-82.

GOUGH, H. C. (1961) Techniques for identifying the creative research scientist. In MACKINNON, D. W. (ed.) *The Creative Person*. Berkeley: Univ. Calif. Press. Ch. 3.

GRAY, J. J. (1969) The effect of productivity on primary process and creativity. *J. Proj. Tech. Pers. Ass.*, **33**, 213-18.

GREEN, B. F. (1956) A method of scalogram analysis using summary statistics. *Psychometrika*, **21**, 79-88.

GREGG, L. W. and SIMON, H. A. (1967) Process models and stochastic theories of simple concept formation. *J. Math. Psychol.*, **4**, 246-76.

GREGORY, R. L. (1971) The social implications of intelligent machines. In MELTZER, B. and MICHIE, D. (eds.) *Machine Intelligence 6*. Edinburgh: Edinburgh Univ. Press. pp. 3-13.

GRIFFITHS, J. A., SCHANTZ, C. A. and SIGEL, I. E. (1967) A methodological problem in conservation studies: the use of relational terms. *Child Devel.*, **38**, 841-8.

GRUEN, G. E. (1965) Experiences affecting the development of number conservation in children. *Child Devel.*, **36**, 963-79.

GRÜNBAUM, A. A. (1908) Über die Abstraktion der Gleichheit. Ein Beitrag zur Psychologie der Relation. *Arch. F.d.ges. Psychol.*, **12**, 340-478.

GUILFORD, J. P. (1966) Intelligence: 1965 Model. *Amer. Psychol.*, **21**, 20-6.

GUILFORD, J. P. (1967) *The Nature of Human Intelligence*. New York: McGraw-Hill.

GUILFORD, J. P., WILSON, R. C., CHRISTENSEN, P. R. and LEWIS, D. J. (1951) A factor analytic study of creative thinking: 1. Hypotheses and description of tests. *Rep. Psychol. Lab., No. 3*. Los Angeles: Univ. South Calif.

GUILFORD, J. P., WILSON, R. C. and CHRISTENSEN, P. R. (1952) A factor analytic study of creative thinking: 2. Administration of tests and analysis of results. *Rep. Psychol. Lab. No. 8*. Los Angeles: Univ. South Calif.

GUTTMAN, L. (1944) A basis for scaling quantitative data. *Amer. Soc. Rev.*, **9**, 139-50.

GUTTMAN, L. (1950) Relation of scalogram analysis to other techniques. In STOUFFER, S. A. *et al. Measurement and Prediction. Studies in Soc. Psych. in World War 2, Vol. 9*. pp. 172-212.

GUY, D. E. (1969) Developmental study of performance on conceptual problems involving a rule shift. *J. Exp. Psychol.*, **82**, 242-9.

HALFORD, G. S. (1968) An experimental test of Piaget's notions concerning the conservation of quantity in children. *J. Exp. Child Psychol.*, **6**, 33-43.

HANDEL, S., DE SOTO, C. and LONDON, M. (1968) Reasoning and spatial representation. *J. Verb. Learn. Verb. Behav.*, **7**, 351-7.

HARDING, R. (1940) *An Anatomy of Inspiration*. London: Cass.

HARGREAVES, D. J. and BOLTON, N. (1972) Selecting creativity tests for use in research. *Brit. J. Psychol.* (in press).

HARMS, E. (1960) *Fundamentals of Psychology: The Psychology of Thinking*. Annals of the New York Academy of Science. Vol. 91, 1-158.

HARONIAN, F. and SUGERMAN, A. A. (1967) Fixed and mobile field independence: review of studies relevant to Werner's dimension. *Psychol. Rep.*, **21**, 41-57.

HARTLEY, D. (1749) *Observations on Man, His Frame, His Duty and His Expectations*. Extract in DENNIS, W. *Readings in the History of Psychology*. New York: Appleton-Century-Crofts. pp. 81-92.

HASAN, P. and BUTCHER, H. J. (1966) Creativity and intelligence: a partial replication with Scottish children of Getzels and Jackson's study. *Brit. J. Psychol.*, **57**, 129-35.

HEAL, L. W., BRANSKY, M. L. and MANKINEN, R. L. (1966) The role of dimension preference in reversal and nonreversal shifts of retardates. *Psychon. Sci.*, **6**, 509-10.

HEBB, D. O. (1949) *The Organization of Behaviour*. New York: Wiley.

HEIDBREDER, E. (1946) The attainment of concepts. I. Terminology and methodology. *J. Gen. Psychol.*, **35**, 173-89.

HELSON, H. (1926) The psychology of Gestalt. *Amer. J. Psychol.*, **37**, 25-62.

HENLE, M. (1962) On the relation between logic and thinking. *Psychol. Rev.*, **69**, 366-78.

HENLE, M. and MICHAEL, M. (1956) The influence of attitudes on syllogistic reasoning. *J. Soc. Psychol.*, **44**, 115-27.

HERTZIG, M. E., BIRCH, H. G., THOMAS, A. and MENDEZ, O. (1968) Class and ethnic differences in the responsiveness of pre-school children to cognitive demands. *Monogr. Soc. Res. Child Devel.*, **33**, 1-69.

HESS, R. D. and SHIPMAN, V. C. (1965) Early experience and the socialization of cognitive modes in children. *Child Devel.*, **36**, 869-86.

HIGGINS, J. and DOLBY, L. L. (1967) Creativity and mediated association: a construct validation study of the RAT. *Educ. Psychol. Meas.*, **27**, 1011-14.

HILGARD, E. R. (1962) Impulsive versus realistic thinking: an examination of the distinction between primary and secondary process in thought. *Psychol. Bull.*, **59**, 477-88.

HILGARD, E. R. and BOWER, G. (1966) *Theories of Learning.* 3rd edn. New York: Appleton-Century-Crofts.

HOOD, H. B. (1962) An experimental study of Piaget's theory of the development of number in children. *Brit. J. Psychol.*, **53**, 273-86.

HOUSE, B. J. and ZEAMAN, D. (1962) Reversal and nonreversal shifts in discrimination learning in retardates. *J. Exp. Psychol.*, **63**, 444-51.

HOUSE, B. J. and ZEAMAN, D. (1963) Miniature experiments in the discrimination learning of retardates. In LIPSITT, L. P. and SPIKER, C. C. (eds.) *Advances in Child Development and Behaviour, Vol. I.* New York: Academic Press. pp. 313-74.

HOUSTON, S. (1970) The re-examination of some assumptions about the language of the disadvantaged child. *Child Devel.*, **41**, 947-63.

HUDSON, L. (1966) *Contrary Imaginations.* London: Methuen.

HUDSON, L. (1968) *Frames of Mind.* London: Methuen.

HULL, C. L. (1920) Quantitative aspects of the evolution of concepts. *Psychol. Monogr.*, **28**, No. 1 (Whole No. 123).

HUME, D. (1739) *A Treatise of Human Nature.* London: Oxford Univ. Press (1888).

HUMPHREY, G. (1963) *Thinking: an Introduction to its Experimental Psychology.* New York: Wiley.

HUNT, E. B. (1962) *Concept Learning: An Information Processing Problem.* New York: Wiley.

HUNT, E. B. (1968) Computer simulation: artificial intelligence studies and their relevance to psychology. *Ann. Rev. Psychol.*, **19**, 135-68.

HUNT, E. B. (1971) What kind of computer is man? *Cognitive Psychol.*, **2**, 57-98.

HUNT, E. B., MARIN, J. and STONE, P. J. (1966) *Experiments in Induction.* New York: Academic Press.

HUNT, J. MCV. (1961) *Intelligence and Experience.* New York: Ronald Press.

HUNTER, I. M. L. (1957) The solving of three-term series problems. *Brit. J. Psychol.*, **48**, 286-98.

HUSSERL, E. (1900) *Logische Untersuchungen. Vol. 1.* Halle: Niemeyer.

HUSSERL, E. (1901) *Logische Untersuchungen. Vol. 2.* Halle: Niemeyer.

HUSSERL, E. (1911) *Philosophy as Rigorous Science.* Logos, 1 (1910-11), 289-341. (New York: Harper Torchbooks, 1965).

HUSSERL, E. (1929) *Formal and Transcendental Logic.* The Hague: M. Nijhoff (1969).

HUSSERL, E. (1954) *Philosophy and the Crisis of European Man.* The Hague: M. Nijhoff. (Eng. transl. New York: Harper Torchbooks, 1965.)

HUSSERL, E. (1960) *Cartesian Meditations.* The Hague: M. Nijhoff.

HUTTENLOCHER, J. (1968) Constructing spatial images: a strategy in reasoning. *Psychol. Rev.*, **75**, 550-60.

HYDE, D. M. (1959) *An investigation of Piaget's theories of the development of the concept of number.* Unpub. Ph.D. thesis, Univ. Lond.

INHELDER, B. and PIAGET, J. (1958) *The Growth of Logical Thinking from Childhood to Adolescence.* London: Routledge & Kegan Paul.

INHELDER, B., BOVET, M., SINCLAIR, H. and SMOCK, C. D. (1966) On cognitive development. *Amer. Psychol.*, **21**, 160-4.

ISAACS, S. (1930) *Intellectual Growth in Young Children.* London: Routledge & Kegan Paul.

JACOBSON, L. I. et al. (1968) Role of creativity and intelligence in conceptualization. *J. Pers. Soc. Psychol.*, **10**, 431-6.

JAMES, W. (1890) *Principles of Psychology. Vols. 1 and 2.* London: Macmillan (1901).

JANIS, I. L. and FRICK, F. (1943) The relationship between attitudes towards conclusions and errors in judging logical validity of syllogisms. *J. Exp. Psychol.*, **33**, 73-7.

JASPERS, K. (1963) *General Psychopathology.* 7th edn. Manchester: Manchester Univ. Press.

JEFFREY, W. E. (1965) Variables affecting reversal shifts in young children. *Amer. J. Psychol.*, **78**, 589-95.

JEFFREY, W. E. (1968) The orienting reflex and attention in cognitive development. *Psychol. Rev.*, **75**, 323-34.

JENKINS, H. M. and WARD, W. C. (1965) Judgment of contingency between responses and outcomes. *Psychol. Monogr.*, **79** (1).

JENKINS, J. J. (1966) Meaningfulness and concepts: concepts and meaningfulness. In KLAUSMEIER, H. J. and HARRIS, C. W. (eds.) *Analyses of Concept Learning.* New York: Academic Press. pp. 65-79.

JOHNSON, E. C. and JOSEY, C. C. (1931) A note on the development of the thought forms of children as described by Piaget. *J. Abnorm. Soc. Psychol.*, **26**, 338-9.

JOHNSON, P. J. and WHITE, R. M. (1967) Concept of dimensionality and reversal shift performance in children. *J. Exp. Child Psychol.*, **5**, 223-7.

JOHNSON-LAIRD, P. N. and TAGART, J. (1969) How implication is understood. *Amer. J. Psychol.*, **82**, 367-73.

JOHNSON-LAIRD, P. N. and WASON, P. C. (1970) A theoretical analysis of insight into a reasoning task. *Cognitive Psychol.*, **1**, 134-48.

JONES, E. (1957) *The Life and Work of Sigmund Freud. 3 Vols.* London: Hogarth.

JONES, S. (1970) Visual and verbal processes in problem-solving. *Cognitive Psychol.*, **1**, 201-14.

KATZ, J. J. (1966) *The Philosophy of Language.* New York: Harper & Row.

KELLEHER, R. I. (1956) Discrimination learning as a function of reversal and nonreversal shifts. *J. Exp. Psychol.*, **51**, 379-84.

KENDLER, H. H. (1964) The concept of the concept. In MELTON, A. W. (ed.) *Categories of Human Learning.* New York: Academic Press. pp. 213-36.

KENDLER, H. H. and KENDLER, T. S. (1961) Effect of verbalization on reversal shifts in children. *Science*, **134**, 1619-20.

KENDLER, H. H. and KENDLER, T. S. (1962) Vertical and horizontal processes in problem solving. *Psychol. Rev.*, **69**, 1-16.

KENDLER, H. H. and KENDLER, T. S. (1966). Selective attention versus mediation: some comments on Mackintosh's analysis of two-stage models of discrimination learning. *Psychol. Bull.*, **66**, 282-8.

KENDLER, H. H., KENDLER, T. S. and LEARNARD, B. (1962) Mediated responses to size and brightness as a function of age. *Amer. J. Psychol.*, **75**, 571-86.

KENDLER, H. H., KENDLER, T. S. and SANDERS, J. (1967) Reversal and partial reversal shifts with verbal materials. *J. Verb. Learn. Verb. Behav.*, **6**, 117-27.

KENDLER, T. S. (1961) Concept formation. *Ann. Rev. Psychol.*, 447-72.

KENDLER, T. S. (1964) Verbalization and optional reversal shifts among kindergarten children. *J. Verb. Learn. Verb. Behav.*, **3**, 428-36.

KENDLER, T. S. and KENDLER, H. H. (1966). Optional shifts of children as a function of number of training trials on the initial discrimination. *J. Exp. Child Psychol.*, **3**, 216-24.

KENDLER, T. S. and KENDLER, H. H. (1970) An ontogeny of optional shift behaviour. *Child Devel.*, **41**, 1-27.

KENDLER, T. S., KENDLER, H. H. and WELLS, D. (1960) Reversal and nonreversal shifts in nursery school children. *J. Comp. Physiol. Psychol.*, **53**, 83-7.

KIERKEGAARD, S. (1846) *Concluding Unscientific Postscript*. London: Oxford Univ. Press (1941).

KLEIN, C. M. (1968) Creativity and incidental learning as functions of cognitive control of attention deployment. *Dissert. Abstr.*, **28**, (11-13), 4747-8.

KNELLER, G. F. (1965) *The Art and Science of Creativity*. New York: Holt, Rinehart & Winston.

KOFFKA, K. (1928) *The Growth of the Mind*. New York: Harcourt, Brace.

KOFFKA, K. (1935). *Principles of Gestalt Psychology*. New York: Harcourt, Brace.

KOFSKY, E. A. (1966) A scalogram study of classificatory development. *Child Devel.*, **37**, 191-204.

KOGAN, N. (1971) A clarification of Cropley and Maslany's analysis of the Wallach-Kogan creativity tests. *Brit. J. Psychol.*, **62**, 113-17.

KOGAN, N. and MORGAN, F. T. (1969) Task and motivational influences on the assessment of creative and intellective ability in children. *Genet. Psychol. Monogr.*, **80**, 91-127.

KÖHLER, W. (1925) *The Mentality of Apes*. Harmondsworth: Pelican (1957).

KÖHLER, W. (1930) *Gestalt Psychology*. London: Bell & Sons.

KÖHLER, W. (1940) *Dynamics in Psychology*. New York: Liveright.

KRIS, E. (1953) *Psycho-analytic Explorations in Art*. London: Allen & Unwin.

KUHN, T. (1970) *The Structure of Scientific Revolutions*. 2nd edn. Chicago: Univ. Chicago Press.

LACHMAN, R. and SANDERS, J. A. (1963) Concept shifts and verbal behaviour. *J. Exp. Psychol.*, **65**, 22-9.

LACKOWSKI, P. (1968) Review of Katz: *The Philosophy of Language*. *Language*, **44**, 606-16.

LANGAN, T. (1966) *Merleau-Ponty's Critique of Reason*. New Haven: Yale Univ. Press.

LANTZ, D. (1963) *Colour naming and colour recognition: a study in the psychology of language.* Unpub. Ph.D. thesis. Harvard Univ.

LAUGHLIN, P. R. (1967) Incidental concept formation as a function of creativity and intelligence. *J. Pers. Soc. Psychol.,* **5,** 115-19.

LAUGHLIN, P. R., DOHERTY, M. A. and DUNN, R. F. (1968) Intentional and incidental concept formation as a function of motivation, creativity, intelligence, and sex. *J. Pers. Soc. Psychol.,* **8,** 401-9.

LAURENDEAU, M. and PINARD, A. (1962) *Causal Thinking in the Child.* New York: Int. Univ. Press.

LAZARUS, R. S. and MCCLEARY, R. A. (1949) Autonomic discrimination without awareness: an interim report. *J. Pers.,* **18,** 171-9.

LAZARUS, R. S. and MCCLEARY, R. A. (1951) Autonomic discrimination without awareness: a study of subception. *Psychol. Rev.,* **58,** 113-22.

LEFFORD, A. (1946) The influence of emotional subject-matter on logical reasoning. *J. Gen. Psychol.,* **34,** 127-51.

LEFRANÇOIS, G. (1968) A treatment hierarchy for the acceleration of conservation of substance. *Canad. J. Psychol.,* **22,** 277-84.

LENNEBERG, E. H. (1961) Colour naming, colour recognition, colour discrimination: a reappraisal. *Percept. Mot. Skills,* **2,** 375-82.

LEONTIEV, A. A. (1971) Social and natural in semiotics. In MORTON, J. (ed.) *Biological and Social Factors in Psycholinguistics.* London: Logos Press. pp. 122-30.

LICHTENWALNER, J. S. and MAXWELL, J. W. (1969) The relationship of birth order and socioeconomic status to the creativity of pre-school children. *Child Devel.,* **40,** 1241-7.

LOCKE, J. (1690) *Essay on the Human Understanding.* Abridged edition. Oxford: Clarendon Press (1924).

LODWICK, A. R. (1959) Logical judgments. In PEEL, E. A. Experimental examination of some of Piaget's schemata concerning children's perception and thinking and a discussion of their educational significance. *Brit. J. Ed. Psychol.,* **29,** 89-103.

LONG, L. (1940) Conceptual relationships in children: the concept of roundness. *J. Genet. Psychol.,* **57,** 289-315.

LOVELL, K. (1959a) Jean Piaget's views on conservation of quantity. *Indian Psychol. Bull.,* **4,** 16-19.

LOVELL, K. (1959b) A follow-up study of some aspects of the work of Piaget and Inhelder on the child's conception of space. *Brit. J. Ed. Psychol.,* **29,** 104-17.

LOVELL, K. (1961) A follow-up study of Inhelder and Piaget's *The Growth of Logical Thinking. Brit. J. Psychol.,* **52,** 143-53.

LOVELL, K. and OGILVIE, E. (1960) A study of the conservation of substance in the junior school child. *Brit. J. Ed. Psychol.*, **30**, 109-18.

LOVELL, K. and OGILVIE, E. (1961a) A study of the conservation of weight in the junior school child. *Brit. J. Ed. Psychol.*, **31**, 138-44.

LOVELL, K. and OGILVIE, E. (1961b) The growth of the concept of volume in junior school children. *J. Child Psychol. Psychiat.*, **2**, 118-26.

LOVELL, K. and SLATER, A. (1960) The growth of the concept of time: a comparative study. *J. Child Psychol. Psychiat.*, **1**, 179-90.

LOVELL, K., HEALEY, D. and ROWLAND, A. D. (1962) Growth of some geometrical concepts. *Child Devel.*, **33**, 751-67.

LOVELL, K., KELLETT, V. L. and MOORHOUSE, E. (1962) The growth of the concept of speed: a comparative study. *J. Child Psychol. Psychiat.*, **3**, 101-10.

LOVELL, K., MITCHELL, B. and EVERETT, I. R. (1962) An experimental study of the growth of some logical structures. *Brit. J. Psychol.*, **53**, 175-88.

LOWES, J. L. (1927) *The Road to Xanadu.* London: Constable.

LUBORSKY, L., BLINDER, B. and SCHIMEK, J. C. (1965) Looking, recalling, and GSR as a function of defense. *J. Abnorm. Psychol.*, **70**, 270-80.

LUCHINS, A. S. (1942) Mechanization in problem solving: the effect of *Einstellung*. *Psychol. Monogr.*, **54**, No. 248.

LUMSDEN, E. A. and KLING, J. K. (1969) The relevance of an adequate concept of 'bigger' for investigations of size conservation: a methodological critique. *J. Exp. Child Psychol.*, **8**, 82-91.

LUMSDEN, E. A. and POTEAT, W. S. (1968) The salience of the vertical dimension in the concept of 'bigger' in five and six year olds. *J. Verb. Learn. Verb. Behav.*, **7**, 404-8.

LUNZER, E. A. (1960) Some points of Piagetian theory in the light of experimental criticism. *J. Child Psychol. Psychiat.*, **1**, 191-202.

LUNZER, E. A. (1968) Children's thinking. In BUTCHER, H. J. (ed.) *Educational Research in Britain.* London: Univ. London Press. pp. 69-100.

LURIA, A. R. (1961) *The Role of Speech in the Regulation of Normal and Abnormal Behaviour.* New York: Liveright.

MCCARTHY, D. (1954) Language development in children. In CARMICHAEL, L. (ed.) *Manual of Child Psychology.* 2nd edn. New York: Wiley. pp. 492-630.

MCCULLOCH, W. S. and PITTS, W. (1943) A logical calculus of the ideas immanent in nervous activity. *Bull. Math. Biophysics,* **5,** 115-37.

MACKAY, C. K. and CAMERON, M. B. (1968) Cognitive bias in Scottish first-year science and arts undergraduates. *Brit. J. Ed. Psychol.,* **38,** 315-18.

MACKAY, D. M. (1951) Mindlike behaviour in artefacts. *Brit. J. Phil. Science,* **2,** 105-21.

MACKAY, D. M. (1955) The epistemological problem for automata. In SHANNON, C. E. and MCCARTHY, J. (eds.) *Automata Studies.* Princeton, N.J.: Princeton Univ. Press. pp. 235-51.

MACKAY, D. M. (1962) The use of behavioural language to refer to mechanical processes. *Brit. J. Phil. Sci.,* **13,** 89-103.

MACKAY, D. M. (1965) From mechanism to mind. In SMYTHIES, J. R. (ed.) *Brain and Mind.* London: Routledge & Kegan Paul. pp. 163-97.

MCKELLAR, P. (1957) *Imagination and Thinking.* London: Cohen & West.

MACKINNON, D. W. (1962) The personality correlates of creativity: a study of American architects. In NIELSEN, G. S. (ed.) *Proceedings 14th Int. Cong. Appl. Psychol., Copenhagen, Vol. 2.* Copenhagen: Munksgaard.

MACKINTOSH, N. J. (1965) Selective attention in animal discrimination learning. *Psychol. Bull.,* **64,** 184-50.

MACKLER, B. and SPOTTS, J. V. (1965) Characteristics of responses to tests of creativity: a second look. *Percept. Mot. Skills,* **21,** 595-9.

MACMURRAY, J. (1957) *The Self as Agent.* London: Faber & Faber.

MACMURRAY, J. (1961) *Persons in Relation.* London: Faber & Faber.

MCNEILL, D. (1970) The development of language. In MUSSEN, P. H. (ed.) *Carmichael's Manual of Child Psychology.* 3rd edn., Vol. 1. New York: Wiley. pp. 1061-1161.

MCWHINNIE, H. J. (1967) Some relationships between creativity and perception in sixth-grade children. *Percept. Mot. Skills,* **25,** 979-80.

MCWHINNIE, H. J. (1969) Some relationships between creativity and perception in fourth-grade children. *Acta Psychol.,* **31,** 169-75.

MADAUS, G. F. (1967) Divergent thinking and intelligence: another look at a controversial question. *J. Educ. Meas.,* **4,** 227-35.

MAIER, N. F. R. (1930) Reasoning in humans: 1. On direction. *J. Comp. Psychol.,* **10,** 115-43.

MAIER, N. F. R. (1931) Reasoning in humans: 2. The solution of a problem and its appearance in consciousness. *J. Comp. Psychol.,* **12,** 181-94.

MALTZMAN, I. (1960) On the training of originality. *Psychol. Rev.*, **67**, 229-42.

MANNIX, J. B. (1960) The number concepts of a group of E.S.N. children. *Brit. J. Ed. Psychol.*, **30**, 180-1.

MARSH, G. (1964) Effect of overtraining on reversal and nonreversal shifts in nursery school children. *Child Devel.*, **35**, 1367-72.

MARSH, R. W. (1964) A statistical re-analysis of Getzels and Jackson's data. *Brit. J. Ed. Psychol.*, **34**, 91-3.

MARX, D. J. (1970) Intentional and incidental concept formation as a function of conceptual complexity, intelligence, and task complexity. *J. Ed. Psychol.*, **61**, 297-304.

MEAD, G. H. (1934) *Mind, Self, and Society* (ed. MORRIS, C. W.). Chicago, Ill.: Univ. Chicago Press.

MEDAWAR, P. B. (1969) *Induction and Intuition in Scientific Thought*. London: Methuen.

MEDNICK, M. T. (1963) Research creativity in psychology graduate students. *J. Consult. Psychol.*, **27**, 265-6.

MEDNICK, M. T., MEDNICK, S. A. and JUNG, C. C. (1964) Continual association as a function of level of creativity and type of verbal stimulus. *J. Abnorm. Soc. Psychol.*, **69**, 511-15.

MEDNICK, S. A. (1962) The associative basis of the creative process. *Psychol. Rev.*, **69**, 220-32.

MEDNICK, S. A. (1968) The Remote Associations Test. *J. Creat. Behav.*, **2**, 213-14.

MEDNICK, S. A. (1969) Reply to Hood's 'On creativity as defined by the Remote Associations Test'. *Psychol. Rep.*, **25**, 194.

MEHLER, J. and BEVER, T. G. (1967) Cognitive capacity of very young children. *Science*, **158**, 141-2.

MEHLER, J. and BEVER, T. G. (1968) Reply to Piaget. *Science*, **162**, 979-81.

MELTZER, B. and MICHIE, D. (eds.) (1971). *Machine Intelligence 6*. Edinburgh: Edinburgh Univ. Press.

MENDELSOHN, G. A. and GRISWOLD, B. B. (1964) Differential use of incidental stimuli in problem solving as a function of creativity. *J. Abnorm. Soc. Psychol.*, **68**, 431-6.

MENDELSOHN, G. A. and GRISWOLD, B. B. (1966) Assessed creativity potential, vocabulary level, and sex as predictors of the use of incidental cues in verbal problem solving. *J. Pers. Soc. Psychol.*, **4**, 423-31.

MERLEAU-PONTY, M. (1962) *The Phenomenology of Perception*. London: Routledge & Kegan Paul.

MERLEAU-PONTY, M. (1964) *Sense and Non-Sense*. Evanston: Northwestern Univ. Press.

MERLEAU-PONTY, M. (1965) *The Structure of Behaviour*. London: Methuen.

MERLEAU-PONTY, M. (1968) *The Visible and the Invisible*. Evanston: Northwestern Univ. Press.

MERMELSTEIN, E. and SHULMAN, L. S. (1967) Lack of formal schooling and the acquisition of conservation. *Child Devel.*, **38**, 39-52.

MICHIE, D. (1970) The intelligent machine. *Science Journal*, **6**, 50-4.

MILGRAM, N. A. and NOCE, J. S. (1968) Relevant and irrelevant verbalization in discrimination and reversal learning by normal and retarded children. *J. Ed. Psychol.*, **59**, 169-75.

MILL, J. (1829) *Analysis of the Phenomena of the Human Mind*. London.

MILL, J. S. (1869) *An Examination of Sir William Hamilton's Philosophy*, 6th edn. London: Longmans, Green.

MILL, J. S. (1874) *A System of Logic*. 6th edn. London: Harper.

MILLER, B. J., RUSS, D., GIBSON, C. and HALL, A. E. (1970) Effects of free association training, retraining, and information on creativity. *J. Exp. Psychol.*, **84**, 226-9.

MILLER, G. A. (1962) Some psychological studies of grammar. *Amer. Psychol.*, **17**, 748-62.

MILLER, G. A. and LENNEBERG, E. (1958) Review of Révész, G.: 'Thinking and Speaking: a symposium' in *Acta Psychol.*, 10 (Whole No.). *Amer. J. Psychol.*, **68**, 696-8.

MILLER, G. A., GALANTER, E. and PRIBRAM, K. H. (1960) *Plans and the Structure of Behaviour*. New York: Holt, Rinehart & Winston.

MILLER, S. A., SHELTON, J. and FLAVELL, J. H. (1970) A test of Luria's hypotheses concerning the development of self-regulation. *Child Devel.*, **41**, 651-65.

MILNER, E. (1951) A study of the relationship between reading readiness in grade one school children and patterns of parent-child interaction. *Child Devel.*, **22**, 95-112.

MINICHIELLO, M. D. and GOODNOW, J. J. (1969) Effect of an 'action' cue on conservation of amount. *Psychon. Sci.*, **16**, 200-1.

MINSKY, M. (1966) Artificial intelligence. *Sci. Amer.*, **215**, 246-63.

MITTLER, M. M. and HARRIS, L. (1969) Dimension preference and performance on a series of concept identification tasks in kindergarten, first-grade, and third-grade children. *J. Exp. Child Psychol.*, **7**, 374-84.

MOHANTY, J. N. (1969) *Edmund Husserl's Theory of Meaning*. The Hague: M. Nijhoff.

MOORE, T. V. (1910) The process of abstraction. *Univ. Calif. Pub. Psychol.*, **1**, 73-197.

MORGAN, J. J. B. and MORTON, J. T. (1944) The distortion of syllogistic reasoning produced by personal convictions. *J. Soc. Psychol.*, **20**, 39-59.

MORRIS, C. W. (1946) *Signs, Language and Behaviour*. New York: Prentice-Hall.

MOYLES, E. W., TUDDENHAM, R. D. and BLOCK, J. (1965) Simplicity/complexity or symmetry/asymmetry? A re-analysis of the Barron-Welsh Art Scales. *Percept. Mot. Skills*, **20**, 685-90.

MÜLLER, M. (1887) *The Science of Thought*. 2 Vols. New York.

MUMBAUER, C. C. and ODOM, R. D. (1967) Variables affecting the performance of preschool children in intradimensional, reversal, and extradimensional shifts. *J. Exp. Psychol.*, **75**, 180-7.

MURDOCK, B. B. (1967) Discussion of papers by Lee W. Gregg and Earl B. Hunt. In KLEINMUNTZ, B. (ed.) *Concepts and the Structure of Memory*. New York: Wiley. pp. 143-52.

MURRAY, F. B. (1968) Cognitive conflict and reversibility training in the acquisition of length conservation. *J. Ed. Psychol.*, **59**, 82-7.

MURRAY, J. P. and YOUNISS, J. (1968) Achievement of inferential transitivity and its relation to serial ordering. *Child Devel.*, **39**, 1259-69.

MUSES, C. A. (1962) *Aspects of the Theory of Artificial Intelligence*. New York: Plenum.

MUSIL, R. (1953) *The Man Without Qualities*. 3 Vols. London: Secker & Warburg.

NASSEFAT, M. (1963) *Élude quantitative sur l'évolution des opérations intellectuelles*. Neuchatel: Delachaux et Niestle.

NEIMARK, E. D. (1970) A preliminary search for formal operations structures. *J. Genet. Psychol.*, **116**, 223-32.

NEISSER, U. (1963) The multiplicity of thought. *Brit. J. Psychol.*, **54**, 1-14.

NEISSER, U. (1967) *Cognitive Psychology*. New York: Appleton-Century-Crofts.

NEISSER, U. and WEENE, P. (1962) Hierarchies in concept attainment. *J. Exp. Psychol.*, **64**, 640-5.

NEWELL, A. and SIMON, H. A. (1961) Computer simulation of human thinking. *Science*, **134**, 2011-7.

NEWELL, A. and SIMON, H. A. (1963) Computers in Psychology. In LUCE, R., BUSH, R. and GALANTER, E. (eds.) *Handbook of Mathematical Psychology. Vol. 1*. New York: Wiley. pp. 361-428.

NEWELL, A. and SIMON, H. A. (1971) *Human Problem Solving*. Englewood Cliffs, N.J.: Prentice-Hall.

NEWELL, A., SHAW, J. C. and SIMON, H. A. (1959) Report on a general problem solving program. In *Proceedings of the International Conference on Information Processing*. Paris: UNESCO House. pp. 256-64.

NEWELL, A., SHAW, J. C. and SIMON, H. A. (1963) Empirical explorations with the Logic Theory machine: a case study in heuristics. In FEIGENBAUM, E. A. and FELDMAN, J. (eds.) *Computers and Thought*. New York: McGraw-Hill. pp. 109-33.

NEWSON, J. and NEWSON, E. (1968) *Four Years Old in an Urban Community*. London: Allen & Unwin.

NUMMEDAL, S. G. and MURRAY, F. B. (1969) Semantic factors in conservation of weight. *Psychon. Sci.*, **16**, 323-4.

O'CONNOR, N. and HERMELIN, B. (1959) Discrimination and reversal learning in imbeciles. *J. Abnorm. Soc. Psychol.*, **59**, 409-13.

OLCZAK, P. V. and KAPLAN, M. F. (1969) Originality and rate of response in association as a function of associative gradient. *Amer. J. Psychol.*, **82**, 157-67.

OLÉRON, P. (1961) L'acquisition des conservations et le langage. *Enfance*, **3**, 201-19.

OSGOOD, C. E. (1953) *Method and Theory in Experimental Psychology*. New York: Oxford Univ. Press.

OSLER, S. F. and SCHOLNICK, E. K. (1968) The effect of stimulus differentiation and inferential experience on concept attainment in disadvantaged children. *J. Exp. Child Psychol.*, **6**, 658-66.

PARSONS, C. (1960) Inhelder and Piaget's *The Growth of Logical Thinking*: 2 – a logician's viewpoint. *Brit. J. Psychol.*, **51**, 75-84.

PASCAL-LEONE, J. and BOVET, M. C. (1966) L'apprentissage de la quantification de l'inclusion et la théorie opérataire. *Acta Psychol.*, **25**, 334-56.

PAVLOV, I. P. (1932) The reply of a physiologist to psychologists. *Psychol. Rev.*, **39**, 81-127.

PELUFFO, N. (1964) La nozione de conservazione del volume e le operazione di combazione come indici di sviluffo del pensiero operatorio in soggete appartenente al ambiente fisici e socioculturali diversi. *Divista di Psicologia Sociale*, **11**, 99-132.

PETERS, D. L. (1970) Verbal mediators and cue discrimination in the transition from nonconservation to conservation of number. *Child Devel.*, **41**, 707-21.

PHILLIPS, V. K. and TORRANCE, E. P. (1971) Divergent thinking, remote associations, and concept attainment. *J. Psychol.*, **77**, 223-8.

PIAGET, J. (1926) *The Language and Thought of the Child*. New York: Harcourt, Brace.

PIAGET, J. (1928) *Judgment and Reasoning in the Child*. New York: Harcourt, Brace.

PIAGET, J. (1932) *The Moral Judgment of the Child*. New York: Harcourt, Brace.

PIAGET, J. (1949) *Traité de Logique*. Paris: Armand Colin.

PIAGET, J. (1950) *The Psychology of Intelligence*. London: Routledge & Kegan Paul.

PIAGET, J. (1951) *Play, Dreams and Imitation in Childhood*. New York: Norton.

PIAGET, J. (1952a) *The Origins of Intelligence in Children*. New York: Int. Univ. Press.

PIAGET, J. (1952b) *The Child's Conception of Number*. New York: Humanities.

PIAGET, J. (1953) *Logic and Psychology*. Manchester: Manchester Univ. Press.

PIAGET, J. (1954a) Le langage et la pensée du point de vue génétique. *Acta psychol.*, **10**, 51-60.

PIAGET, J. (1954b) *The Construction of Reality in the Child*. New York: Basic Books.

PIAGET, J. (1956) Les stades du développement intellectuel de l'enfant et de l'adolescent. In OSTERRIETH, P. *et al. Le Problème des stades en psychologie de l'enfant*. Paris: Presses Univ. France, pp. 33-41.

PIAGET, J. (1957) Logique et équilibre dans les comportements du sujet. In APOSTEL, L., MANDELBROT, B. and PIAGET, J. (eds.) *Logique et équilibre. Études d'épistémologie génétique. Vol. 2*. Paris: Presses Univ. France. pp. 27-117.

PIAGET, J. (1962) *Comments on Vygotsky's critical remarks concerning 'The Language and Thought of the Child' and 'Judgment and Reasoning in the Child'*. Cambridge, Mass: M.I.T. Press.

PIAGET, J. (1967) *Biologie et connaissance. Essai sur les relations entre les régulations organiques et les processus cognitifs*. Paris: Gallimard.

PIAGET, J. (1968a) Quantification, conservation and nativism: quantitative evaluations of children aged two to three years are examined. *Science*, **162**, 976-81.

PIAGET, J. (1968b) *On the Development of Memory and Identity*. Worcester, Mass: Clark Univ. Press.

PIAGET, J. (1969) *The Mechanisms of Perception*. London: Routledge & Kegan Paul.

PIAGET, J. (1970a) *Introduction* to LAURENDEAU, M. and PINARD, A.

The Development of the Concept of Space in the Child. New York: Int. Univ. Press.

PIAGET, J. (1970b) *Genetic Epistemology.* New York: Columbia Univ. Press.

PIAGET, J. and INHELDER, B. (1956) *The Child's Conception of Space.* London: Routledge & Kegan Paul.

PIAGET, J. and INHELDER, B. (1958) *The Growth of Logical Thinking from Childhood to Adolescence.* London: Routledge & Kegan Paul.

PIAGET, J. and INHELDER, B. (1966) *L'image mentale chez l'enfant.* Paris: Presses Univ. France.

PIAGET, J., FRAISSE, P. and REUCHLIN, M. (1968) *Experimental Psychology: Its Scope and Method. Vol. 1.* London: Routledge & Kegan Paul.

PIAGET, J., INHELDER, B. and SINCLAIR, H. (1968) *Memoire et intelligence.* Paris: Presses Univ. France.

PIAGET, J., INHELDER, B. and SZEMINSKA, A. (1960) *The Child's Conception of Geometry.* New York: Basic Books.

PIAGET, J., VINH-BANG, and MATALON, B. (1958) Note on the law of the temporal maximum of some optico-geometric illusions. *Amer. J. Psychol.,* **71,** 277-82.

PIERS, E. V. and KIRCHNER, E. P. (1971) Productivity and uniqueness in continued word association as a function of subject creativity and stimulus properties. *J. Pers.,* **39,** 264-76.

PIKAS, A. (1966) *Abstraction and Concept Formation.* Cambridge, Mass: Harvard Univ. Press.

PINARD, A. and LAURENDEAU, M. (1969) 'Stage' in Piaget's cognitive-developmental theory: exegesis of a concept. In ELKIND, D. and FLAVELL, J. H. (eds.) *Studies in Cognitive Development.* New York: Oxford Univ. Press. pp. 121-70.

PINE, F. and HOLT, R. R. (1960) Creativity and primary process: a study of adaptive regression. *J. Abnorm. Soc. Psychol.,* **61,** 370-9.

PIVCEVIC, E. (1970) *Husserl and Phenomenology.* London: Hutchinson.

POLANYI, M. (1958) *Personal Knowledge.* London: Routledge & Kegan Paul.

POLANYI, M. (1959) *The Study of Man.* London: Routledge & Kegan Paul.

POLANYI, M. (1967) *The Tacit Dimension.* London: Routledge & Kegan Paul.

POPPER, K. R. (1950) Indeterminism in classical and quantum physics. *Brit. J. Phil. Sci.,* **1,** 117-33 and 173-95.

POPPER, K. R. (1959) *The Logic of Scientific Discovery.* London: Hutchinson.

PRICE, H. H. (1962) *Thinking and Experience.* 2nd edn. London: Hutchinson.

PRICE-WILLIAMS, D. R. (1962) Abstract and concrete modes of classification in a primitive society. *Brit. J. Ed. Psychol.,* 32, 50-61.

PRICE-WILLIAMS, D. R., GORDON, W. and RAMIREZ, M. (1969) Skill and conservation: a study of pottery-making children. *Devel. Psychol.,* 1, 769.

PRIOR, A. N. (1955) *Formal Logic.* Oxford: Clarendon Press.

RAINWATER, J. M. (1964) *Effects of set on problem solving in subjects of varying levels of assessed creativity.* Unpub. Ph.D. diss. Univ. Calif.

RAPAPORT, D. (1951) Toward a theory of thinking. In: *Organization and Pathology of Thought.* New York: Columbia Univ. Press. pp. 689-730.

RAY, W. S. (1967) *The Experimental Psychology of Original Thinking.* London: Macmillan.

RAYNER, E. H. (1958) A study of evaluative problem-solving: Part 1, Observations on adults. *Quart. J. Exp. Psychol.,* 10, 155-65.

REESE, H. W. (1962) Verbal mediation as a function of age level. *Psychol. Bull.,* 59, 502-9.

REESE, H. W. (1968) *The Perception of Stimulus Relations.* New York: Academic Press.

REEVES, J. W. (1965) *Thinking about Thinking.* London: Secker & Warburg.

REITMAN, W. (1965) *Cognition and Thought.* New York: Wiley.

RESTLE, E. (1961) Statistical methods for a theory of cue learning. *Psychometrika,* 26, 291-306.

RESTLE, F. (1962) The selection of strategies in cue learning. *Psychol. Rev.,* 69, 329-43.

RÉVÉSZ, G. (1954) Denken und sprachen. *Acta Psychol.,* 10, 3-50.

RICHARDS, P. N. (1970) *A study of some of the effects on children's creative thinking of the discovery approach to mathematics in the primary school.* Unpub. M.Ed. thesis, Univ. Durham.

RIEGEL, K. F., RIEGEL, R. M. and LEVINE, R. S. (1966) An analysis of associative behaviour and creativity. *J. Pers. Soc. Psychol.,* 4, 50-6.

RIVERS, W. H. R. (1905) Vision. In HADDON, A. C. *Report of the Cambridge Anthropological Expedition to the Torres Straits.* London: Cambridge Univ. Press.

ROBINSON, J. A. (1967) A review of automatic theorem-proving.

Annual Symposia in Applied Mathematics, **19**. Providence: Rhode Island: Amer. Math. Soc.

ROE, A. (1951a) A psychological study of eminent biologists. *Psychol. Monogr.*, **65**, No. 14 (Whole No. 331).

ROE, A. (1951b) A psychological study of physical scientists. *Genet. Psychol. Monogr.*, **43**, 121-235.

ROE, A. (1953) *The Making of a Scientist*. New York: Dodd, Mead.

ROGOLSKY, M. M. (1968) Artistic creativity and adaptive regression in third-grade children. *J. Proj. Tech. Pers. Ass.*, **32**, 53-62.

ROLL, S. (1970) Reversibility training and stimulus desirability as factors in conservation of number. *Child Devel.*, **41**, 501-7.

ROSENSTEIN, J. (1960) Cognitive abilities of deaf children. *J. Speech Hearing Res.*, **3**, 108-19.

ROSENSTEIN, J. (1961) Perception, cognition and language in deaf children. *Excep. Child.*, **27**, 276-84.

ROTHENBERG, B. and OROST, J. H. (1969) The training of conservation of number in young children. *Child Devel.*, **40**, 707-26.

RUSSELL, B. (1940) *An Inquiry into Meaning and Truth*. London: Allen & Unwin.

RYLE, G. (1949) *The Concept of Mind*. London: Hutchinson.

SAPIR, E. (1927) *Language*. New York: Harcourt, Brace.

SARAVO, A. (1967) Effect of number of variable dimensions on reversal and non-reversal shifts. *J. Comp. Physiol. Psychol.*, **64**, 93-7.

SAUGSTAD, P. and RAAHEIM, K. (1960) Problem solving, past experience and availability of functions. *Brit. J. Psychol.*, **51**, 97-104.

SCHAEFFER, B. and ELLIS, S. (1970) The effects of overlearning on children's non-reversal and reversal learning using unrelated stimuli. *J. Exp. Child Psychol.*, **10**, 1-7.

SCHNEIDER, G. E. (1968) Contrasting visuomotor functions of tectum and cortex in the golden hamster. *Psychol. Forsch.*, **31**, 52-62.

SCHUTZ, A. (1967) *Collected Papers, Vol.* 1. The Hague: M. Nijhoff.

SCHWARTZ, M. M. and SCHOLNICK, E. K. (1970) Scalogram analysis of logical and perceptual components of conservation of discontinuous quantity. *Child Devel.*, **41**, 695-705.

SEGGIE, J. L. (1969) Levels of learning involved in conjunctive and disjunctive concepts. *Aust. J. Psychol.*, **21**, 325-33.

SEGGIE, J. L. (1970) The utilization by children and adults of binary propositional thinking in concept learning. *J. Exp. Child Psychol.*, **10**, 235-47.

SELLS, S. B. (1936) The atmosphere effect: an experimental study of reasoning. *Arch. Psychol.*, **200**.

SHAFER, R. (1958) Regression in the service of the ego: the relevance of a psycho-analytic concept for personality assessment. In LINDZEY, G. (ed.) *Assessment of Human Motives*. New York: Rinehart. pp. 119-48.

SHANNON, C. E. (1950) Automatic chess player. *Sci. Amer.*, **182**, 48.

SHAPIRO, B. J. and O'BRIEN, T. C. (1970) Logical thinking in children ages six through thirteen. *Child Devel.*, **41**, 823-9.

SIEGELMAN, E. and BLOCK, J. (1969) Two parallel scalable sets of Piagetian tasks. *Child Devel.*, **40**, 951-6.

SIGEL, I. E., ROEPER, A. and HOOPER, F. H. (1966) A training procedure for acquisition of Piaget's conservation of quantity: a pilot study and its replication. *Brit. J. Ed. Psychol.*, **36**, 301-11.

SILVERMAN, I. W. (1966) Effect of verbalisation on reversal shifts in children: additional data. *J. Exp. Child Psychol.*, **4**, 1-8.

SILVERMAN, L. H. (1965) Regression in the service of the ego: a case study. *J. Proj. Tech. Pers. Assess.*, **29**, 232-47.

SIMON, H. A. (1969) *The Science of the Artificial*. Cambridge, Mass.: M.I.T. Press.

SIMON, H. A. and BARENFELD, M. (1969) Information-processing analysis of perceptual processes in problem solving. *Psychol. Rev.*, **76**, 473-83.

SIMON, H. A. and KOTOVSKY, K. (1963) Human acquisition of concepts for sequential patterns. *Psychol. Rev.*, **70**, 534-46.

SIMON, H. A. and NEWELL, A. (1971) Human problem solving: the state of the theory in 1970. *Amer. Psychol.*, **26**, 145-59.

SINCLAIR-DE-ZWART, M. (1967) *Acquisition de langage et développement de la pensée*. Paris: Dunod.

SLACK, C. W. (1955) Feedback theory and the reflex arc concept. *Psychol. Rev.*, **62**, 263-7.

SLAMECKA, N. J. A. (1968) A methodological analysis of shift paradigms in human discrimination learning. *Psychol. Bull.*, **69**, 423-38.

SMEDSLUND, J. (1961a) The acquisition of conservation of substance and weight in children: 2. External reinforcement of conservation of weight and of the operations of addition and subtraction. *Scand. J. Psychol.*, **2**, 71-84.

SMEDSLUND, J. (1961b) The acquisition of conservation of substance and weight in children: 3. Extinction of conservation of weight acquired 'normally' and by means of empirical controls on a balance. *Scand. J. Psychol.*, **2**, 85-7.

SMEDSLUND, J. (1961c) The acquisition of conservation of substance and weight in children: 4. Attempt at extinction of the visual components of the weight concept. *Scand. J. Psychol.*, **2**, 153-5.

SMEDSLUND, J. (1961d) The acquisition of conservation of substance and weight in children: 5. Practice in conflict situations without external reinforcement. *Scand. J. Psychol.*, **2**, 156-60.

SMEDSLUND, J. (1961e) The acquisition of conservation of substance and weight in children: 6. Practice on continuous versus discontinuous material in problem situations without external reinforcement. *Scand. J. Psychol.*, **2**, 203-10.

SMEDSLUND, J. (1963a) The development of concrete transitivity of length in children. *Child Devel.*, **34**, 389-405.

SMEDSLUND, J. (1963b) The concept of correlation in adults. *Scand. J. Psychol.*, **4**, 167-73.

SMEDSLUND, J. (1964) Concrete reasoning: a study in intellectual development. *Monogr. Soc. Res. Child Devel.*, **29**, No. 2.

SMEDSLUND, J. (1965) The development of transitivity of length: a comment on Braine's reply. *Child Devel.*, **36**, 577-80.

SMEDSLUND, J. (1969) Meanings, implications and universals: towards a psychology of man. *Scand. J. Psychol.*, **10**, 1-5.

SMILANSKY, S. (1968) *The Effects of Sociodramatic Play on Disadvantaged Preschool Children.* New York: Wiley.

SMILEY, S. S. and WEIR, M. W. (1966) The role of dimensional dominance in reversal and nonreversal shift behaviour. *J. Exp. Child Psychol.*, **4**, 211-16.

SMITH, I. D. (1968) The effects of training procedures upon the acquisition of conservation of weight. *Child Devel.*, **39**, 515-26.

SMOKE, K. L. (1932) An objective study of concept formation. *Psychol. Monogr.*, **42**, No. 4.

SMOKE, K. L. (1933) Negative instances in concept learning. *J. Exp. Psychol.*, **16**, 583-8.

SOKOLOV, Y. N. (1963) *Perception and the Conditioned Reflex.* London: Pergamon.

SPENCE, K. W. (1940) Continuous versus noncontinuous interpretations of discrimination learning. *Psychol. Rev.*, **47**, 271-88.

SPENCER, H. (1855) *The Principles of Psychology.* 2 Vols. London: Williams & Norgate (1885).

SPERLING, S. E. (1965) Reversal learning and resistance to extinction: a review of the rat literature. *Psychol. Bull.*, **63**, 291-7.

SPIEGELBERG, H. (1965) *The Phenomenological Movement.* 2 Vols. (2nd edn.). The Hague: M. Nijhoff.

SPOTTS, J. V. and MACKLER, B. (1967) Relationships of field-dependent and field-independent cognitive styles to creative test performance. *Percep. Mot. Skills*, **24**, 239-68.

STAATS, A. W. (1961) Verbal habit-families, concepts, and the operant conditioning of word classes. *Psychol. Rev.*, **68**, 190-204.

STEFFERUD, E. (1963) *The Logic Theory Machine: a Model Heuristic Program*. Rand Corp. Tech. Rept. RM-3731-CC (Rand Corp., Santa Monica, Calif.).

STEWART, D. K. (1961) Communication and logic: evidence for the existence of validity patterns. *J. Gen. Psychol.*, **64**, 297-305.

STEWART, D. K. (1965) Communication, ideas and meaning. *Psychol. Rep.*, **16**, 885-92.

STONE, M. A. and AUSUBEL, D. P. (1969) The intersituational generality of formal thought. *J. Genet. Psychol.*, **115**, 169-80.

STRAUSS, M. E. (1969) Cognitive style and the use of incidental cues in problem solving. *J. Psychol.*, **73**, 69-74.

STRAUSS, S. and LANGER, J. (1970) Operational thought inducement. *Child Devel.*, **41**, 163.

STROOP, J. R. (1953a) The basis of Logon's theory. *Amer. J. Psychol.*, **47**, 499-504.

STROOP, J. R. (1935b) Studies of interference in serial verbal reaction. *J. Exp. Psychol.*, **18**, 643-72.

SUCHMAN, R. G. and TRABASSO, T. (1966) Stimulus preference and cue function in young children's concept attainment. *J. Exp. Child Psychol.*, **3**, 188-98.

SULLIVAN, E. V. (1967) Acquisition of conservation of substance through film modeling techniques. *Ontario Institute for Studies in Education, Educational Research Series, No. 2*, 11-23.

SULLIVAN, E. V. (1969) Transition problems in conservation research. *J. Genet. Psychol.*, **115**, 41-54.

SUZUKI, S. (1961) Study on shifts of discrimination learning in children. *Jap. J. Ed. Psychol.*, **9**, 84-91, 127-8.

TANNER, J. M. and INHELDER, B. (1956a) *Discussions on Child Development*. Vol. 1. London: Tavistock.

TANNER, J. M. and INHELDER, B. (1956b) *Discussions on Child Development*. Vol. 4. London: Tavistock.

TAUB, M. (1961) *Computers and Common Sense. The Myth of Thinking Machines*. New York: Columbia Univ. Press.

THISTLETHWAITE, D. (1950) Attitude and structure as factors in the distortion of reasoning. *J. Abnorm. Soc. Psychol.*, **45**, 442-58.

THORNDIKE, E. L. (1922) The effect of changed data upon reasoning. *J. Exp. Psychol.*, **5**, 33-8.

THORNDIKE, R. L. (1963) The measurement of creativity. *Teachers College Rec.*, **64**, 422-4.

TIGHE, L. S. (1965) Effect of perceptual pretraining on reversal and nonreversal shifts. *J. Exp. Psychol.*, **70**, 379-85.

TIGHE, L. S. and TIGHE, T. J. (1965) Overtraining and discrimination shift behaviour in children. *Psychon. Sci.*, **2**, 365-6.

TIGHE, L. S. and TIGHE, T. J. (1966) Discrimination learning: two views in historical perspective. *Psychol. Bull.*, **66**, 353-70.

TIGHE, L. S. and TIGHE, T. J. (1969). Transfer from perceptual pretraining as a function of number of task dimensions. *J. Exp. Child Psychol.*, **8**, 495-502.

TIGHE, T. J. (1964) Reversal and nonreversal shifts in monkeys. *J. Comp. Physiol. Psychol.*, **58**, 324-6.

TIGHE, T. J. and TIGHE, L. S. (1966) Overtraining and optional shift behaviour in rats and children. *J. Comp. Physiol. Psychol.*, **62**, 49-54.

TIGHE, T. J. and TIGHE, L. S. (1967) Discrimination shift performance of children as a function of age and shift procedure. *J. Exp. Psychol.*, **74**, 466-70.

TIGHE, T. J. and TIGHE, L. S. (1968a) Differentiation theory and concept shift behaviour. *Psychol. Bull.*, **70**, 756-61.

TIGHE, T. J. and TIGHE, L. S. (1968b) Perceptual learning in the discrimination processes of children: an analysis of five variables in perceptual pretraining. *J. Exp. Psychol.*, **77**, 125-34.

TIGHE, T. J. and TIGHE, L. S. (1969a) Perceptual variables in the transposition behaviour of children. *J. Exp. Child Psychol.*, **7**, 566-77.

TIGHE, T. J. and TIGHE, L. S. (1969b) Facilitation of transposition and reversal learning in children by prior perceptual training. *J. Exp. Child Psychol.*, **8**, 366-74.

TIGHE, T. J. and TIGHE, L. S. (1970) Optional shift behaviour of children as a function of age, type of pretraining, and stimulus salience. *J. Exp. Child Psychol.*, **9**, 272-85.

TIGHE, T. J., BROWN, P. L. and YOUNGS, E. A. (1965) The effect of overtraining on the shift behaviour of albino rats. *Psychon. Sci.*, **2**, 141-2.

TORRANCE, E. P. (1962) *Guiding Creative Talent*. Englewood Cliffs, N.J.: Prentice-Hall.

TORRANCE, E. P. (1968) Examples and rationales of test tasks for assessing creative abilities. *J. Creat. Behav.*, **2**, 165-78.

TRABASSO, T., DEUTSCH, J. A. and GELMAN, R. (1966) Attention and discrimination learning of young children. *J. Exp. Child Psychol.*, **4**, 9-19.

TRABASSO, T., STAVE, M. and EICHBERG, R. (1969) Attribute preference and discrimination shifts in young children. *J. Exp. Child Psychol.*, **8**, 195-209.

TREVARTHEN, C. B. (1968) Two mechanisms of vision in primates. *Psychol. Forsch.*, **31**, 299-337.

TURING, A. M. (1936) On computable numbers, with an application to the 'Entscheidungsproblem'. *Proc. London Math. Soc. (ser. 2)*, **42**: 230-65, **43**: 544.

TURING, A. M. (1950) Computing machinery and intelligence. *Mind*, **59**, 433-60.

TURRISI, F. D. and SHEPP, B. E. (1969) Some effects of novelty and overtraining on the reversal learning of retardates. *J. Exp. Child Psychol.*, **8**, 389-401.

UNDERWOOD, B. J. (1952) An orientation for research on thinking. *Psychol. Rev.*, **59**, 209-19.

UNDERWOOD, B. J. (1966) Some relationships between concept learning and verbal learning. In KLAUSMEIER, H. J. and HARRIS, C. W. (eds.) *Analyses of Concept Learning*. New York: Academic Press. pp. 51-63.

UZGIRIS, I. C. (1964) Situational generality of conservation. *Child Devel.*, **35**, 831-41.

VAN DE GEER, J. P. (1957) *A Psychological Study of Problem Solving*. Haarlem: Utgeverij de Toorts.

VAN DE GEER, J. P. and JASPARS, J. M. F. (1966) Cognitive Functions. In *Annual Review of Psychology*. Palo Alto: Ann. Reviews Inc. pp. 145-76.

VAN MONDFRANS, A. P., FELDHUSEN, J. F., TREFFINGER, D. J. and FERRIS, D. R. (1971) The effects of instructions and response time on divergent thinking test scores. *Psychol. in the Schools*, **8**, 65-71.

VARELA, J. A. (1969) Elaboration of Guilford's SI model. *Psychol. Rev.*, **76**, 332-6.

VERNON, M. (1967) Relationship of language to the thinking process. *Arch. Gen. Psychiat.*, **16**, 325-33.

VERNON, P. E. (1950) *The Structure of Human Abilities*. London: Methuen.

VERNON, P. E. (1969) *Intelligence and Cultural Environment*. London: Methuen.

VERNON, P. E. (ed.) (1970) *Creativity: Selected Readings*. Harmondsworth: Penguin.

VYGOTSKY, L. S. (1962) *Thought and Language*. New York: Wiley.

WACHTEL, P. (1967) Conceptions of broad and narrow attention. *Psychol. Bull.*, **68**, 417-29.

WAGHORN, L. and SULLIVAN, E. V. (1970) The exploration of transition rules in conservation of quantity (substance) using film mediated modeling. *Acta Psychol.*, **32**, 65-80.

WALKER, H. E. (1962) *Relationships between predicted school behaviour and measures of creative potential.* Unpub. Doctorial diss., Univ. Michigan.

WALLACE, J. G. (1965) *Concept Growth and the Education of the Child.* Windsor: N.F.E.R.

WALLACH, L. (1969) On the bases of conservation. In ELKIND, D. and FLAVELL, J. H. (eds.) *Studies in Cognitive Development.* New York: Oxford Univ. Press. pp. 191-219.

WALLACH, L. and SPROTT, R. L. (1964) Inducing number conservation in children. *Child Devel.*, **35**, 1057-71.

WALLACH, L., WALL, A. J. and ANDERSON, L. (1967) Number conservation: the roles of reversibility, addition-subtraction, and misleading perceptual cues. *Child Devel.*, **38**, 425-42.

WALLACH, M. A. (1970) Creativity. Ch. 17 in MUSSEN, P. H. (ed.) *Carmichael's Manual of Child Psychology.* 3rd edn. Vol. 1. New York: Wiley. pp. 1211-72.

WALLACH, M. A. and KOGAN, N. (1965) *Modes of Thinking in Young Children.* New York: Holt, Rinehart & Winston.

WALLACH, M. A. and WING, C. W. (1969) *The Talented Student: a Validation of the Creativity-Intelligence Distinction.* New York: Holt, Rinehart & Winston.

WALLAS, G. (1926) *The Art of Thought.* London: Jonathan Cape.

WARD, J. (1967) An oblique factorization of Wallach and Kogan's 'creativity' correlations. *Brit. J. Ed. Psychol.*, **37**, 380-2.

WARD, W. C. (1968) Creativity in young children. *Child Devel.*, **39**, 737-54.

WARD, W. C. (1969) Creativity and environmental cues in nursery school children. *Devel. Psychol.*, **1**, 543-7.

WARR, P. B. (1970) *Thought and Personality.* Harmondsworth: Penguin.

WASON, P. C. (1959) The processing of positive and negative information. *Quart. J. Exp. Psychol.*, **11**, 92-107.

WASON, P. C. (1961) Response to affirmative and negative binary statements. *Brit. J. Psychol.*, **52**, 133-42.

WASON, P. C. (1966) Reasoning. In FOSS, B. M. (ed.) *New Horizons in Psychology.* Harmondsworth: Penguin.

WASON, P. C. (1968) Reasoning about a rule. *Quart. J. Exp. Psychol.*, **20**, 273-81.

WASON, P. C. (1969) Regression in reasoning? *Brit. J. Psychol.*, **60**, 471-80.

WASON, P. C. and JOHNSON-LAIRD, P. N. (1970) A conflict between selecting and evaluating information in an inferential task. *Brit. J. Psychol.*, **61**, 509-15.

WASON, P. C. and JONES, S. (1963) Negatives: denotation and connotation. *Brit. J. Psychol.*, **54**, 299-307.

WATT, W. C. (1970) On two hypotheses concerning psycholinguistics. In HAYES, J. R. (ed.) *Cognition and the Development of Language.* New York: Wiley. pp. 137-220.

WEISSMAN, P. (1967) Ego functions in creativity. *Psychother. Psychosom.*, **15**, 273-85.

WELLS, H. (1963) Effects of transfer and problem structure in disjunctive concept formation. *J. Exp. Psychol.*, **56**, 63-9.

WERNER, H. (1948) *The Comparative Psychology of Mental Development.* New York: Wiley.

WERTHEIMER, M. (1923) Untersuchungen zur Lehre von der Gestalt. *Psychol. Forsch.*, **4**, 301-50.

WERTHEIMER, M. (1945) *Productive Thinking.* London: Tavistock (1961).

WHITE, B. (1969) The initial coordination of sensori-motor schemas in human experience – Piaget's ideas and the role of experience. In ELKIND, D. and FLAVELL, J. H. (eds.) *Studies in Cognitive Development.* New York: Oxford Univ. Press. pp. 237-56.

WHITE, R. M. and JOHNSON, P. J. (1968) Concept of dimensionality and optional shift performance in nursery school children. *J. Exp. Child Psychol.*, **6**, 113-19.

WHITE, S. H. (1965) Evidence for a hierarchical arrangement of learning processes. In LIPSITT, L. P. and SPIKER, C. C. (eds.) *Advances in Child Development and Behaviour.* Vol. 2. New York: Academic Press.

WHITEHEAD, A. N. (1938) *Modes of Thought.* New York: Cambridge Univ. Press.

WHITEHEAD, A. N. and RUSSELL, B. (1927) *Principia Mathematica.* 3 Vols. Cambridge: Cambridge Univ. Press.

WHORF, B. L. (1956) *Language, Thought, and Reality: Selected Writings of Benjamin Lee Whorf.* (Edited by CARROLL, J. B.) New York: Wiley.

WICKELGREN, W. A. (1962) A simulation program for concept attainment by conservative focussing. *Behav. Sci.*, **7**, 245-7.

WICKELGREN, W. A. and COHEN, D. H. (1962) An artificial language and memory approach to concept attainment. *Psychol. Rep.*, **10**, 815-27.

WIENER, N. (1948) *Cybernetics*. New York: Wiley.

WILD, C. (1965) Creativity and adaptive regression. *J. Pers. Soc. Psychol.*, **2**, 161-9.

WILKINS, M. C. (1928) The effect of changed material on ability to do formal syllogistic reasoning. *Arch. Psychol.*, **16**, 1-83.

WILLIAMS, G. F. (1971) A model of memory in concept learning. *Cognitive Psychol.*, **2**, 158-84.

WINER, G. A. (1968) Induced set and acquisition of number conservation. *Child Devel.*, **39**, 196-205.

WISDOM, J. (1952) Symposium: mentality in machines. In *Men and Machines. Aristotelian Society, Supplementary Volume 26.* pp. 1-26.

WITKIN, H. A. *et al.* (1954) *Personality through Perception.* New York: Harper.

WITKIN, H. A. *et al.* (1962) *Psychological Differentiation.* New York: Wiley.

WITTGENSTEIN, L. (1953) *Philosophical Investigations.* Oxford: Basil Blackwell.

WOERNER, M. G. (1963) *Verbal mediation and reversal shifts in children.* Unpub. Ph.D. thesis, New York University.

WOHLWILL, J. F. (1959) Un essai d'apprentissage dans le domaine de la conservation du nombre. In PIAGET, J. (ed.) *L'apprentissage des structures logiques. Études d'épistémologie génétique*, **9.** Paris: Presses Univ. pp. 125-35.

WOHLWILL, J. F. (1960) A study of the development of the number concept by scalogram analysis. *J. Genet. Psychol.*, **97**, 345-77.

WOHLWILL, J. F. and LOWE, R. C. (1962) An experimental analysis of the development of the conservation of number. *Child Devel.*, **33**, 153-67.

WOLFF, J. L. (1966) The role of dimensional preferences in discrimination learning. *Psychon. Sci.*, **5**, 455-6.

WOLFF, J. L. (1967) Concept-shift and discrimination-reversal learning in humans. *Psychol. Bull.*, **68**, 369-408.

WOODWARD, M. (1959) The behaviour of idiots interpreted by Piaget's theory of sensori-motor development. *Brit. J. Ed. Psychol.*, **29**, 60-71.

WOODWORTH, R. S. and SELLS, S. B. (1935) An atmosphere effect in formal syllogistic reasoning. *J. Exp. Psychol.*, **18**, 451-60.

WUNDT, W. (1894) *Logik: Eine Untersuchung der Prinzipien der Ekenntnis.* 2 Vols. Stuttgart: Ferdinand Enke.

WYCKOFF, L. B. (1952) The role of observing responses in discrimination learning. *Psychol. Rev.*, **59**, 431-42.

YAMAMOTO, K. (1964) Threshold of intelligence in academic achievement of highly creative students. *J. Exp. Ed.*, **32**, 401-4.

YAMAMOTO, K. (1965a) Effects of restriction of range and test unreliability on correlation between measures of intelligence and creative thinking. *Brit. J. Ed. Psychol.*, **35**, 300-5.

YAMAMOTO, K. (1965b) Validation of tests of creative thinking: a review of some studies. *Excep. Child.*, **31**, 281-90.

YOUNISS, J. (1964) Concept transfer as a function of shifts, age and deafness. *Child Devel.*, **35**, 695-700.

YOUNISS, J. and MURRAY, J. P. (1970) Transitive inference with nontransitive solutions controlled. *Devel. Psychol.*, **2**, 169-75.

ZEAMAN, D. and HOUSE, B. J. (1963) The role of attention in retardate discrimination learning. In ELLIS, N. R. (ed.) *Handbook of Mental Deficiency*, New York: McGraw-Hill. pp. 159-223.

ZERN, D. (1969) Some trends in the development of concrete reasoning in children: a note to Jan Smedslund's 'Concrete Reasoning: a study in intellectual development.' *J. Genet. Psychol.*, **115**, 3-5.

Indexes

Name Index

K

General Index